THINGS
THAT DIFFER

THE FUNDAMENTALS
OF DISPENSATIONALISM

THINGS THAT DIFFER

THE FUNDAMENTALS OF DISPENSATIONALISM

by

CORNELIUS R. STAM

Founder of the Berean Bible Society
and
Prolific Author of over Thirty Bible Study Books

BEREAN BIBLE SOCIETY
N112 W17761 Mequon Road
Germantown, WI 53022
(Metro Milwaukee)

Previous Copyrights, 1959, 1961, 1982, 1985

by

CORNELIUS R. STAM

Copyright, 1996

by

BEREAN BIBLE SOCIETY
N112 W17761 Mequon Road
Germantown, WI 53022
(Metro Milwaukee)

Sixteenth Printing

PRINTED IN U.S.A.

ISBN 1-893874-25-7

EERDMANS PRINTING COMPANY
GRAND RAPIDS, MICHIGAN

CONTENTS

CHAPTER V

CHAPTER VI

CHAPTER VII

CHAPTER VIII

CHAPTER XIII

CHAPTER XIV

CHAPTER XV

PREFACE

Great strides have already been taken in dispensational Bible study by such men of God as Darby, Scofield and Larkin, but it would be a mistake to suppose, as some seem to, that the ground has now been completely covered, for in "rightly dividing the Word of truth" the field is as large as the Book itself. Indeed, for the past years the need for another, systematic book on dispensationalism has been increasingly felt as it has become evident that the popular writings now in existence on the subject fall short in at least one significant respect; namely, their failure to present clearly and *consistently* the distinctive character of Paul's message and ministry as the apostle of the present dispensation.

Most of our Bible teachers have seen *to a limited degree* the distinction between Paul's ministry and that of the twelve, but have taught *at the same time* that Paul labored under the so-called "great commission" given to the other apostles, that the church of this age began at Pentecost with Peter and the eleven, that "the gospel of the grace of God" was proclaimed before Paul, etc. This failure to grasp fully the distinctive character of Paul's apostleship has contributed much to the confusion that exists among fundamental believers and has left a great deal still to be clarified for those who desire "the full assurance of understanding."

11

The re-discovery of Paul's special place in God's program, and the increased emphasis laid in late years upon what he calls *"my gospel, and the preaching of Jesus Christ according to the revelation of the mystery,"* have provided God's people with the key to many problems which, because they have remained so long unanswered, have caused the great dispensational Bible conferences of a generation ago to all but disappear.

In the study of the dispensations we enjoy true Bible *analysis.* We take the Book apart,* so to speak; not to cast *any* of it aside, but to examine its separate parts and to note the differences.

But we also enjoy true Bible *synthesis* in the study of the dispensations and see the perfect harmony of the whole Word of God. Many Bible schools advertise courses in Bible synthesis which really amount to nothing more than brief summaries of its sixty-six books. Any such course should be characterized as *synopsis,* not synthesis. Bible synthesis is a systematic study of the *progressive unfolding* of God's revelation and of *the development* of His dealings with men, as well as of *the unity of His purpose* in those dealings. It is a study of the dispensations *in their relation to each other.* Hence no study which denies or ignores the doctrine of dispensations is true Bible synthesis.

The present volume does not deal with the dispensations consecutively but rather with dispensationalism in its relation to God's message and program for today. Capital letters are used in some Scripture quotations to emphasize connections

---

*"Rightly dividing" in II Tim. 2:15 means *to cut straight or right.*

12

which might otherwise be overlooked. While single clauses are frequently quoted, we have not, we trust, used these in violation of their true sense in the light of their contexts. Sub-headings have been liberally used as an aid to clear thinking and at the close of each chapter we have added a list of twenty questions as a further help to the Bible student to consider and retain what he has read.

We gratefully acknowledge the help of others in the preparation of this volume. Of these, three have submitted *doctrinal* criticisms: Pastor Charles F. Baker of Milwaukee and Pastor Donald Elifson of Chicago; both well qualified to deal with dispensational matters, and Pastor J. C. O'Hair of Chicago, who has probably contributed more to the recovery of dispensational truth than any man living today. We do not, of course, imply that these brethren necessarily endorse every detail of this volume as it now appears, but their criticisms have been prayerfully considered and many of their suggestions have been adopted.

Though we have sought to make this book as comprehensive as possible, it is not presumed to be exhaustive for, as we say, the field of dispensational study is as great as the Bible itself. Should there still be some time remaining before the Lord returns to catch His own away, the Spirit will enlighten the hearts and minds of others to see what we have missed and other writers will doubtless improve upon what has here been written.

As we send these studies forth we humbly pray that they may prove a substantial contribution to our readers' understanding and enjoyment of the

Scriptures, and a distinct help in their service for Christ.

As the days grow darker may God lead us all further into the light of His truth so that we may be more intelligently and effectively used, "to the glory of His grace."

CORNELIUS R. STAM.

MILWAUKEE, WISCONSIN
February 1, 1951

ALL CHARTS BY CORNELIUS R. STAM

ARTIST: WAYNE A. WEBB

INTRODUCTION

RIGHTLY DIVIDING THE WORD
OF TRUTH

"Study to show thyself approved unto God, a work-man that needeth not to be ashamed, rightly dividing the Word of truth."

—II Tim. 2:15.

*   *   *   *

Those who seek to teach the Word rightly divided frequently encounter the objection that *"All* [or *every*] *Scripture is given by inspiration of God, and is profitable . . ."* (II Tim. 3:16). It is argued from this passage that it is dishonoring to God to divide the Bible into dispensations and emphasize the differences between them, since it is *all* for us, from Genesis 1 to Revelation 22.

Does this mean, then, that II Tim. 2:15 and II Tim. 3:16 contradict each other? Surely they do not. The fact is that, written only a few paragraphs apart, by the same author, to the same person, about the same Book, these two verses *complement* each other. II Tim. 2:15 explains *how* God's work-man may get most out of the Bible, while II Tim. 3:16 declares that *all* of it was given for his profit. All Scripture is indeed profitable when "rightly divided," but when wrongly divided or not divided at all, the truth is changed into a lie and becomes most *un*profitable. Thus II Tim. 2:15 is the key to

15

II Tim. 3:16 and to the understanding and enjoyment of the Word of truth.

One difficulty is that multitudes of Christians shrink from the *effort* involved in *studying* the Scriptures with a view to rightly dividing them. And, alas, their spiritual leaders often encourage them in their lethargy.

Some years ago we heard a preacher exclaim: "Some say, 'This is for the Jew and that is for the church. This is for us and that is not for us.' *I* take a *whole* Bible!"

Did he mean that we should *not* distinguish between God's program for Israel in Old Testament times and His program for the body of Christ today? Certainly not, but it sounded so. Did he mean that those who *do* thus divide the Word do *not* believe the whole Bible? No, but he gave that impression. He discouraged his hearers from endeavoring to rightly divide the Word of truth by implying that those who do so discard parts of the Bible as not for them. And this preacher was representative of a large proportion of the spiritual leaders in the church today.

Is it any wonder that the Christian masses use the Bible merely for devotional reading and often neglect even that? How can they be expected to have an interest in the *study* of the Scriptures when their leaders themselves fail to set the example? And one need but look about him to see the delinquency here. Where are the Bible teachers of yesterday? What has happened to the great Bible conferences that were held all over the land? How many pastors *teach* the Word to their congregations? And the missionaries and evangelists: is there not a widespread feeling that they do not need to study the Scriptures too thoroughly since "their business is to win souls"?

As a result, the vast majority of believers really *understand* very little of God's Word. They know the basic facts of salvation but seem quite satisfied to remain ignorant of precious truths which, if they but searched to find them, would make them *workmen* whom God could approve, not needing to be ashamed of their service for Him.

But rather than *study* to attain to a better *understanding* of the Word and become proficient in its *use*, many actually boast that they are satisfied with "the simple things"!

And this after all the earnest prayers of Paul that believers might have the spirit of *wisdom* and *revelation* in the *knowledge* of Christ (Eph. 1:17), that they might *know* what is theirs in Christ (Eph. 1:18-23) and *comprehend* the breadth and length and depth and height of it! (Eph. 3:18). This after all his *labor* and *strife* and *conflict* that they might have *"the full assurance of understanding"*! (Col. 1:28-2:2). This after all his prayers that they might "be *filled* with the *knowledge* of His will in all *wisdom* and *spiritual understanding"* (Col. 1:9). This after his stern rebuke of those carnal babes to whom he could preach no more than Christ *crucified*; whom he had to feed with milk alone because they were not able to digest solid food! (I Cor. 2 and 3).

Slothful Christians often consider themselves quite spiritual merely because their *emotions* are easily aroused. They boast of their contentment with "the simple things" while they should be

17

ashamed of their indifference to the written Word of God. They claim great devotion to God, yet neglect the one great means of knowing Him better. They profess fervent faith in Him, yet scarcely trouble to find out *just what He has said.* They do not, like David, meditate upon God's Word day and night nor, like the prophets, "enquire and search diligently" as to its true meaning.

The results of this attitude toward the Word are appalling, for such may trust Christ for salvation, but beyond this they exercise, in most cases, a blind, superstitious faith that cannot but *dis*honor God. *Feelings* are taken for *facts* and their own *wishes* for God's *Word.* They go into wrong paths, saying, "But I prayed very earnestly about it and now feel perfectly at peace." They say, "The Lord spoke to me," and refer to some *feeling* rather than to some passage of Scripture consistently applied. Thoughtlessly they say, *"If it's in the Bible I believe it,"* yet as they read the Bible they take to themselves only what warms their hearts and leave the rest unapplied, not knowing exactly why.

But those who boast of their contentment with "the simple things" and oppose dispensational Bible study on the ground that all the Bible is for us, have certainly missed the fact that all Scripture was given that the *man* of God might be *perfectly fitted and fully equipped for his work* (See II Tim. 3:17).

There is a great difference between the "child of God" and the *"man* of God" and no one who remains an infant in the truth can be approved as a *workman* for God or as a *soldier* of Jesus Christ, for the workmen God approves must know how to rightly divide the Word of truth and the soldiers

He honors must know how to wield the Sword of the Spirit.

We can sympathize with those who have *begun* to study the Bible dispensationally and have found it confusing. The study of almost any subject is confusing at first, but as we persevere we begin to *understand* and to reap the fruits of our toil. Indeed, to any thoughtful person the Scriptures must continue to be confusing until he learns to rightly divide and so to *understand* them. And what joy can compare with that of coming into a fuller understanding of God's Word?

It is written concerning the great spiritual revival under Ezra, when the law was read and explained to the people of Israel:

"And all the people went their way to eat, and to drink, and to send portions, and to make great mirth, BECAUSE THEY HAD UNDERSTOOD THE WORDS THAT WERE DECLARED UNTO THEM" (Neh. 8:12).

On the resurrection morning two disciples trudged wearily toward Emmaus, heart-broken because their Master had been crucified. They did not understand that according to the prophetic Word He *must* suffer and die before entering into His glory. Then the Lord Jesus Himself drew near and, unrecognized, explained this to them from the Scriptures until they understood and believed and rejoiced.

"And they said one to another, DID NOT OUR HEART BURN WITHIN US, WHILE HE TALKED WITH US BY THE WAY, AND WHILE HE OPENED TO US THE SCRIPTURES?" (Luke 24:32).

Studying the Bible dispensationally may seem confusing at first but actually it dispels confusion,

19

explains difficult problems, reconciles seeming contradictions and lends power to the believer's ministry.

If I should step inside a modern United States Post Office all would doubtless seem very confusing to me. But it would be a mistake to suggest piling all the mail neatly in one corner and handing it out promiscuously to all comers as some would do with the Bible. The postal employees must "rightly divide" the mail so that each person receives what is addressed to him. What seems like confusion to the novice is really a simplification of the work to be done in getting each person's private mail to him.

It is granted that in the Bible even that which was addressed to those of other dispensations is given to us for our learning and profit, but we must not confuse this with our own private mail or make the mistake of carrying out instructions meant particularly for others.

While I am reading mail addressed personally to me, a friend may hand *me*, for my interest or information, mail addressed to *him*. His mail and mine may all prove informative and profitable, but I must still be careful not to confuse the two, expecting to receive things promised to him or carrying out instructions addressed to him.

Thus all the Bible is *for* us, but it is not all addressed to us or written about us, and if we would really understand and enjoy it; if we would really know how to use it effectively in service for Christ, we must be careful always to note who is addressing whom, about what and when and why.

Chapter I.

THE PRINCIPLES AND DISPENSATIONS OF GOD

One of the first lessons the Bible student should learn is the difference between the principles and the dispensations of God.

The opponents of dispensationalism have often charged us with teaching, for example, that under the Old Testament men were saved by the works of the law, whereas today they are saved by grace through faith.

This charge is at least misleading, for no thinking dispensationalist would teach that the works of the law *in themselves* could ever save, or even help save, anyone.

We understand clearly that *"by the deeds of the law there shall no flesh be justified in His sight: for by the law is the knowledge of sin"* (Rom. 3:20). Nor do we suppose that the works of the *ceremonial* law had any essential power to save. We have not forgotten that the Scriptures also teach that *"it is not possible that the blood of bulls and of goats should take away sins"* (Heb. 10:4).

We have no illusions as to man's utter inability to please God by works *as such* in any age. Man has always been saved essentially by the grace of

God, through faith. There could be no other way to be saved. This is a fixed principle to which Hebrews 11 bears abundant testimony and it should be self-evident to those who accept as facts the utter depravity of man and the infinite holiness of God.

But this does not alter the fact that God's dealings with men and the stated terms of acceptance with Him have changed again and again down through the ages and that faith in Him would therefore be expressed in different ways. Hebrews 11 also bears consistent testimony to this fact.

Faith would most assuredly approach God in God's way at any time, and to seek to gain acceptance with Him in any other way would, of course, be *unbelief* and self-will. Thus, while works never did or could save *as such,* they did once save as *expressions of faith.*

THE PRINCIPLES OF GOD

A *principle,* as we have used the word above, is a settled rule of morality or conduct. We respect men with principles; men who stand for the right, whatever the cost. God, of course, has the very highest principles and never deviates from them. He always did and always will hate sin. Sin always was and always will be contrary to His holy nature. In no age has this been any less so than in any other age. In like manner, God always did and always will delight in righteousness, mercy and love. God never has and never will deviate in the slightest degree from these principles.

The *principle* of law or justice, for example, has continued unchanged through the ages. No matter

22

what the dispensation, when wrong is done God's sense of *justice* is offended. This may be simply demonstrated by three Scriptural examples:

Cain lived *before* the dispensation of the law by Moses. Cain murdered his brother Abel. Was this right or wrong? Did he get into trouble over it? He did, although the written law had not yet been given.

David lived *under* the law of Moses. He also committed murder. Was this right or wrong? Wrong, of course, and he also got into trouble over it.

You and I live *after* the law, under the dispensation of grace. Suppose we should commit murder, would that be right or wrong? Would we get into trouble over it—*with God?* Would the fact that Christ bore our sins on Calvary, make murder any more right? Would God look upon it as less sinful because it took place under the dispensation of grace?

You say, in the case of the true believer today, the full legal penalty for the sin would still have been borne by Christ and, though he knew it not, David too was forgiven on this ground. But does not the very fact that David's sins and ours were *paid for,* rather than overlooked, *prove* that the principles of law and justice remain fixed?

The principle of grace is equally unchangeable. This may be simply demonstrated by one passage of Scripture: Rom. 4:1-6:

Abraham lived *before* the dispensation of the law. How was he justified? *"Abraham believed*

23

God, and it was counted unto him for righteousness" (Rom. 4:3).

David lived *under* the law. How was he justified? *"David also describeth the blessedness of the man unto whom God imputeth righteousness without works"* (Rom. 4:6).

You and I live *after* the law, under the dispensation of grace. How are we justified? *"To him that worketh not, but believeth on Him that justifieth the ungodly, his faith is counted for righteousness* (Rom. 4:5).

Now in the cases of Abraham and David, works were *required* for salvation, whereas in our case works for salvation are distinctly *forbidden*; yet it is clear from the passages above that Abraham, David and we were *all* saved *essentially* by grace through faith and that works *as such* have never had any saving value.

THE DISPENSATIONS OF GOD

WHAT IS A DISPENSATION?

While the principles of God have to do with His *character,* His *nature*, the dispensations of God concern His *dealings* with those under Him, especially with man.

Many people have been frightened away from dispensationalism by the length of the word itself, especially since some who seek to rightly divide the Word have been called *Ultradispensationalists!* The root of this long word, however, has a very simple meaning, for the word *dispense* means simply *to deal out.* The word *dispensation,* then, means *the act of dispensing or dealing out,* or, *that which is dispensed or dealt out.* There are medical *dispensaries,* for example, where medicines are *dispensed* to the poor. Sometimes these *dispensations* are conducted on a particular day of each week. Now such a dispensation of medicine may take a full twelve hours each week, but it does not follow from this that a dispensation is a period of twelve hours! Yet there are some who, when they think of dispensations, can think of nothing but periods of time! Indeed, one of the greatest Bible teachers of the past generation defined a dispensation as follows: "A dispensation is a period of time during which man is tested in respect of obedience to some specific revelation of the will qf God."

This is incorrect, for a dispensation is *not* a period of time but *the act of dealing out* or *that which is dealt out.* The Bible teacher above referred to doubtless meant that a dispensation *covers* a period of time.

The word *dispensation* is not a mere theological term. It is used many times in the Bible, though not always translated thus. In Eph. 3:2, for example, Paul writes of *"the dispensation of the grace of God, which is given me to you-ward."* Just as the dispensation of the law was committed to Moses (John 1:17), so the dispensation of the grace of God was committed to Paul.

The organic meaning of the original word for *dispensation* (*oikonomia*) is *house management,* though its usage conforms closely to the English word dispensation. Sometimes this word is trans-

25

lated *stewardship* in the Authorized Version. This is interesting because the word *steward* (*oikonomos*), rather than meaning *servant,* as some have supposed, means *house manager.* The steward was the *head* servant, the one into whose hands the management of the house was committed. He dealt out the money for the household necessities, dispensed the food and clothing to the servants and children, paid the wages, etc. All was entrusted to him to dispense faithfully and wisely. He was the appointed *dispenser* of his Lord's goods and of the business of the household.*

Thus we read in Luke 12:42:

"And the Lord said, Who then is that faithful and wise steward [oikonomos] whom his lord shall make ruler over his household, to give them their portion of meat in due season?"

In Luke 16:1,2, where again the words *oikonomos* and *oikonomia* are translated *steward* and *stewardship,* we have the same idea:

"And He said also unto His disciples, There was a certain rich man, which had a steward; and the same was accused unto him that he had wasted his goods.

"And he called him, and said unto him, How is it that I hear this of thee? Give an account of thy steward-ship; for thou mayest be no longer steward."

In I Cor. 9:16,17 this same word is again translated *dispensation,* but once more it conveys the same idea:

"For though I preach the gospel, I have nothing to glory of: for NECESSITY IS LAID UPON ME; yea, woe is unto me if I preach not the gospel!

---

*Eliezer and Joseph were such stewards (Gen. 15:2, 24:2, 39:4).

26

"For if I do this thing willingly, I have a reward; but [even] if against my will [I MUST do it, for] A DISPENSATION OF THE GOSPEL IS COMMITTED UNTO ME."

Note that in each of these cases the idea of *responsibility* is involved. It was "a *faithful* and *wise* steward" the Lord sought to set over his household. The rich man discharged his steward because he had wasted his goods. Necessity, or responsibility, was laid upon Paul because "a dispensation of the gospel" had been committed to him.

One of the clearest passages of all in this connection is found in I Cor. 4:1,2, where the Apostle Paul says:

"LET A MAN SO ACCOUNT OF US AS OF THE MINISTERS [SERVANTS] OF CHRIST AND STEWARDS [DISPENSERS] OF THE MYSTERIES OF GOD.

"MOREOVER, IT IS REQUIRED IN STEWARDS THAT A MAN BE FOUND FAITHFUL."

Let us get this meaning of the word *dispensation* clearly fixed in our minds. When we see that a dispensation involves *responsibility* rather than merely denoting a period of time, we will, if sincerely desirous to be in the will of God, seek to understand clearly and to carry out faithfully, the dispensation of the grace of God committed to us.

CHANGES IN THE DISPENSATIONS
OF GOD

It must be evident to the most casual reader of the Scriptures that a great change in God's dealings with man took place at the fall. Previous to that Adam and Eve had enjoyed unbroken fellowship with God, dwelling in blissful innocence in the beautiful garden of Eden.

But now all was changed. Sin had caused a separation from God. Adam and Eve were driven from the garden. A sense of blameworthiness overcame them which, from then on, was to play a large part in their actions. Ashamed, now, to appear before God as they were, they had to be clothed. Adam had to earn a living for himself and his family by hard toil and Eve was to bring forth children in sorrow. Worst of all, sin had entered into the world, and death by sin. All this, of course, involved a change in man's responsibilities to God and to others.

From this point on God's dealings with men changed again and again. Human Government was instituted after the flood, with Noah (Gen. 9:6), the dispensation of promise began with Abram (Gen. 12:1-3), "the law was given by Moses" (John 1:17), "grace and truth came by Jesus Christ" (John 1:17) and was dispensed by Paul, the chief of sinners, saved by grace (Eph. 3:1-3).

The foregoing are some of the most prominent dispensational changes to date, but these may be sub-divided and there are still others to come.

Thus, while the principles of God never change, His dispensations, His dealings with men, do change from time to time. This includes even the terms of acceptance with God. At first blood sacrifices were required (Gen. 4:3-5, Heb. 11:4); then, later, circumcision was added (Gen. 17:14); then obedience to the whole Mosaic law was demanded (Ex. 19:5, 6, Rom. 10:5); then "the baptism of repentance for the remission of sins" (Mark 1:4, Acts 2:38) and today it is

"TO HIM THAT WORKETH NOT, BUT BELIEVETH ON HIM THAT JUSTIFIETH THE UNGODLY; HIS FAITH IS COUNTED FOR RIGHTEOUSNESS" (Rom. 4:5).

ADAM	ADAM	NOAH	ABRAHAM	MOSES	PAUL	CHRIST
Created In God's Image	Fallen In Sin	First Civil Ruler	Father Of Believers	The Law Giver	Chief of Sinners Saved	The Shepherd King
Gen. 1:26,27	Rom. 5:12	Gen. 9:1-7	Rom. 4:9-12	John 1:17	I Tim. 1:13-16	Jer. 23:5,6

THE PRINCIPLES OF GOD
ETERNAL AND UNCHANGEABLE
Salvation, always essentially by Grace through faith

The DISPENSATION of INNOCENCE	The DISPENSATION of CONSCIENCE	The DISPENSATION of HUMAN GOVERNMENT	The DISPENSATION of PROMISE	The DISPENSATION of LAW	The DISPENSATION of GRACE	The DISPENSATION of THE KINGDOM
Gen. 2:8-17 Gen. 2:25	Gen. 3:8-10 Rom. 2:11-15	Gen. 9:6 Rom. 13:1	Gen. 12:1-3 Gen. 22:17,18	Ex. 20:1-26 Gal. 3:19	Rom. 5:20,21 Eph. 3:1-4	Isa. 9:6,7 Isa. 11:1-9

This chart is not meant to indicate the *close* of any dispensation, but rather the changes or advances in God's dealings with men, for some of the dispensations have not yet closed. For example: while the call of Abraham ushered in the dispensation of promise, it did not bring the preceding dispensation to a close, for human government is still in force today.

Note carefully that while God *refuses* works for salvation today, He *required* them under other dispensations. This was not, as we have explained, because works *in themselves* could ever save, but because they were the necessary expression of faith when so required.

Tradition has it that men have always been saved through faith in the shed blood of Christ; that even those who lived before the cross had to look forward in faith to the death of a coming Christ for salvation.

It is high time that this false notion, so deeply rooted in the minds of even sincere believers, be shattered, for it does not have one single line of Scriptural support.

Let us not be misunderstood. It is true that all the saints of past ages were saved through the *merits* of Christ's shed blood, but not through their *faith* in that shed blood. Those of past ages were expected to believe only what God had thus far revealed, or what He had revealed to *them*. In other words, they were saved simply because they trusted God and believed what He said. The full plan of salvation has since been unfolded, but the Scriptures make it crystal clear that these believers were saved without even understanding that Christ would die for them.

I Pet. 1:10,11 alone makes this clear:

"OF WHICH SALVATION THE PROPHETS HAVE INQUIRED AND SEARCHED DILIGENTLY, who prophesied of the grace that should come unto you:

"SEARCHING WHAT, or what manner of time, THE SPIRIT OF CHRIST WHICH WAS IN THEM DID SIGNIFY, WHEN IT [HE] TESTIFIED BEFOREHAND THE SUFFERINGS OF CHRIST, AND THE GLORY THAT SHOULD FOLLOW."

Mark well, they did not search merely concerning the "manner of time," i.e., the character of the times, during which these things should transpire. They searched and inquired diligently to discover "WHAT . . . the Spirit . . . did signify," i.e., *what He meant,* "when He testified beforehand the sufferings of Christ and the glory that should follow." And the next verse goes on to explain that God revealed to them that they were ministering, not to themselves, but to those of a future time.

Could anything be clearer from this than that they did *not even understand* what the Spirit meant when He predicted the sufferings of Christ? How, then, could they have been saved through faith in His shed blood?

An indignant opponent of dispensationalism once asked us: "Do you mean to tell us that Moses commanded the building of the tabernacle with its gate and curtains, its brazen altar and laver, its table of shewbread, its golden lampstand and altar of incense, its ark of the covenant and mercy seat, *and did not tell them that all these were types of Christ and His finished work?*"

Our reply was simply, *"What saith the Scripture?"* Is there any hint whatever that Moses told them that these things pointed to Christ or that he even had any idea of this himself? We *now* know that these things were typical of Christ and His work of redemption, and rejoice to see that God had this in mind all the while; that the cross was neither an accident nor an afterthought, but this revelation is conspicuously *absent* from the Old Testament record. There is no hint that Moses

31

even knew, much less taught, that these things were typical of Christ.*

If it is true that Moses and the prophets knew and understood about the coming death of Christ and had to trust in His shed blood for salvation, would this not also be true of the twelve apostles? Yet they had labored with Christ Himself for a considerable length of time, preaching the gospel of the kingdom, before He even *began* to tell them that He must suffer and die, and when He did tell them Peter rebuked Him for His "defeatist" attitude!

Matt. 16:21,22: "From that time forth began Jesus to show unto His disciples, how that He must go unto Jerusalem, and suffer many things of the elders and chief priests and scribes, and be killed, and be raised again the third day.

"Then Peter took Him, and began to rebuke Him, saying, Be it far from Thee, Lord: this shall not be unto Thee."

Later, when He told them again that these things must come to pass as predicted by the prophets, they did not have the slightest idea what He was talking about. This fact is impressed upon us by a three-fold emphasis in Luke 18:34:

1. "AND THEY UNDERSTOOD NONE OF THESE THINGS:

2. "AND THIS SAYING WAS HID FROM THEM,

---

*It is sometimes presumed from Deut. 18:15-19 that Moses must have known a good deal about the coming Redeemer, but this is reading things into the Scriptures. There is nothing about a *Redeemer* here. This passage merely states that God would raise up to Israel a *Prophet* to whom they should give heed or suffer the consequences. Shall it be assumed from this that Moses taught his people to trust in the future death of Christ for salvation? And if the very prophets who later *predicted* the death of Christ were not permitted to understand their own and each other's predictions, are we to suppose that Moses understood *more* than was revealed to them? Let us be careful about assuming that the Old Testament saints "must have understood" these things, and always ask, *"What saith the Scripture?"*

3. "NEITHER KNEW THEY THE THINGS WHICH WERE SPOKEN."

By this time they had been associated with Christ, preaching the gospel of the kingdom and working miracles, for at least two years, yet they did not even know that He would suffer and die. Does this mean that none of them were saved? Certainly not. It simply confirms what Peter says about the prophets searching and inquiring diligently what the Spirit, who spoke through them, meant when He testified beforehand the sufferings of Christ and the glory that should follow.

It may surprise some of our readers to find that even after the resurrection, at Pentecost, Peter himself did not see in the death of Christ what we see in it today. He now knew about the crucifixion, of course, as a historical fact, but he did not base any offer of salvation upon it. Indeed, he *blamed* Israel for it and when his hearers were convicted of their sins and asked what they should do, he replied:

"REPENT, AND BE BAPTIZED EVERY ONE OF YOU IN THE NAME OF JESUS CHRIST FOR THE REMISSION OF SINS . . ." (Acts 2:38).

Was this because he was out of the will of God or blinded by unbelief? No; he was "filled with the Holy Spirit" (Acts 2:4). It was simply that the "due time" had not yet arrived to make these things known.

This brings us again to the importance of a recognition of the distinctive ministry of Paul. It is not until Paul that we have what is properly called *"the preaching of the cross."* It is he who first says:

33

"BUT NOW THE RIGHTEOUSNESS OF GOD WITHOUT THE LAW IS MANIFESTED . . . .

"Even the righteousness of God which is by faith of Jesus Christ unto all and upon all them that believe . . . .

"BEING JUSTIFIED FREELY BY HIS GRACE THROUGH THE REDEMPTION THAT IS IN CHRIST JESUS:

"Whom God hath set forth to be a propitiation THROUGH FAITH IN HIS BLOOD, to declare HIS RIGHTEOUSNESS FOR THE REMISSION OF SINS THAT ARE PAST,* through the forbearance of God;

"To declare, I say, AT THIS TIME, His righteousness: that He might be just, and THE JUSTIFIER OF HIM WHICH BELIEVETH IN JESUS" (Rom. 3:21-26).

This is what the Apostle Paul meant by

"THE FAITH WHICH SHOULD AFTERWARDS BE REVEALED" (Gal. 3:23).

This is what he meant when he wrote of Christ:

"Who gave Himself a ransom for all, TO BE TESTIFIED IN DUE TIME.

"WHEREUNTO I AM ORDAINED A PREACHER, AND AN APOSTLE, (I SPEAK THE TRUTH IN CHRIST, AND LIE NOT;) A TEACHER OF THE GENTILES IN FAITH AND VERITY" (I Tim. 2:6,7).

But this will be further discussed in a later lesson. All we are seeking to establish here is the fact of *progressive revelation* and the utter unscripturalness of the tradition that those who lived before Christ were saved by looking forward in faith to His finished work.

This is not only established in a negative way in the Scriptures; it is also established in a positive way. It is not merely made plain that the saints

---

*i.e., "the transgressions that were under the first testament" (Heb. 9:15).

of past ages did *not* understand about Christ's death, but in many cases we are told exactly what they *did* know and believe to find acceptance with God.

We have stated that Hebrews 11 makes it clear that salvation has always been the reward of faith. There is one *constant* that runs all down through the chapter: *"By faith . . . By faith . . . By faith."* At the introduction to the long list of acts of faith wrought by individuals, we read that *"By it [faith] the elders obtained a good report"* and that *"without faith it is impossible to please [God]"* and the whole long list closes with the statement: *"These all . . . obtained a good report through faith"* (Verses 2,6,39).

But there are *variables* in Hebrews 11 too, for in almost every case these heroes of faith believed some different revelation of God and expressed their faith in some different way. But nowhere in this list of saints do we read of one who was saved by faith in the death of a coming Christ. It is *we* who *now* know that they were saved through the death of Christ. And when Christ is preached to *us, we* show *our* faith by ceasing our works and accepting with humble thanks what *He* has done for us.

In Heb. 11:4 we are told precisely how Abel obtained divine witness that he was righteous:

"BY FAITH ABEL OFFERED UNTO GOD A MORE EXCELLENT SACRIFICE THAN CAIN, BY WHICH HE OBTAINED WITNESS THAT HE WAS RIGHT-EOUS, GOD TESTIFYING OF HIS GIFTS; and by it he, being dead, yet speaketh."

This agrees with the record in Gen. 4:4,5:

"And the Lord had respect unto ABEL AND to HIS OFFERING,

"But unto CAIN AND to HIS OFFERING He had not respect."

There is not one word here about faith in the death of Christ. Abel obtained witness that he was righteous *because he brought the required sacrifice* and God testified, not of his faith in Christ, but of *his gifts*.

In Heb. 11:7 we are further told exactly how Noah became an heir of *"the righteousness which is by faith."*

"BY FAITH NOAH, being warned of God of things not seen as yet, moved with fear, PREPARED AN ARK, to the saving of his house [from the flood]; BY WHICH HE CONDEMNED THE WORLD AND BECAME HEIR OF THE RIGHTEOUSNESS WHICH IS BY FAITH."

Could anything be plainer than this? How did Noah become an heir of the righteousness which is by faith? By trusting in the death of a coming Christ? No, by believing what God had said about the flood, and building an ark.

And so on down the chapter. Each of these elders obtained a good report because he believed God's word to *him*.

What about Abraham, God's great example of faith? How was he justified?

"What saith the Scripture? ABRAHAM BELIEVED GOD AND IT WAS COUNTED UNTO HIM FOR RIGHTEOUSNESS" (Rom. 4:3).

But what had God said that Abraham believed? Had God told him about a coming Christ who would die on a cross for him? Read the record and see, for this passage in Romans is quoted from Gen. 15:5,6:

"And [the Lord] brought him forth abroad, and said, look now toward heaven, and tell [count] the stars, if thou be able to number them: and He said unto him, So shall thy seed be.

"AND HE BELIEVED IN THE LORD; AND HE COUNTED IT TO HIM FOR RIGHTEOUSNESS."

Again we ask: could anything be plainer than this? Is there one word here about the death of Christ? Certainly not. God simply promised here to multiply Abraham's seed, and Abraham believed God and trusted Him to keep His word. It was this simple faith in God that God counted to him for righteousness. We *now* know that it was on the *basis* of the coming death of Christ that God could justly do this, but that was not yet revealed to Abraham.

Later God gave the law and demanded perfect obedience for acceptance with Him (Ex. 19:5,6, Rom. 10:5). He knew, of course, that no man could keep it perfectly, but He knew too that true believers would earnestly seek to keep it and He would honor their faith in Him. Also, *He* had Christ in mind to pay the penalty for a broken law so that His righteousness might be imputed to those who had taken His word seriously.

That *He* had the plan of redemption in mind all the while is indicated by the fact that He had them put the covenant of the law in a coffin* and met them, through their high priest, at the blood sprin-

---

*The *ark* of the covenant was really the *coffin* of the covenant. The original word is translated *coffin* in Gen. 50:26.

kled mercy seat, but He did not explain the significance of all this to them. He must first *demonstrate* historically man's utter inability to keep God's holy law.

We know, for example, that David was really saved by God's grace, not by his own feeble works, but suppose he had proclaimed salvation *"without the law"* or, like Paul, had said: *"Let no man therefore judge you in meat, or in drink, or in respect of an holy day, or of the new moon, or of the sabbath days"* (Col. 2:16)! He would soon have been forced to abdicate his throne and would have been put to death for despising the written law of God.

Again we are told exactly how John the Baptist's hearers received the remission of sins. Was it by faith in the death of Christ, who had by then already appeared on the scene? Read the Scriptures and see:

"John did baptize in the wilderness, and preach THE BAPTISM OF REPENTANCE FOR THE REMISSION OF SINS" (Mark 1:4).

If these words do not mean what they say, then the Scriptures serve no purpose whatever as a revelation from God to man.*

Suppose while John preached the baptism of repentance for remission of sins, some Israelite had risen to say: *"To him that worketh not, but believeth on Him that justifieth the ungodly, his faith is counted for righteousness"* (Rom. 4:5)! He would have been taken out and stoned in accordance with the law.

---

*Had John understood all that we now see in his inspired statement in John 1:29, his whole message would have been different, but the time for this had not yet come.

Yes, and on the positive side we are even told how the 3,000 at Pentecost found the remission of sins:

"Now when they heard this, they were pricked in their heart, and said unto Peter and to the rest of the apostles, Men and brethren, what shall we do?

"Then Peter said unto them . . ."

What did he say? Note it carefully. Did he say: "Christ died for your sins. Simply trust Him and eternal life is yours"? He did not. His entire Pentecostal address will be searched in vain for any such statement. Indeed, Peter's hearers had become convicted because he had *charged* them with the guilt of Christ's death. And when they asked what they must do, Peter replied:

"REPENT, AND BE BAPTIZED EVERY ONE OF YOU IN THE NAME OF JESUS CHRIST FOR THE REMISSION OF SINS, AND YE SHALL RECEIVE THE GIFT OF THE HOLY GHOST" (Acts 2:37,38).

This was in perfect conformity with the requirements of the so-called "great commission," which the church of today seeks, in a half-hearted way, to carry out:

"And He said unto them, Go ye into all the world, and preach the gospel* to every creature.

"HE THAT BELIEVETH AND IS BAPTIZED SHALL BE SAVED; BUT HE THAT BELIEVETH NOT° SHALL BE DAMNED [CONDEMNED]" (Mark 16:15,16).

We are aware that some, to uphold their own baptism theories, have interpreted this to mean,

---

*Here many anticipate revelation. They suppose the eleven were sent out to preach "the gospel of the grace of God," which is not even mentioned until we come to Paul.

°Whether baptized or not.

"He that believeth and is saved ought to be baptized," but such wresting of the clear words of Scripture cannot but displease God and pervert our understanding of His program.

On the positive side, as on the negative, we again wait for the raising up of Paul before we learn of *"the gospel of the grace of God"* (Acts 20:24), *"the dispensation of the grace of God"* (Eph. 3:1,2) and *"the preaching of the cross,"* i.e., as glad news to be accepted by faith for salvation (I Cor. 1:18,23, Gal. 6:14, Rom. 3:25,26).

It is evident, then, that the saints of past ages were not all saved by believing the same things, for God did not reveal the same things to them all. Indeed, even the stated terms of salvation were changed from time to time.

ANTICIPATING REVELATION

It is one of the first principles of sound Bible interpretation not to anticipate revelation, yet how many unconsciously do this! They read the Old Testament and the gospel records as though the saints of those times must have understood all about the death of Christ as it is presented in Romans, Galatians and Ephesians!

Think a moment: Had Abel understood about the death of Christ for sin, would a blood sacrifice have been required of him? Should he not, in such a case, have rested in the complete redemption to be wrought by Christ? Would not the bringing of a blood sacrifice, in such a case, have indicated *unbelief* rather than faith?

40

Now that the death of Christ has been proclaimed for salvation, does God command *us* to offer animals in sacrifice? Suppose we should offer such sacrifices only as symbolic of His death, to help us worship Him better, would that be merely *unnecessary* or would it be *wrong*? In the light of Paul's epistles it would, of course, be wrong.* Yet many have a hazy idea that those who lived before Christ offered their sacrifices with the full understanding that they typified the death of Christ on Calvary. The fact is that these types were not understood until *after* the Antitype had appeared. We *now* rejoice, as we consider them, in the proof that God had Calvary in mind all the while; that the death of Christ was not an accident or an after-thought. But God was teaching one lesson at a time: first the shadows, then the substance; first the sacrifices, then later, Christ the great, all-sufficient Sacrifice.

THE HARMONY BETWEEN THE PRINCIPLES AND DISPENSATIONS OF GOD

But do not the principles and the dispensations of God conflict? No indeed. Men in every age have been saved simply by *believing God* and approaching Him in His appointed way. When works were required for salvation, they did not save *as such,* but only as the required expression of faith. With the Old Testament saints the bringing of the required sacrifices, etc., constituted "the obedience of faith." With us, resting in the finished work of

---

*And in the light of Paul's epistles it is equally *wrong* to observe any ceremony once required for salvation. See Col. 2:14,20.

Christ for salvation is "the obedience of faith." See Rom. 1:5, 6:17, 15:18, 16:26, Heb. 5:9, 11:8.

When God says, "Offer an animal in sacrifice and I will accept you," what will faith do? Faith will offer an animal in sacrifice, of course. Abel did this and was accepted, not because the blood of beasts can take away sins, but because he approached God in *God's* way. This is "the obedience of faith."

In the case of Cain we have a clear indication that God is not satisfied with mere works, as such, for Cain offered a more attractive-looking sacrifice than Abel, but was rejected because he did not bring the sacrifice which God had required (Gen. 4:5).

When God says: "Build an ark and I will save you and yours from the flood," what will faith do? Faith will build an ark, of course. And when Noah did this he showed his faith in God and "became an heir of the righteousness which is by faith."

When God says, "Obey my voice indeed and you will be Mine," what will faith do? Faith will try earnestly to obey. You say: But they could not obey perfectly, therefore would be rejected by God. We reply that we have already proved that works in themselves cannot save. It was only as Israelites recognized the law as *the Word of God* to them and *therefore* sought to obey it that they were saved. Such an effort to keep the law represented "the obedience of faith."

When God says, "Repent and be baptized for the remission of sins," what will faith do? Just one thing: repent and be baptized. We know that oceans of water cannot wash away one sin, yet when John the Baptist and Peter preached repentance and baptism for remission not one of their hearers would have interpreted their words to mean: "Trust in the death of Christ for salvation." Indeed, when God required water baptism for salvation the *only* way to manifest faith was to be baptized, and those who refused to do so were condemned for their unbelief:

"But the Pharisees and lawyers REJECTED THE COUNSEL OF GOD AGAINST THEMSELVES, BEING NOT BAPTIZED OF HIM" (Luke 7:30).

But when God says, *"BUT NOW the righteousness of God without the law is manifested"* (Rom. 3:21); *"To him that worketh not, but believeth on Him that justifieth the ungodly, his faith is counted for righteousness"* (Rom. 4:5); *"Being justified freely by His grace, through the redemption that is in Christ Jesus"* (Rom. 3:24); *"In whom we have redemption through His blood, the forgiveness of sins according to the riches of His grace"* (Eph. 1:7); *"Not by works of righteousness which we have done, but according to His mercy He saved us"* (Tit. 3:5); *"Not of yourselves: it is the gift of God: not of works, lest any man should boast"* (Eph. 2:8,9)— when God now says this, what will faith do? Faith will say, "This is the most wonderful offer ever made by God to man. I cannot refuse it. I will trust Christ as my Savior and accept salvation as the free gift of God's grace."

So the dispensations of God in no way conflict with His principles, for the Old Testament saints,

43

though saved instrumentally* by works, were saved essentially by grace through faith." But now the righteousness of God without the law has been *manifested* (Rom. 3:21). It was *"testified in due time"* through the Apostle Paul (I Tim. 2:6,7). He says it was given to him to *"declare,* I say, *at this time,* His righteousness: that He might be just, and the justifier of Him which believeth in Jesus" (Rom. 3:26). Thus, to bring works to God for salvation today would be *unbelief.*

A prominent opponent of these truths has argued that truth is *horizontal,* not vertical, i.e., that it runs on through the ages unchanged and unchangeable. This is true. *Truth* is horizontal, but *the revelation of truth is vertical,* i.e., God has *revealed* truth to man, not all at once, but a little at a time, *historically.* Noah knew more of God's revelation than Adam, Abraham than Noah, Moses than

---

*If I drive a screw into a piece of wood with a screwdriver, does the screwdriver do the work, or do I? Shall we say that we each did part of it? No. In one sense the screwdriver did it *all,* for I did not even touch the screw in the operation. But then, the screwdriver was merely the *instrument* I used, so *essentially* it was I who did it all.

So it was with salvation before the dispensation of grace was ushered in. When God required water baptism for the remission of sins, for example, men could get their sins remitted only by submitting to baptism. Thus *instrumentally* it was their baptism that procured for them the remission of sins, yet *essentially* it was *God* who saved them by grace when He saw their faith.

It may be argued that the believer in such a case had exercised faith in his heart *before* being baptized, so that baptism had nothing whatever to do with his salvation. The answer is that he believed that *being baptized* he would be accepted, and so was, in his heart, already baptized.

This is the answer to problems where impossibilities to fulfil the stated requirements are involved. Suppose, for example, a man, exercising true faith, was on his way to offer a sacrifice or to be baptized and, on his way, suddenly fell dead. Would he not be accepted? Surely he would; simply because he had come in faith to fulfil the requirement. Thus the thief on the cross was saved without water baptism in a day when baptism was required for the remission of sins, but who can doubt that he would have rejoiced at the opportunity to be baptized had he not been nailed to a cross?

Abraham, the twelve than Moses, Paul than the twelve.

Thus too, the *principles* of God are horizontal; they go on unchanged through every age. But the *dispensations* are *vertical* and follow one after another as God imparts new revelations to man.*

QUIZ

1. What is a dispensation? 2. What other word (besides *dispensation*) is sometimes used in the Authorized Version to translate *oikonomia*? 3. Prove by Scripture that the *moral* law could not, in itself, save from sin. 4. Prove by Scripture that the *ceremonial* law could not, in itself, save from sin. 5. In what sense did works once save? 6. Were men of past dispensations saved by the death of Christ? 7. Was this *preached* to them? 8. Were they *offered* salvation by faith in the death of a coming Christ? 9. Prove by Scripture that salvation by the blood of Christ, apart from works, was not *proclaimed* in Old Testament times. 10. Draw a chart or state in geometrical terms the difference between truth and the *revelation* of truth. 11. Explain how the dispensation of law did not violate God's principle of saving men by grace through faith. 12. Would it be wrong today to observe ordinances once required for salvation? 13. Would it be wrong to observe an ordinance once required for salvation, if we acknowledged that it had no saving value? 14. Prove this by Scripture . 15. What statement by our Lord concerning baptism has been changed by most Fundamentalists to make it correspond with their views on baptism? 16. Through whom did God first begin to dispense His message and program for today? 17. Prove this by Scripture. 18. Could any Old Testament person, refusing to bring sacrificial offerings, be saved? 19. Could any under John the Baptist or at Pentecost, refusing to be baptized, be saved? 20. Give Scriptural examples.

---

*See chart on page 29. This subject is furthed discussed in the author's booklet, *God's Plan of Salvation Made Plain*.

Chapter II

PROPHECY AND THE MYSTERY

THE MOST IMPORTANT DIVISION
OF THE BIBLE

The supposition that the most important division of the Bible is that between the Old and New Testaments has often been expressed in the statement: "The Old Testament is for the Jews; the New Testament is for us."

This is quite incorrect, however. First of all, the titles *Old Testament* and *New Testament* are not accurate designations of the two sections of the Bible which they are supposed to represent.

The covenant of the law (later called *the old covenant,* or *testament*) was not made until 2500 years of human history had elapsed. *"The law was given by Moses"* (John 1:17), about 1500 B.C., as recorded in Exodus 19 and 20. We are told concerning this period of time *"from Adam to Moses"* that "there [was] no law" (Rom. 5:13,14), i.e., *the* law had not yet been given.

This means that there is actually not one word of the old testament in Genesis. Indeed, Israel did not even emerge as a nation until her deliverance from Egypt described in Exodus. If, therefore, the

Old Testament is for the Jews and the New Testament for us, for whom is the book of Genesis?

As to the new covenant; this was not made until the death of Christ.

"... **He is the Mediator of the new testament [covenant] that by means of death . . . they which are called might receive the promise of eternal inheritance" (Heb. 9:15).**

It was in the shadow of the cross, as our Lord communed with His disciples, that He said:

"**This cup is the new testament in my blood, which is shed for you" (Luke 22:20).**

This means that the greater part of the four gospel records actually covers old testament rather than new testament history and that our Lord and His disciples all lived under the old covenant at that time.*

It should be noted too that both the actual old and new testaments, though they *affect* us, were *made* with *the nation Israel,* and that the new covenant simply promises that Israel will one day render spontaneously the obedience required of her under the old covenant. (Deut. 5:1-3, Jer. 31:31).

The most important division in the Bible, then, is not that between the so-called Old and New Testaments.

The most important division in the Bible is that between *prophecy* and the great *mystery* proclaimed by the Apostle Paul.

It is a striking fact that the very opening words of the Bible read: "In the beginning God created

---

*Hereinafter we nevertheless use the terms *Old Testament* and *New Testament* in the accepted sense by way of accommodation.

the heaven and *the earth.*" It does not say that He created the universe, but *the heaven* and *the earth.* This is because He had a purpose concerning the earth quite distinct from His purpose concerning heaven. His purpose concerning *the earth* and Christ's reign upon it is the subject of prophecy (II Pet. 1:16-19). His purpose concerning *heaven* and our exaltation there with Christ is the subject of *"the mystery"* (Eph. 2:4-10, 3:1-4). Into these two great subjects the Bible is basically divided.*

Concerning the kingdom on earth Zacharias said:

"Blessed be the Lord God of Israel; for He hath visited and redeemed His people,

"And hath raised up an horn of salvation for us in the house of His servant David;

"AS HE SPAKE BY THE MOUTH OF HIS HOLY PROPHETS, WHICH HAVE BEEN SINCE THE WORLD BEGAN" (Luke 1:68-70).

Again at Pentecost, Peter, speaking of the absence of Christ and of the signs of His return, said:

"Whom the heaven must receive until the times of restitution of all things, WHICH GOD HATH SPOKEN BY THE MOUTH OF ALL HIS HOLY PROPHETS SINCE THE WORLD BEGAN."

"YEA, AND ALL THE PROPHETS FROM SAMUEL AND THOSE THAT FOLLOW AFTER, AS MANY AS HAVE SPOKEN, HAVE LIKEWISE FORETOLD OF THESE DAYS" (Acts 3:21,24).

But concerning the body of Christ, with its heavenly calling and position, not one word is to be found in the pages of prophecy. Indeed, God kept

---
*See the author's book entitled, *The Two-fold Purpose of God.*

48

this great purpose a secret until He was ready to bring the body itself into being, and then He revealed it first to the Apostle Paul. The apostle says of this great purpose, that it was:

"KEPT SECRET SINCE THE WORLD BEGAN" (Rom. 16:25).

"A MYSTERY . . . ORDAINED BEFORE THE WORLD UNTO OUR GLORY" (I Cor. 2:7).

"IN OTHER AGES ... NOT MADE KNOWN" (Eph. 3:5).

"FROM THE BEGINNING OF THE WORLD . . . HID IN GOD" (Eph. 3:9).

"HID FROM AGES AND FROM GENERATIONS" (Col. 1:26).

Manifestly there is a great difference between that which was *"spoken by the mouth of all [God's] holy prophets since the world began"* and that which was *"kept secret since the world began."*

PROPHECY AND THE MESSIANIC KINGDOM

As we have seen, God's plan to establish the Messianic kingdom was no secret to the Jews of Christ's day. The kingdom is the very theme of Old Testament prophecy and is described there in great detail. Some of the principal facts to be noted in regard to it are as follows:

1. It will be set up on earth: *"I shall give Thee . . . the uttermost parts of THE EARTH for Thy possession"* (Psa. 2:8). *"THE EARTH shall be full of the knowledge of the Lord"* (Isa. 11:9). *"A King shall reign and prosper, and shall execute judgment and justice in THE EARTH"* (Jer. 23:5).

"He shall not fail nor be discouraged, till He have set judgment in THE EARTH" (Isa. 42:4).

The angels confirmed this when, at His birth, they praised God, saying: *"Glory to God in the highest, and ON EARTH peace, good will toward men"* (Luke 2:14).

Our Lord, too, confirmed it when He said: *"Blessed are the meek: for they shall inherit THE EARTH"* (Matt. 5:5), and taught His disciples to pray: *"Thy kingdom COME. Thy will be done IN EARTH, as it is in heaven"* (Matt. 6:10).

The kingdom which John the Baptist, our Lord and the twelve proclaimed "at hand" was indeed "the kingdom *of* heaven" (Matt. 3:1,2, 4:17, 10:5-7), but it was to be set up *on earth.* Now, while its *establishment* is held in abeyance, it is vested in Christ Himself in heaven (Col. 1:13), but *the goal of prophecy* is the *establishment* of the kingdom *on earth* (Rom. 11:25-29).

2. It will be a theocracy. God Himself will reign, in the person of Christ: *"They shall call His name Emmanuel, which being interpreted is, God with us"* (Isa. 7:14, Matt. 1:23). *"And His name shall be called . . . The mighty God"* (Isa. 9:6). *"The Lord shall be king over all the earth"* (Zech. 14:9). *"The King, the Lord of hosts"* (Zech. 14:16).

3. It will be centered at Jerusalem, Israel's capital city: *"Out of Zion shall go forth the law, and the Word of the Lord from Jerusalem"* (Isa. 2:3). *"The Lord of hosts shall reign in mount Zion, and in Jerusalem"* (Isa. 24:23). *"At that time they*

50

shall call Jerusalem the throne of the Lord" (Jer. 3:17). Thus He will reign primarily over Israel (Mic. 5:2).

This was confirmed by the angel Gabriel (Luke 1:32,33), by the Magi (Matt. 2:1,2) and by the Lord Himself (Matt. 19:28).

4. It will extend to all the earth: *"Yea, all kings shall fall down before Him: all nations shall serve Him"* (Psa. 72:11). *"And there was given Him dominion, and glory, and a kingdom, that all people, nations, and languages, should serve Him"* (Dan. 7:14). *"Yea, many people and strong nations shall come to seek the Lord of hosts in Jerusalem, and to pray before the Lord"* (Zech. 8:22).

5. All Israel will then be saved: *"They shall all know Me, from the least of them unto the greatest of them"* (Jer. 31:34). *"I will save them . . . and will cleanse them: so shall they be My people, and I will be their God"* (Ezek. 37:23).

This was confirmed by Paul in Romans 11:26, etc.

6. Israel's suffering and sorrow will then be over: *"Speak ye comfortably [comfortingly] to Jerusalem . . . that her warfare is accomplished, that her iniquity is pardoned"* (Isa. 40:2). *"Give unto them beauty for ashes, the oil of joy for mourning, the garment of praise for the spirit of heaviness"* (Isa. 61:3). *"They shall obtain joy and gladness, and sorrow and sighing shall flee away"* (Isa. 35:10).

7. Israel will then become a blessing to all nations:

51

"'And the Gentiles shall come to thy light, and kings to the brightness of thy rising" (Isa. 60:3). *"And it shall come to pass, that as ye were a curse among the heathen, O house of Judah, and house of Israel; so will I save you, and ye shall be a blessing"* (Zech. 8:13). *"In those days it shall come to pass, that ten men shall take hold, out of all languages of the nations, even shall take hold of the skirt of him that is a Jew, saying, We will go with you: for we have heard that God is with you"* (Zech. 8:23).

These promises date back to the covenant which God made with Abraham: *"I will multiply thy seed . . . and in thy seed shall all the nations of the earth be blessed"* (Gen. 22:17,18).

8. Government will be purified: *"With righteousness shall He judge the poor, and reprove with equity for the meek of the earth"* (Isa. 11:4). *"As the earth bringeth forth her bud, and as the garden causeth the things that are sown in it to spring forth; so the Lord God will cause righteousness and praise to spring forth before all the nations"* (Isa. 61:11). *"A King shall reign and prosper, and shall execute judgment and justice in the earth"* (Jer. 23:5).

9. War and bloodshed will be abolished.* *"His name shall be called . . . The Prince of Peace"* (Isa. 9:6). *"And He shall judge among the nations, and shall rebuke many people: and they shall beat their swords into plowshares, and their spears into prun-*

---

*When Satan is "loosed for a little season" at the close of the millennium, he will deceive many and gather an army together against Jerusalem, but ere his soldiers even begin to fight, fire from heaven will devour them and Satan himself will be cast into the lake of fire (Rev. 20:7-10).

inghooks: *nation shall not lift up sword against nation, neither shall they learn war any more"* (Isa. 2:4).

10. Health and long life will be restored to the human race: *"Then the eyes of the blind shall be opened, and the ears of the deaf shall be unstopped. Then shall the lame man leap as an hart, and the tongue of the dumb sing"* (Isa. 35:5,6). *"There shall be no more thence an infant of days, nor an old man that hath not filled his days: for the child shall die an hundred years old; but the sinner being an hundred years old shall be accursed"* (Isa. 65: 20).*

11. The animal creation will be tamed: *"The wolf also shall dwell with the lamb, and the leopard shall lie down with the kid; and the calf and the young lion and the fatling together; and a little child shall lead them. And the cow and the bear shall feed; their young ones shall lie down together: and the lion shall eat straw like the ox. And the sucking child shall play on the hole of the asp, and the weaned child shall put his hand on the cockatrice' den. They shall not hurt nor destroy in all my holy mountain"* (Isa. 11:6-9).

12. The curse will be removed from the vegetable creation: *"The desert shall rejoice, and blossom as a rose. It shall blossom abundantly . . . for in the wilderness shall waters break out, and streams in the desert. And the parched ground shall become a pool, and the thirsty land springs of water"* (Isa. 35:1,2,6,7).

---

*i.e., He who dies at 100 years old will be considered a child and will have been accursed because of sin, which will not be tolerated at that time.

THE PROPHETIC WORD AND THE
BELIEVER TODAY

All Scripture is, of course, equally important *as the Word of God,* and all profitable to the man of God. Yet the thoughtful student of the Word soon discovers that certain passages have a more *direct* bearing upon others than upon himself and are in that sense more important to those *directly* involved.

The command to keep the Passover, for example, *directly* involved the Israelites under the law and was, in that sense, of greater importance to them than to us.

In the same way prophecy (except Paul's) deals *directly* with Israel and the nations, not with the body of Christ.

While a deep interest in the prophetic word is commendable, we must not forget that there is nevertheless another great body of truth which more *directly* concerns us.

When God finally set the nation Israel aside He said, through the Apostle Paul:

"Be it known therefore unto you, that THE SALVA-TION OF GOD IS SENT UNTO THE GENTILES, and that they will hear it" (Acts 28:28).

Therefore Paul says, by inspiration:

". . . I SPEAK TO YOU GENTILES, INASMUCH AS I AM THE APOSTLE OF THE GENTILES, I MAGNIFY MINE OFFICE" (Rom. 11:13).

Thus, while Israel and the prophetic program are temporarily set aside, the church is made up predominantly of Gentiles in the flesh, with Paul as their apostle.

54

This is why the apostle speaks of *"this mystery among the Gentiles"* (Col. 1:27) and explains to the Gentile believers of this day:

"For I would not, brethren, that ye should be ignorant of THIS MYSTERY, lest ye should be wise in your own conceits; THAT BLINDNESS IN PART IS HAPPENED TO ISRAEL, UNTIL THE FULNESS OF THE GENTILES BE COME IN" (Rom. 11:25).

When the period here referred to has run its course, God will again resume His dealings with Israel and bring the prophetic program to a conclusion, as the next verses state:

"And so ALL ISRAEL SHALL BE SAVED: AS IT IS WRITTEN, There shall come out of Sion the Deliverer, and shall turn away ungodliness from Jacob:

"FOR THIS IS MY COVENANT UNTO THEM . . ." (Rom. 11:26,27).

This interruption of the prophetic program must be borne in mind in any consideration of the importance of the prophetic word. While *as the Word of God,* prophecy is fully as important as any other part of the Scripture, it deals *directly* with Israel and the nations, not with the body of Christ.

Thus it is Peter, not Paul, who says:*

"We have also a more sure word of prophecy;° whereunto ye do well that ye take heed [(] as unto a light that shineth in a dark place, until the day dawn and the day star arise [)] in your hearts" (II Pet. 1:19).

---

*We believe that these apostles of the circumcision were inspired to write particularly for a future day. When the body of Christ has been caught up and the time of tribulation begins, Israel will be "scattered" (I Pet. 1:1, James 1:1) and *"the* end of all things" will again be "at hand" (I Pet. 4:7), (I John 2:18).

°We regret the rendering which reads: *"We have also the word of prophecy made more sure,"* i.e., by Peter's personal vision of the transfigured Christ. How could *anything* make the Word of God more sure?

55

Again it is John, not Paul, who writes in his introduction to *The Revelation*:

"Blessed is he that readeth, and they that hear the words of this prophecy, and keep those things which are written therein: for the time is at hand" (Rev. 1:3).

A blessing, of course, comes to any one who reverently studies *any* part of the blessed Book, but this special blessing will be the portion of those who study *the Book of the Revelation* and keep its precepts in that day when the revelation of Christ in glory will again be at hand.

Hence it is important to remember that while all Scripture is indeed for us, Paul's epistles constitute our *private mail*. It is Paul who was specially chosen of God as the apostle of the Gentiles and the one through whom the mystery was to be revealed.

What a pity, in this dispensation of the grace of God, that the church abounds with "prophetic experts," while "experts" in "this mystery among the Gentiles" are so rare!

THE REVELATION OF THE MYSTERY

Many "mysteries" are to be found in the Scriptures, but one stands out pre-eminently as *"The Mystery:"* the great body of truth committed by revelation to the Apostle Paul.

When Messiah first appeared on earth, God did not immediately establish His kingdom by force. The kingdom was first proclaimed "at hand" and offered for acceptance. This proclamation and offer was, of course, made to Israel, for the Gentiles had long been given up, "even as they did not like to retain God in their knowledge" (Rom. 1:28). But Israel proved herself no better than the Gentiles as she took the heaven-sent King, nailed Him to a tree and then, when God raised Him from the dead, still stood by her awful deed, defying the resurrected and glorified Christ and waging relentless war against those who dared to acknowledge Him as Messiah.

"He was in the world, and the world was made by Him, and the world knew Him not.

"He came unto His own, and His own received Him not" (John 1:10,11).

And so, before the actual bringing in of the glorious reign of Christ, man was allowed to demonstrate his own moral failure and see for himself that the establishment of the long-promised kingdom would not be the result of his own efforts or character but of the grace and power of God, for man had done everything in his power to *hinder* the bringing in of the kingdom.

But *"where sin abounded, grace did much more abound"* (Rom. 5:20). When Israel rejected her Messiah, God cast her aside (temporarily) along with the other nations, that He might offer to all His enemies everywhere reconciliation by grace alone, through faith in the rejected Christ. Thus "the dispensation of the grace of God" was ushered in (Eph. 3:2) so that those willing to accept God's grace might be reconciled to Him in one body by the cross (Eph. 2:16).

"FOR GOD HATH CONCLUDED THEM ALL IN UNBELIEF, THAT HE MIGHT HAVE MERCY UPON ALL" (Rom. 11:32).

"AND THAT HE MIGHT RECONCILE BOTH [JEWS AND GENTILES] UNTO GOD IN ONE BODY BY THE CROSS, HAVING SLAIN THE ENMITY THEREBY.

"And came and preached peace to you [Gentiles] which were afar off, and to them [Israelites] that WERE nigh" (Eph. 2:16,17).

Nothing of this is to be found anywhere in prophecy. It was a surprise of grace, so to speak, "hid from ages and from generations"; "kept secret since the world began."

The main features of this hitherto unrevealed program were as follows:

1. Israel set aside, temporarily, along with the Gentiles: *"Israel hath not obtained that which he seeketh for"* (Rom. 11:7). *"The fall of them"* (Rom. 11:12). *"The casting away of them"* (Rom. 11:15). *"Because of unbelief they were broken off"* (Rom. 11:20). *"For God hath concluded them all in unbelief"* (Rom. 11:32).

2. Mercy shown to all alike: *"For God hath concluded them all in unbelief THAT HE MIGHT HAVE MERCY UPON ALL* (Rom. 11:32). *"For there is NO DIFFERENCE between the Jew and the Greek: for THE SAME LORD OVER ALL is RICH UNTO ALL THAT CALL UPON HIM. For whosoever shall call upon the name of the Lord shall be saved"* (Rom. 10:12,13). *"For there is one God, and one Mediator between God and men, the Man Christ Jesus"* (I Tim. 2:5).

58

3. The gospel of the grace of God, through Christ's finished work, proclaimed: Hence Paul's claims concerning *"the ministry which I have received of the Lord Jesus, to testify THE GOSPEL OF THE GRACE OF GOD"* and *"THE DISPENSATION OF THE GRACE OF GOD which is given me to you-ward"* (Acts 20:24, Eph. 3:2).

4. Believers reconciled to God by the cross: *"God was in Christ, RECONCILING the world unto Himself"*,(II Cor. 5:19). *"That He might RECONCILE both [Jews and Gentiles] unto God . . . BY THE CROSS"* (Eph. 2:16). *"When we were enemies, we were RECONCILED to God BY THE DEATH OF HIS SON"* (Rom. 5:10). *"And you, that were sometime alienated and enemies . . . yet now hath He RECONCILED in the body of His flesh THROUGH DEATH"* (Col. 1:21,22).

5. Jewish and Gentile believers thus baptized into one body: *"That He might reconcile both unto God in ONE BODY by the cross"* (Eph. 2:16). *"That the Gentiles should be fellowheirs [joint heirs], and of THE SAME BODY [of a joint body], and partakers [joint partakers] of His promise in Christ by the gospel"* (Eph. 3:6). *"There is ONE BODY"* (Eph. 4:4). *"For by one Spirit are we all baptized into ONE BODY, whether we be Jews or Gentiles"* (I Cor. 12:13). *"Now ye are THE BODY OF CHRIST, and members in particular"* (I Cor. 12:27). *"So we, being many, are ONE BODY in Christ, and every one members one of another"* (Rom. 12:5). *"For as many of you as have been baptized into Christ have put on Christ. There is*

neither Jew nor Greek . . . for ye are all one in Christ Jesus" (Gal. 3:27,28).

6. This body of believers given a position in Christ in the heavenlies: *"And [God] hath raised us up together and made us sit together in heavenly places in Christ Jesus"* (Eph. 2:6). *"[God] hath blessed us with all spiritual blessings in heavenly places in Christ"* (Eph. 1:3). *"For our conversation [citizenship] is in heaven"* (Phil. 3:20). *"If ye then be risen with Christ, seek those things which are above, where Christ sitteth on the right hand of God. Set your affection on things above . . . for . . . your life is hid with Christ in God"* (Col. 3:1-3).

How vastly different this is from the reigning of Christ on earth at Jerusalem over Israel and the nations! How different from peace on earth with all Israel saved, war and disease abolished, the animal creation tamed and the curse removed from the vegetable creation!

What a pity that these great distinctions between prophecy and the mystery have not been more generally observed!

TAKING GOD AT HIS WORD

Because of a failure to recognize the mystery, some have supposed it necessary to alter prophecy to account for the present condition of Israel and the presence of the predominantly Gentile church of this age.

Seeing that the fulfillment of prophecy apparently ceased shortly after the crucifixion of Christ, and realizing that there was still much left to be fulfilled, these have supposed that God could not have meant exactly what He said when He prophesied that Christ would sit on the throne of David in Jerusalem as King of Israel. They have supposed that these things must have been intended in a *"spiritual"* sense and so have concluded that Christ is *now* seated on "David's throne" at God's right hand, thus confusing earthly Jerusalem with "the Jerusalem which is above." They have further concluded that the church of today is "spiritual" Israel, that heaven is Canaan, etc.

But there is in fact nothing spiritual about this interpretation of the Scripture. It is *carnal,* not spiritual, to fail to take God at His Word and to seek to explain away difficulties by arbitrarily altering what has been plainly written.

We vigorously object to this whole system of interpretation because:

1. *It leaves us at the mercy of theologians.* If the Scriptures do not mean what they obviously, naturally seem to mean, who has the authority to decide just what they do mean? If theologians have that authority, then we must agree with Rome that the Church, not the Bible, is the final and supreme authority. Nor will it any longer avail us to turn to the Scriptures for light, for the Word of God does not mean what it says and only trained theologians can tell us what it does mean.

2. *It affects the veracity of God.* It is a thrust at His very honor. If the obvious, natural meaning of the Old Testament promises is not to be depended upon, how can we depend upon *any* promise of God?

61

Then, when He says: "Whosoever shall call upon the name of the Lord shall be saved," He may also mean something else. This is unthinkable of God, for it is *only just* that the promisee should have a fair understanding of the promise, for promised something, he will have a right to *claim* exactly what he has been promised. A little child is supposed to have said: "If God didn't mean what He said, why didn't He say what He meant?"

3. *It endorses apostasy.* Indeed, it is the *mother* of apostasy. When Luke 1:32,33 is "spiritualized" the Modernist agrees wholeheartedly. He agrees that the throne of David and the house of Israel in this passage must be viewed in a "spiritual sense"—*and so must the next few verses!* Thus Christ was not *really* born of a virgin. This picture is merely drawn to impress us with the purity of His person, etc.!

And the Modernist denies the resurrection in the same way. Concerning Acts 2:30-32 it is argued that since Christ will not really occupy the throne of David, *neither was He really raised from the dead!* The Scriptures which say so must be "spiritually" interpreted!

And here comes one of "Jehovah's Witnesses," claiming to belong to the 144,000. Ask what tribe he is from and he will explain that not physical, but "spiritual" Israelites are referred to in the prophecy of the 144,000! Yet we are distinctly told that there are to be 12,000 *from each tribe, and the tribes are named!*

Rome employs the same reasoning. She is seeking to establish the kingdom of Christ on earth!

Because the Church of Rome is really a political system, with a state and a ruler on earth it may seem at first that she leans rather to a literal interpretation of prophecy, but this is not so, for the Church of Rome is not literal Israel, Rome is not Jerusalem, and Christ Himself is not reigning.

Those who have resorted to the "spiritualization" of the prophetic Scriptures because they cannot account for the seeming cessation in their fulfillment, will find the solution to their problem in the recognition of the mystery. Recognize the mystery and there will be no need to alter prophecy.

THE IMPORTANCE OF THE MYSTERY TO US

Before further considering this great body of truth let us note the surpassing importance of it *to us*. We say *to us* because Paul was sent particularly to the *Gentiles* with this revelation (Eph. 3: 1-3).

1. God has made it known:

"HAVING MADE KNOWN UNTO US THE MYSTERY OF HIS WILL" (Eph. 1:9).

2. It is His will that all see it:

"AND TO MAKE ALL MEN* SEE WHAT IS THE FELLOWSHIP [Gr. oikonomia, DISPENSATION] OF THE MYSTERY" (Eph. 3:9).

3. Paul asked prayers for open doors to make it known:

"PRAYING . . . THAT GOD WOULD OPEN UNTO US A DOOR OF UTTERANCE TO SPEAK THE MYSTERY OF CHRIST" (Col. 4:3).

---

*The word *men* is not found in the original. Cf. Eph. 3 :10.

4. He asked prayers for an open mouth and boldness to proclaim it:

"THAT I MAY OPEN MY MOUTH BOLDLY, TO MAKE KNOWN THE MYSTERY OF THE GOSPEL" (Eph. 6:19).

5. A knowledge of it imparts spiritual encouragement and enlightenment:

"THAT THEIR HEARTS MIGHT BE COMFORTED [ENCOURAGED] . . . UNTO ALL RICHES OF THE FULL ASSURANCE OF UNDERSTANDING . . . THE ACKNOWLEDGEMENT [Gr. epignosis, FULL KNOWLEDGE] OF THE MYSTERY" (Col. 2:2).

6. Believers are established by it:

"NOW TO HIM THAT IS OF POWER TO STABLISH YOU ACCORDING TO MY GOSPEL, AND THE PREACHING OF JESUS CHRIST ACCORDING TO THE REVELATION OF THE MYSTERY" (Rom. 16:25).

7. Proclaimed for the obedience of faith:

"NOW . . . MADE MANIFEST, AND BY THE SCRIPTURES OF THE PROPHETS [Gr. PROPHETIC SCRIPTURES*] . . . MADE KNOWN TO ALL NATIONS FOR THE OBEDIENCE OF FAITH" (Rom. 16:26).

BASIC DISTINCTIONS BETWEEN PROPHECY AND THE MYSTERY

PROPHECY	THE MYSTERY°
Concerns a *kingdom*; a political organization (Dan. 2:44, Matt. 6:10).	Concerns a *body*; a living *organism* (I Cor. 12:12,27, Eph. 4:12-16).
The kingdom to be established *on earth* (Jer. 23:5, Matt. 6:10).	The body given a position *in heaven* (Eph. 1:3, 2:5-6, Col. 3:1-3).

*i.e., Paul's own writings. Certainly not the Old Testament Scriptures. See the *"now"* in Eph. 3:5.

°Those who question whether the items listed under this heading are associated with the mystery have but to search and see whether they can find them in prophecy.

Christ to be its *King* (Jer. 23.5, Isa. 9:6,7).

Christ its living *Head* (Eph. 1:19-23, Col. 1:18).

The kingdom *prophesied "since the world began"* (Luke 1:68-70, Acts 3:21).

The body chosen in Christ before the world began, but *"kept secret since the world began"* (Rom. 16:25, Eph. 1:4-11, 3:5-9).

Israel to be given *supremacy* over the nations (Isa. 60:10-12, 61:6).

Jew and Gentile placed on the *same level* before God (Rom. 10:12, 11:32, Eph. 2:16,17).

The Gentiles to be blessed through Israel's *instrumentality* (Gen. 22:17,18, Zech. 8:13).

The Gentiles blessed through Israel's *obstinacy* (Acts 13:44-46, Rom. 11:28-32).

The Gentiles to be blessed through Israel's *rise* (Isa. 60:1-3, Zech. 8:22,23).

The Gentiles blessed through Israel's *fall* (Acts 28:27,28, Rom. 11:11,12,15).

Prophecy mainly concerns *nations* as such (Isa. 2:4, Ezek. 37:21,22).

The mystery concerns *individuals* (Rom. 10:12,13, II Cor. 5:14-17).

Prophecy concerns blessings, both material and spiritual, *on earth* (Isa. 2:3, 4, 11:1-9, etc.).

The mystery concerns "all spiritual blessings *in the heavenlies"* (Eph. 1:3, Col. 3:1-3).

Prophecy concerns Christ's *coming to the earth* (Isa. 59:20, Zech. 14:4).

The mystery explains Christ's present *absence from the earth* (Eph. 1:20-23, Col. 3:1-3).

In prophecy salvation by grace through faith *alone* is not contemplated.

Salvation by grace through faith alone lies at the very heart of the mystery (Rom. 3:21-26, 4:5, Eph. 2:8,9).

65

The proclamation of the prophetic program committed particularly to *the twelve* (Matt. 10:5-7, Acts 1:6-8, 3:19-26).

The proclamation of the mystery committed particularly to *Paul* (Eph. 3:1-3, 8,9, Col. 1:24-27).

The prophetic program revealed through *many* of God's servants (Luke 1:70, II Pet. 1:21).

The mystery revealed through *one* man: Paul (Gal. 1:1,11,12, 2:2,7,9, Eph. 3:2,3).*

Old testament writers frequently did not understand the prophecies made known through them (Dan. 12:8-10, I Pet. 1:10-12).

Paul both understood and longed that others might understand the mystery revealed through him. (Eph. 1:15-23, 3:14-21, Col. 1:9-10, 2:1-3).

QUIZ

1. Which is the most important division of the Bible?
2. When and through whom was the old covenant (or testament) made? 3. When and through whom was the new covenant made? 4. What is the main subject of prophecy? 5. What form of government will prevail in the Messianic kingdom? 6. Where will the kingdom be set up? 7. What great change will take place in Israel with the establishment of this kingdom? 8. What will be the relation of the Gentiles to Israel in the Messianic kingdom? 9. What is the main subject of the mystery? 10. At what point in Israel's history did God begin to reveal the mystery? 11. What is the relative status of Gentiles

---

*It is sometimes argued from Eph. 3:5 that Paul was only one of many "apostles and prophets" to whom the mystery was revealed. The words "by the Spirit" are significant in this connection. Paul first received the truth of the mystery "by the revelation of Jesus Christ" (Gal. 1:12, Eph. 3:3, etc.). He then "went up by revelation" and communicated it to the leaders at Jerusalem (Gal. 2:2) and they "saw" and "perceived" it and gave Paul and Barnabas, his companion, "the right hands of fellowship" (Gal. 2:7,9). It was "by the Spirit," of course, that they "saw" and "perceived" these truths, but not until Paul had communicated them to them.

to Jews before God today? 12. What is the relation between Jewish and Gentile *believers* today? 13. Where is the believer's position and citizenship today? 14. What erroneous method of interpretation have some theologians applied to the kingdom prophecies? 15. What has caused them to adopt this method? 16. How does this method of interpretation affect the rest of Scripture? 17. What is the relation of this method to the prevailing heresies of our day? 18. What is the solution to the problem which has caused some theologians to adopt this method? 19. Name five basic distinctions between prophecy and the mystery. 20. Give five Scriptures to show the importance of the mystery.

Chapter III.

THE TWO-FOLD ASPECT OF
THE MYSTERY

THE TWO-FOLD MEANING OF
THE TERM

The Greek word *musterion,* rendered *mystery* in the Authorized Version, has a two-fold meaning. It may mean merely *what is kept hidden,* or it may mean *something understood only by the initiated.* It may also mean both at the same time.

The original word is perhaps closer in meaning to our word *secret* than it is to *mystery* in its modern usage. We may speak of *keeping a thing a secret,* i.e., not telling it out, or we may speak of *the secret* of a man's success, i.e., the *key,* the *clue* to his success.

The great mystery revealed through Paul is spoken of in both ways—sometimes both together:

1. *The mystery* is a truth which was *intentionally kept hidden* until revealed to and through the Apostle Paul: He says it was *"kept secret since the world began"* (Rom. 16:25), *"in other ages . . . not made known," "from the beginning of the world . . . hid in God"* (Eph. 3:5,9), *"hid from ages and from generations"* (Col. 1:26).

2. Now that it has been revealed it is still *comprehended only by the initiated*: Hence the apostle

prays *"that the God of our Lord Jesus Christ, the Father of glory, may give unto you the spirit of wisdom and revelation in the knowledge of Him"* (Eph. 1:17 and cf. Ver. 9), *"that ye might be filled with the knowledge of His will in all wisdom and spiritual understanding," "The mystery . . . now . . . made manifest to His saints: to whom God would make known what is the riches of the glory of this mystery among the Gentiles," "the full assurance of understanding . . . the acknowledgment* [Gr. *epignosis, full knowledge] of the mystery"* (Col. 1:9, 26,27, 2:2). It is therefore of the utmost importance that we seek light and understanding from the Holy Spirit in the study of this great subject.

THE MYSTERY OF THE GOSPEL

or

THE SECRET OF THE GOOD NEWS

In closing the most sublime of all his letters, the Apostle Paul writes:

"And [pray] for me, that utterance may be given unto me, that I may open my mouth boldly, to make known THE MYSTERY OF THE GOSPEL,

"For which I am an ambassador in bonds: that therein I may speak boldly, as I ought to speak" (Eph. 6:19,20).

The precise wording of the phrase *"mystery of the gospel"* should be carefully noted. The apostle is not speaking here of the good news of a secret, but of the *secret* of, or *key* to, the *good news.**

---

*The term *gospel* (Gr. *evangelion*) means simply *good news* and should always be thought of in this way.

GOOD NEWS PROCLAIMED EVER
SINCE THE FALL

Along with the idea that the Old Testament saints trusted in the coming death of Christ for salvation, goes the notion, equally unscriptural, that there never has been more than one gospel.

This will be thoroughly discussed in a later chapter, but here it is necessary to point out the simple fact that ever since the fall God has proclaimed gospel, or good news, to sinners.

Was it not gospel, or good news, God announced to fallen Adam and Eve when He promised that Eve's seed would eventually crush the Serpent's head (Gen. 3:15)? Was it not good news God proclaimed to Abram when He said that in him all the families of the earth would be blessed (Gen. 12:3, cf. Gal. 3:8)? Was it not good news God made known to David when He promised to establish his house and throne and kingdom forever (II Sam. 7:16)? Was it not good news God revealed through the prophets, that peace and prosperity and blessing should prevail in the coming kingdom (Isa. 2:2-4, 11:6-9, 35:1-7, Jer. 23:5)? Was it not good news John the Baptist proclaimed when he introduced Christ and announced the kingdom "at hand" (Matt. 3:2,3)? Was it not good news Peter preached when later he actually *offered* the kingdom to Israel, crying: *"Repent . . . the times of refreshing shall come from the presence of the Lord; and He shall send Jesus Christ, which before was preached unto you"* (Acts 3:19,20)?

All this was *gospel,* or good news, but what was *"the mystery of the gospel;"* what was the *secret* of

70

the good news? How could a holy and righteous God proclaim *good news* to *sinners?* How could He *justly* offer them good things to come when, as sinners, they *deserved* His wrath?

The answer to this is found in the epistles of Paul.

THE SECRET OF THE GOSPEL
PROCLAIMED BY PAUL

If anything is made clear in the Pauline epistles it is the fact that the secret of all God's good news to man is centered in *Calvary.* It was because Christ was to die for sin that God could proclaim good news to sinners, whether it concerned the bringing in of the millennial kingdom, the blessing of the nations through Abraham's seed or the final defeat of Satan.

It was not until some time after the crucifixion, however, that the secret of the gospel was revealed to and through the Apostle Paul, and with it the best news of all: *"the gospel of the grace of God."*

The proclamation of "the gospel of the grace of God" was the natural accompaniment to the revelation of the cross as the secret of God's good news. Indeed, the apostle calls his distinctive message both *"the gospel of the grace of God"* (Acts 20:24) and *"the preaching of the cross"* (I Cor. 1: 18), for "the gospel of the grace of God" *is* "the preaching of the cross," i.e., *as good news.* It is the proclamation of the over-abounding grace of God to man through the shed blood of Christ, and in the Pauline message everything centers in the cross.

According to the Pauline epistles "we have redemption *through His blood"* (Eph. 1:7), we are justified *by His blood"* (Rom. 5:9), "reconciled to God *by the death of His Son"* (Romans 5:10), "made nigh *by the blood of Christ"* (Eph. 2:13) and "made the righteousness of God in Him" because *"God hath made Him to be sin for us"* (II Cor. 5:21).

The covenant of the law was abolished *by the cross* (Col. 2:14), the curse of the law was removed *by the cross* (Gal. 3:13), the "middle wall of partition" was broken down *by the cross* (Eph. 2:14,15) and believing Jews and Gentiles are reconciled to God in one body *by the cross* (Eph. 2:16).

Little wonder the apostle calls his message "the preaching of the cross"!

To the believer it is thrilling to see the cross as God's reply to Satan when, at first glance, it had appeared that the cross was Satan's greatest triumph.

Satan had, of course, worked long behind the scenes to prevent the coming of the Redeemer. He had opposed it by seeking the destruction of all Hebrew males in Egypt (Ex. 1:16,22), by seeking the annihilation of the whole nation by Pharaoh (Ex. 14), by seeking to wipe out "all the seed royal" through Athaliah (II Chron. 22:10), by seeking the destruction of the race again through Haman (Esth. 3:12,13).

When the deceiver was overruled in these and other attempts on Christ, and the Lord, after all, appeared on earth, Satan redoubled his efforts to destroy Him. When but an infant, Herod sought the young child's life (Matt. 2); at Nazareth, His neighbors tried to throw Him over a cliff (Luke 4:

29); a fierce storm on Galilee would have engulfed Him (Mark 4:37), etc.

Finally it seemed Satan was winning. He had succeeded in turning Israel's rulers against Christ (John 7:48), then the masses (Matt. 13:13-15), then many of His own disciples (John 6:66,67) and finally even one of the twelve (Matt. 26:14-16).

Some suppose that Satan sought to *prevent* the crucifixion, but we must not presume that Satan understood how the cross would accomplish his defeat and our redemption. We read distinctly that *"Satan entered into"* Judas (John 13:27). Satan thought that the crucifixion of Christ would *destroy* Him. How he must have congratulated himself on his success as our Lord died in shame and disgrace on Calvary's cross!

Doubtless it was a great shock and disappointment to him when Christ arose from the dead, but imagine his dismay when he discovered that he had tricked himself by crucifying Christ—that God had actually paid for man's sins by the death of Christ so that He might save the chief of sinners and send him forth to offer *"redemption through His blood, the forgiveness of sins, according to the riches of His grace"!* (Eph. 1:7).

Thus Satan reached the climax of his career of deception when he deceived *himself* at Calvary.

In the light of this it is not strange that Satan hates and opposes the message of grace, the preaching of the cross, more bitterly than he ever hated or opposed the prophetic program. Nor is it strange that it is God's purpose:

". . . that now unto the principalities and powers

73

in heavenly places might be known by the church the manifold wisdom of God" (Eph. 3:10).

THE SECRET OF THE GOSPEL NOT
REVEALED BEFORE PAUL

We must be careful not to assume that *predictions* concerning the *crucifixion* are the same as "the preaching of the cross" or that "the preaching of the cross" has nothing to do with the mystery simply because the crucifixion itself was prophesied.

Predictions concerning the death of Christ are to be found in numerous Old Testament passages as well as in the four records of our Lord's earthly ministry, but *never were the merits of Christ's death proclaimed as the ground of salvation until Paul.* The difficulty is that so much has been *read into* these passages which is not there.

How much, for example, could Adam and Eve have understood about the plan of salvation from the statement recorded in Gen. 3:15? If they even understood from this that the coming Redeemer would die, they understood more than the twelve apostles did 4000 years later while working with the Lord Himself and preaching "the gospel of the kingdom (Luke 9:1-6, 18:31-34).*

Does some reader *suppose* that the plan of salvation *must* have been explained to Adam and Eve? Such a supposition would be entirely gratuitous. In fact, the record would rather indicate the opposite.

It is *now* clear that the Holy Spirit had the

---

*It has been brought out that our Lord upbraided two of His followers for not believing all that the prophets had written concerning His death and resurrection, but this was *after* His resurrection. Moreover, the prophets had not predicted the preaching of the cross for the remission of sins.

death of Christ in mind in Psa. 22, but who would have dreamed, until Christ died, that it depicted His crucifixion or that its opening cry would be that of our crucified Savior? Indeed, the passage was not even written in the form of a prediction!

And what about Isaiah 53? Is Christ not portrayed here as bearing the sins of the world? Those who suppose so have again read something *into* the passage. Verse 6 reads: *"All WE like sheep have gone astray . . . and the Lord hath laid on Him the iniquity of US all."*

Since the prophet says "all *we*", the thoughtful student of Scripture will naturally inquire, "all *who?*" And he will find in verse 8 that Isaiah speaks as a Hebrew prophet concerning *his own people*:

"For the transgression of MY PEOPLE was He stricken."

So, first of all, the prophet speaks here of Messiah's death only as it relates to *the nation Israel.**

It is true, of course, that we Gentiles have *also* gone astray and that the Lord has *also* laid our iniquities upon Christ, but that is not the question here.

The *tone* of Isaiah 53 is another factor which must not be overlooked. The prophet does not proclaim the death of Christ as good news, or *offer* salvation through its merits, as it is our joy to do today. On the contrary, he begins with a tone of disappointment. *Who will believe his report? A tender plant . . . a root out of a dry ground . . . no form nor comeliness . . . no beauty that we should desire Him . . . despised . . . rejected . . . a man of sorrows and acquainted with grief."*

---

*For the manner in which the crucifixion of Christ will bring about Israel's salvation see the author's book entitled, *The Two-fold Purpose of God.*

Who wants tender plants or roots out of dry ground? Dress a man in gorgeous apparel, put a crown on his head, set him on a throne in a palace with a thousand rooms, and men will come from the ends of the earth to kiss his feet. But such a character as Isaiah describes; who would do homage to him?

But, continues the prophet, He is bearing *our* sins. *We* are the guilty ones, yet *He* goes as a lamb to the slaughter.

Note, in all of Isaiah's prediction there is nothing about trusting in the merits of the Crucified for salvation. There is *substitution*, to be sure, (which some consider the very acme of Christian truth) but substitution *in itself* is not good news. Many an innocent victim has unjustly borne the penalty for the crime of another. Was this something to be rejoiced in or boasted about?

Isaiah points out, indeed, that when Messiah comes He will be rejected and slain, taking the blame for Israel's sins, but this is still quite different from proclaiming the merits of Christ's death in an offer of salvation to be accepted by faith.*

Finally, we remind our readers that even this was but a *prediction*, which the prophet himself obviously did not understand (I Peter 1:10-12) or he would surely have filled his book with the glad message.

But did not John the Baptist know the secret of the gospel when he said of Christ:

"Behold the Lamb of God, which taketh [beareth] away the sin of the world" (John 1:29).

*The phrase *"By His knowledge shall My righteous Servant justify many"* (Verse 11) is translated in Darby's *New Translation*: *"By His knowledge shall My righteous Servant instruct many in righteousness."*

If he did, why then did he proclaim *"the baptism of repentance for the remission of sins"?* (Mark 1:4).

In Matt. 3:1,2 we are given the *theme* of John's message:

"In those days came John the Baptist, preaching in the wilderness of Judaea,

"And saying, REPENT YE: FOR THE KINGDOM OF HEAVEN IS AT HAND."

If John understood what we now do about the death of Christ, why was not *that* his theme?

We must not forget the background of John 1:29. John had been baptizing repentant sinners, and Jesus had come among them, also to be baptized.

"But John forbad Him, saying, I have need to be baptized of Thee, and comest Thou to me?" (Matt. 3:14).

But Jesus insisted on being baptized. Though perfectly sinless, He came *as a sinner* and was *"numbered with the transgressors."* Is it strange that John, who realized that he himself and the multitude were the ones who needed repentance and cleansing, should describe Christ as the Lamb of God, bearing away the sin of the world?

We say again that if John the Baptist even understood that Christ would die he knew more than the twelve did after working with Christ Himself for the greater part of His earthly ministry. But the fact that John preached what he did indicates that he probably knew no more than they did.

Even after the crucifixion, the apostles did not immediately see the death of Christ as the secret of the gospel. Peter, as we have seen, *referred* to the crucifixion, but did not *offer* it for salvation. He

77

blamed his hearers for the death of Christ and demanded repentance and water baptism for the remission of their sins (Acts 2:36,38).

No, even Philip did not preach the cross to the eunuch as the secret of the gospel. The eunuch had been reading Isa. 53. Philip then preached *Christ* from that passage, proving from it that the crucified Jesus was the Messiah, whose coming Isaiah had predicted.

Read the record carefully. Nowhere does it say that Philip instructed the eunuch that Christ had died for him, or that the eunuch should trust in His death for salvation. Philip simply *identified* Jesus as the Messiah from that passage, and baptized the eunuch when he confessed:

"I believe that Jesus Christ is the Son of God" (Acts 8:37).

But it may still be objected: Does not Paul say, "Christ died for our sins *according to the Scriptures?"* Yes, Christ's death for sin was in accordance with the Scriptures, but we insist that it was not until Paul that His death for sin was proclaimed as good news and seen as the secret of all the good news that had gone before. The fact is, simply, that the *prophesied* death of Christ turned out to be *the secret of the gospel.*

Thus the *fact* of Christ's death for the sins of others was *"testified beforehand"* (I Peter 1:11), but Paul, by revelation, makes it very clear that the eternal purpose of God in that death and the offer of salvation to all through its merits was to be

". . . TESTIFIED IN DUE TIME, whereunto I am ordained a preacher, and an apostle . . ." (I Tim. 2:6,7).

Whereas Peter at Pentecost had *accused* his hearers of crucifying Christ and had demanded repentance and baptism for the remission of sins (Acts 2:23,36,38), Paul proclaimed the crucifixion of Christ *as good news* (I Cor. 1:18). With Peter at Pentecost it was a matter of *shame*; Paul *gloried* in it (Gal. 6:14).

It was through Paul, and no one before Paul, that Christ was *"set forth to be a propitiation THROUGH FAITH IN HIS BLOOD"* (Rom. 3:25).

It was Paul who first explained how men had been

". . . **kept under the law, shut up unto THE FAITH WHICH SHOULD AFTERWARDS BE REVEALED"** (Gal. 3:23).

And it was Paul who was first sent forth to proclaim that faith.

It was Paul who first said:

"BUT NOW the righteousness of God without the law is manifested . . ."

"[We] declare, I say, AT THIS TIME, [Christ's] righteousness: that [God] might be just, and the justifier of him which believeth in Jesus" (Rom. 3:21,26).

It was Paul who first said:

". . . **One died for all . . . wherefore HENCEFORTH KNOW WE NO MAN AFTER THE FLESH . . ."** (II Cor. 5:14,16).

Paul, the chief of sinners, saved by grace, *offers* the cross as the sole ground of remission (Rom. 3:24); he *boasts* in it (Gal. 6:14); he exclaims: *"[He] loved ME and gave Himself for ME!"* (Gal. 2:20), *"[He] loved THE CHURCH and gave Himself for it!"* (Eph. 5:25), *"The love of Christ constraineth us . . . He died for ALL"* (II Cor. 5:14,15).

THE MYSTERY (OR SECRET) OF GOD'S WILL

We proceed now from "the mystery of the gospel" (Eph. 6:19) to "the mystery of God's *will*" (Eph. 1:9); from *the secret of the good news* to *the good news of "the secret,"* i.e., the *purpose* kept secret until revealed to and through the Apostle Paul. This is what he refers to in the words:

"Having made known unto us THE MYSTERY OF HIS WILL, according to His good pleasure which He hath purposed in Himself:

"That in the dispensation of the fulness of times He might gather together in one all things in Christ, both which are in heaven, and which are on earth; even in Him" (Eph. 1:9,10).

In this passage, as in many others by Paul, the *will* of God refers to His *eternal purpose*, not merely His will in some particular detail, or His will for our lives. Thus he exhorts: *"Be ye not unwise, but understanding what the will of the Lord is"* (Eph. 5:17. See also Eph. 1:5,11, Col. 1:9).

As we have pointed out, the mystery of God's will is the gathering together of all in heaven and earth *in Christ*. This, however, is His *ultimate* purpose. All God's own were not gathered together in Christ at once. Thus the mystery of God's will involved the unfolding of a new program, a new dispensation.

In brief, the mystery as it relates to the present, is the glorious truth that God has concluded both Jew and Gentile in unbelief that He might have mercy upon all (Rom. 11:32) and that He might reconcile both unto God in one body by the Cross (Eph. 2:16).

80

The heavenly position of this "one body," its spiritual blessings, its present responsibilities, etc., will be discussed in subsequent chapters, but it should here be stated that God's eternal *purpose,* so long kept secret, is directly bound up with *the secret of the gospel,* for the carrying out of this purpose is the historical demonstration of the fact that the Christ who was crucified on Calvary is Himself the secret of all God's good news. Indeed, it was by the unfolding of His long-hidden *purpose* that God made known the secret of the gospel.

GOD'S SECRET PURPOSE NOT REVEALED UNTIL PAUL

It is important to notice that not until Paul do we read of God's *"having made known unto us the mystery of His will."*

It is this secret *purpose,* as well as the secret of the gospel, that he labels *"my gospel,"* insisting that it was *"kept secret since the world began"* (Rom. 16:25).

It is he who first proclaims *"the hidden [mystery] which God ordained before the world unto our glory"* (I Cor. 2:7). It is he, referring again to this secret purpose, who explains *"How that by revelation He made known unto me the mystery,"* insisting again .that *"in other ages [it] was not made known,"* that it was *"unsearchable,"* i.e., not to be found in the Scriptures thus far written, and *"from the beginning of the world . . . hid in God"* (Eph. 3:3-9). It is he who speaks of:

"THE DISPENSATION OF GOD WHICH IS GIVEN TO ME FOR YOU, TO FULFIL [make full, complete] THE WORD OF GOD:

81

"EVEN THE MYSTERY WHICH HATH BEEN HID FROM AGES AND FROM GENERATIONS, BUT NOW IS MADE MANIFEST TO HIS SAINTS:

"TO WHOM GOD WOULD MAKE KNOWN WHAT IS THE RICHES OF THE GLORY OF THIS MYSTERY AMONG THE GENTILES; WHICH IS CHRIST IN YOU,* THE HOPE OF GLORY" (Col. 1:25-27).

QUIZ

1. What is the two-fold meaning of the word translated "mystery" in the Authorized Version? 2. How could the term "mystery of the gospel" be translated in modern, every-day English? 3. What is meant by this phrase? 4. When was *gospel* first preached to sinners? 5. In what great event do we find "the mystery of the gospel"? 6. When and by whom was "the mystery of the gospel" first proclaimed? 7. What did Satan hope to accomplish by the crucifixion of Christ? 8. How did God over-rule him? 9. What is the difference between *predictions* about the cross and *"the preaching of the cross"*? 10. What Scripture indicates that the prophets themselves did not understand their predictions concerning the sufferings of Christ? 11. What Scriptures indicate that Christ's own apostles, after preaching "the gospel" for some time, did not even know that He would die? 12. How can you prove that Isaiah 53 does *not* speak of Christ dying for the sins of all men? 13. What was the *theme* of John the Baptist's message? 14. Did he offer the death of Christ for the remission of sins? 15. How did the cross figure in Peter's Pentecostal message and what did he demand for the remission of sins? 16. How did Philip use Isaiah 53 when preaching to the eunuch? 17. Who first proclaimed, as a message, salvation by grace, through faith in the death of Christ? 18. What is meant by "the mystery of God's will"? 19. Explain how "the mystery of the gospel" and "the mystery of God's will" are related in the great revelation made to and through the Apostle Paul. 20. Give three Scripture passages to prove that "the mystery" was *first* revealed to Paul.

---

*Collectively, as the One in whom the **Body is joined together.**

Chapter IV.

THE UNFOLDING OF THE MYSTERY

ISRAEL'S FORMER GLORY

The nation Israel, with all her shortcomings, was once the only bright spot in a dark world. God had promised that through her, as Abraham's multiplied seed, the other nations should be blessed (Gen. 22:17,18). Ruth, the Moabitess, and others like her, found shelter under the wings of God by coming to Israel (Ruth 2:12).

Our Lord said to the Samaritan woman:

"Ye worship ye know not what: we know what we worship: for SALVATION IS OF THE JEWS" (John 4:22).

Paul, in Rom. 3:1,2, asks the question: *"What advantage then hath the Jew?"* and answers:

"Much every way: CHIEFLY, BECAUSE THAT UNTO THEM WERE COMMITTED THE ORACLES OF GOD."

In Rom. 9:4,5, he says:

". . . TO [ISRAEL] PERTAINETH THE ADOPTION, AND THE GLORY, AND THE COVENANTS, AND THE GIVING OF THE LAW, AND THE SERVICE OF GOD, AND THE PROMISES;

"WHOSE ARE THE FATHERS, AND OF WHOM, AS CONCERNING THE FLESH, CHRIST CAME . . ."

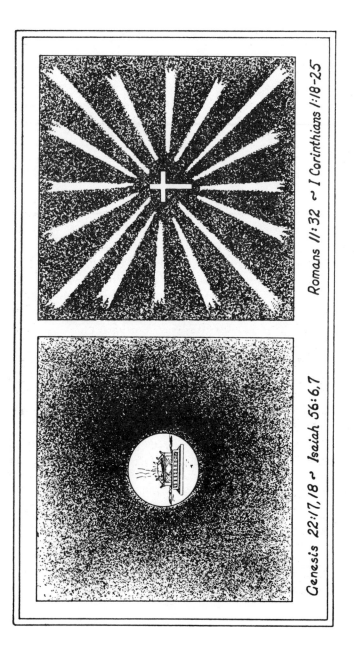

Romans 11:32 ~ I Corinthians 1:18-25

Genesis 22:17,18 ~ Isaiah 56:6,7

THE HEART OF ISRAEL'S RELIGION

This honor was not bestowed upon Israel, however, because she was better or more deserving than others. Israel's own King David had written by inspiration:

"The Lord looked down from heaven upon the children of men, to see if there were any that did understand, and seek God.

"They are ALL gone aside, they are ALL together become filthy: THERE IS NONE THAT DOETH GOOD, NO, NOT ONE" (Psa. 14:2,3).

This is why, at the heart of Israel's religion, we find a blood sacrifice. We know that *"It is not possible that the blood of bulls and of goats should take away sins"* (Heb. 10:4), but these sacrifices *atoned** for sins until such time as Christ should come to *"put away sin by the sacrifice of Himself"* (Heb. 9:26).

Israel's blood sacrifices were meanwhile a confession of sin, a testimony to the fact that "the wages of sin is death" and an acknowledgment that were it not for God's grace she too would stand outside His favor. Thus it is written:

"For the life of the flesh is in the blood: and I have given it to you upon the altar to make an atonement for your souls: for it is the blood that maketh an atonement for the soul" (Lev. 17:11).

"And almost all things are by the law purged with blood; AND WITHOUT SHEDDING OF BLOOD IS NO REMISSION" (Heb. 9:22).

These means of approach to God, while they indicated that Israel was no better than the Gentiles,

---

*The word *atone* (Hebrew: *kapher*) means *to cover.*

gave them, at the same time, a distinct advantage over the Gentiles—and a great responsibility toward them.

Israel was not to keep these blessings to herself, for God had said to Abraham: *"And in thy seed shall all the nations of the earth be blessed"* (Gen. 22:18).* They were to be the *agents,* not merely the *objects* of God's blessing.

ISRAEL'S FAILURE

The Word and worship of God were committed to Israel that *through her* the Gentiles might find God.

When our Lord cast the money-changers out of the temple, He said:

"Is it not written. My house shall be called of all nations the house of prayer?" (Mark 11:17).

The Lord was, of course, referring to Isa. 56:6, 7, where we read:

"Also the sons of the stranger, that join themselves to the Lord, to serve Him, and to love the name of the Lord, to be His servants, every one that keepeth the sabbath from polluting it, and taketh hold of my covenant;

"Even them will I bring to my holy mountain, and make them joyful in my house of prayer: their burnt-offerings and their sacrifices shall be accepted upon mine altar; FOR MINE HOUSE SHALL BE CALLED AN HOUSE OF PRAYER FOR ALL PEOPLE."

Israel's covenant relationship with God and her God-given religion, of course, constituted a "middle wall of partition" between her and the ungodly Gen-

---

*It should be noted that in the covenant promises to Israel there is generally, besides the future aspect, the challenge of present fulfillment (Deut. 1:8, Heb. 3:19, etc.).

ties, but this did not mean that Israel was to leave the Gentiles in their ungodly state and keep them outside that wall. The Abrahamic Covenant indicated otherwise and from the passage just quoted from Isaiah, it is clear that any Gentiles, willing to become proselytes to Judaism were to be welcomed to the temple, where a covenant people found access to God.

But did the people of Israel make this known among the nations? They did not. They would have left the Gentile world in darkness forever. Indeed, the temple, meant to be a house of prayer for all nations, had become a center of villainy and fraud. Hence our Lord was forced to add to His quotation from Isaiah, the words: "BUT YE HAVE MADE IT A DEN OF THIEVES."

THE THREE CALLS TO
REPENTANCE

It was after 1500 years of failure under the law, with the coming Messianic kingdom in view, that God issued to Israel her three greatest calls to repentance.

The first was by John the Baptist, of whom our Lord said, *"There is not a greater prophet"* (Luke 7:28).

John's ministry was to bring Israel back to God, and so make the way smooth for the coming King. The cry was:

". . . Prepare ye the way of the Lord, make His paths straight.

87

"Every valley shall be filled, and every mountain and hill shall be brought low; and the crooked shall be made straight, and the rough ways shall be made smooth" (Luke 3:4,5).

John labored earnestly to fulfill his mission. His ministry reached into every department of Israel's national life. He dealt with "the people," with the tax gatherers, with the soldiers (Luke 3:10-14). He dared to send the proud Pharisees and Sadducees away, calling them a "generation of vipers," asking them: *"Who hath warned you to flee from the wrath to come?"* and saying: *"Bring forth therefore fruits meet for repentance"* (Matt. 3:7,8). He even entered the court of King Herod, rebuking him for living with his brother's wife "and for all the evils which Herod had done" (Luke 3:19).

But with all this Israel as a nation did not repent. Indeed, the great reformer was "shut up in prison" (Luke 3:20) and finally beheaded (Matt. 14:10) by Israel's wicked and licentious king—a crime which would hardly have been tolerated had there been a real reformation in the nation.

So, the way for our Lord was made anything but smooth. He had to take up the cry where John had left off. Nor was the response to our Lord's message any more satisfactory than the response to John's. They despised Him, heckled Him, plotted against Him. When He wrought mighty miracles among them they had the impudence to ask: *"By what authority doest Thou these things? and who gave Thee this authority?"* (Matt. 21:23).

Finally they brought Him to trial on various

false charges. And, while under examination and trial, they subjected Him to the most cruel and inhuman treatment. They mocked Him; they scourged Him; they spat in His face. They pulled His beard and His hair; they blindfolded Him, buffetted Him and called upon Him to prophesy who had smitten Him. They crowned Him with thorns; they put a purple robe upon Him and a reed (instead of a sceptre) in His hand, kneeling before Him in mockery. Then, taking the reed from His hand, they smote Him on the head with it.

So intense was their hatred against the Son of God that when the Roman governor, Pilate, finding no fault in Him, would have chastised Him and released Him, *"they cried out all at once, saying, Away with this man . . ."* (Luke 23:18). *"And they were instant with loud voices, requiring that He might be crucified"* (Luke 23:23).

And thus Israel, rather than heeding Christ's call to repentance, actually persuaded Pilate to have Him nailed to a cross, where, writhing in pain, He suffered shame and disgrace for *their* sins.

All this, of course, had not taken God by surprise. Indeed, He had predicted it. The Spirit, through the prophets, had *"testified beforehand the sufferings of Christ, and the glory that should FOLLOW"* (I Peter 1:11). Thus Israel's Messiah, while hanging on the cross, cried: *"Father, forgive them; for they know not what they do"* (Luke 23:34).

And now the stage, it seemed, was being set for the glory to follow. Fifty days after the resurrection the Holy Spirit was "poured out" upon the disciples and the signs of the "last days" began to appear (Acts 2). Amid these miraculous signs Israel (of that day) was given her third and last opportunity to repent, with the offer of Christ's return and "the times of refreshing" if she did so.

It was the Apostle Peter, chiefly, whom God used to call Israel to repentance at Pentecost. To those who were convicted by His message and inquired what they should do, he answered:

"REPENT, AND BE BAPTIZED EVERY ONE OF YOU IN THE NAME OF JESUS CHRIST FOR THE REMISSION OF SINS, AND YE SHALL RECEIVE THE GIFT OF THE HOLY GHOST" (Acts 2:38).

A short while later, to the multitudes gathered at Solomon's porch, Peter cried:

"REPENT YE THEREFORE, AND BE CONVERTED, THAT YOUR SINS MAY BE BLOTTED OUT, WHEN [THAT SO] THE TIMES OF REFRESHING SHALL [MAY] COME FROM THE PRESENCE OF THE LORD;

"AND HE SHALL SEND JESUS CHRIST, WHICH BEFORE WAS PREACHED UNTO YOU" (Acts 3:19,20).

But still Israel (as a nation) refused to repent. Instead, her rulers forbad the apostles to speak in Christ's name; threatening them, scourging them, imprisoning them. Finally they could not refrain from shedding blood again and Stephen, a man "full of faith and power," was dragged out and stoned to death.

Thus Israel responded to God's three gracious calls to repentance by three brutal murders: those of John the Baptist, Christ and Stephen. And mark well that their guilt increased with each successive murder. In the case of John the Baptist they *permitted* it; in the case of Christ they *demanded* it; in the case of Stephen they *committed* it. They had turned a deaf ear to the Father (through John), to the Son Himself, while on earth, and to the Holy Spirit (through the Pentecostal believers). They had resisted the Father before Christ's coming; they despised Christ Himself while He was among them; they blasphemed the Holy Spirit after Christ was gone. Now there was no excuse. They had committed the unpardonable sin, of which the Lord had warned them (Matt. 12:31,32).

ISRAEL JOINS THE WORLD'S
REBELLION

It must not be supposed that Israel's enmity against Christ spent itself in the murder of Stephen. This was but the beginning of a prolonged and intense persecution of Christ and His followers:

"And at that time there was a great persecution against the church which was at Jerusalem; and they were all scattered abroad throughout the regions of Judaea and Samaria, except the apostles" (Acts 8:1).

Saul of Tarsus was the leader of this persecution:

"As for Saul, he made havock of the church, entering into every house, and haling men and women committed them to prison" (Acts 8:3).

The Gentiles had long before rebelled against God at the tower of Babel (Gen. 11:3,4), *"even as they did not like to retain God in their knowledge"* (Rom. 1:28). For this God finally "gave them up" (Rom. 1:24,26,28) and scattered them over the face

91

of the earth (Gen. 11:9). Now Israel had joined the rebellion and God would give them up and scatter them too.

It is sometimes supposed that the scattering of the Jerusalem disciples to Judaea and Samaria was in fulfillment of the "great commission," as recorded in Acts 1:8. The very opposite, however, is the case. These disciples had not left Jerusalem in response to any command of our Lord. They had *fled for their lives.* And the twelve apostles, the very ones our Lord had commanded to go from Jerusalem to all the world, *stayed at Jerusalem!*

It was natural, of course, for the believers at Jerusalem to flee when the fearful persecution broke out, but how shall we regard the conduct of the twelve apostles in staying there?

Were they delinquent in their duty to evangelize the world? The Scriptures answer plainly that they were not. The reason the twelve stayed at Jerusalem was because the kingdom, in which they were to have twelve thrones (Matt. 19:28), was to be established *at Jerusalem,* and blessing and salvation was to flow *from there* to the ends of the earth; hence their work there was not yet done.

Thus the continuance of the apostles at Jerusalem and the flight of the believing multitude indicated the same thing—that Israel was *not* turning to Christ. Looking back *now* we can see that this great persecution was "the secret crisis in Israel's history," as Sir Robert Anderson called it, and that the kingdom was not, for the time being, to be set up, unless it were by force.

But what about God's plan to send salvation and blessing to the world? Must the nations now remain in darkness because of Israel's refusal to become the channel of blessing?

According to prophecy God's response to the world's rejection of Christ was to be the outpouring of His wrath. He was to *make* Israel (and so the Gentiles) willing in the day of His power. Israel, with the Gentiles had declared war on Him and His Anointed One; He would make a counter-declaration, as it is written:

"Why do the heathen rage, and the people [OF ISRAEL, see Acts 4:25-27] imagine a vain thing?

"The kings of the earth set themselves, and the rulers take counsel together, against the Lord, and against His Anointed, saying,

"Let us break their bands asunder, and cast away their cords from us.

"HE THAT SITTETH IN THE HEAVENS SHALL LAUGH: THE LORD SHALL HAVE THEM IN DERISION.

"THEN SHALL HE SPEAK UNTO THEM IN HIS WRATH, AND VEX THEM IN HIS SORE DISPLEASURE" (Psa. 2:1-5).

"THE LORD SAID UNTO MY LORD, SIT THOU AT MY RIGHT HAND, UNTIL I MAKE THINE ENEMIES THY FOOTSTOOL.

"THE LORD SHALL SEND THE ROD OF THY STRENGTH OUT OF ZION: RULE THOU IN THE MIDST OF THINE ENEMIES.

"THY PEOPLE SHALL BE WILLING IN THE DAY OF THY POWER . . ." (Psa. 110:1-3).

These words of David are the consistent testimony of Old Testament prophecy. Was the judgment now to fall?

No, it was against the dark background of man's failure and sin that God was now to reveal the riches of His grace.

THE SECRET PURPOSE UNFOLDED

The first intimation of God's purpose concerning the dispensation of grace was the salvation of Saul, the chief of sinners, and the leader of Israel's —yea, the world's—rebellion against Christ (I Tim. 1:13-16).

To him the Lord revealed what He could not yet reveal to the other apostles when He gave them their great commission: i.e., that Israel would be set aside and salvation sent by grace to all directly through the crucified, risen, exalted Christ.

One of the first lessons Paul learned was that God was to conclude Israel, along with the Gentiles, in unbelief. He, like the twelve, would have launched his ministry from Jerusalem but when, after His conversion, he returned there, the Lord appeared to him and said:

"Make haste, and get thee quickly out of Jerusalem: FOR THEY WILL NOT RECEIVE THY TESTIMONY CONCERNING ME" (Acts 22:18).

Compare this statement with Luke 24:47 and see what God was now doing. He was concluding Israel in unbelief along with the Gentiles. And why? In order that He might offer salvation to *all* men by grace, *solely and directly through the merits of Christ.*

"FOR GOD HATH CONCLUDED* THEM ALL IN

*Gr. sunkleio: to shut up together, to include together.

94

UNBELIEF, THAT HE MIGHT HAVE MERCY UPON ALL" (Rom. 11:32).

Thus, through the *fall* of Israel, salvation was now to be preached to the Gentiles (Rom. 11:11, 12,15). With the raising up of Paul to replace the twelve as "the apostle of the Gentiles" (Rom. 11:13), God began to bring Jewish religion to an end and to usher in the "reign" of grace.*

Here the reader should turn to the foregoing chart and note how God, having fully demonstrated that *"there is no difference"* between Jew and Gentile (Rom. 3:22,23), now magnifies the *cross* and its power to save (Eph. 1:7).

"FOR HE IS OUR PEACE, WHO HATH MADE BOTH ONE, AND HATH BROKEN DOWN THE MIDDLE WALL OF PARTITION BETWEEN US;

"HAVING ABOLISHED IN HIS FLESH THE ENMITY . . .

". . . THAT HE MIGHT RECONCILE BOTH UNTO GOD IN ONE BODY BY THE CROSS, HAVING SLAIN THE ENMITY THEREBY" (Eph. 2:14-16).

Thus the middle wall of partition has been broken down (see chart) and Jewish and Gentile believers are reconciled to God in one body *by the cross. The cross, the finished work of Christ,* is what God would have us proclaim to the world today (I Cor. 1:18, II Cor. 5:14-21, Gal. 6:14, Eph. 1:7, etc.), for therein lies the secret of "His purpose and grace."

Mark well, however, that *reconciliation* postulates *alienation*; hence *reconciliation* could not be

---

*See Rom. 5:20,21 and I Tim. 1:13-16 and note the phrases: *"grace," "much more abound," "exceeding abundant," "that grace might reign"* and *"in me first"* (or, *chiefly*).

proclaimed until Israel had been cast away along with the Gentiles and the alienation of *all* from God had been fully demonstrated, *"The casting away of them"* opened the way for *"the reconciling of the world"* (Rom. 11:15).

The *"dispensation of the grace of God,"* the reconciliation of Jews and Gentiles to God *in one body* by the cross, is the great mystery which was hid in God until revealed to and through the Apostle Paul.

Paul was the natural representative of God's purpose concerning the body because he was himself a Hebrew and a Roman in one person (See Acts 26:16-18, New Tr.), an enemy *reconciled* to God and His Christ, the "pattern" whom God chose to "show forth all longsuffering" (I Tim. 1:16) and "one born out of [before the] due time" (I Cor. 15.8) as *both* Jews and Gentiles are today. All this will be discussed further in another lesson.

God's prophesied purpose to bless the nations *through Israel* will, of course, still be carried out, but while Israel remains in her unrepentant state God is blessing Jews *and* Gentiles *through Christ, Abraham's Seed,* in spite of the failure of Abraham's *multiplied* seed (Gal. 3:16,19,22, Eph. 3:5,6). This is in accordance with His "eternal purpose," and is a living demonstration of the fact that *all* blessing flows from Calvary; that even millennial blessing will flow *from Christ,* through Israel, to the Gentiles.

"O the depth of the riches, both of the wisdom and knowledge of God! How unsearchable are His judgments, and His ways past finding out!" (Rom. 11:33).

QUIZ

1. Show from Scripture what *chief* advantage Israel had over the Gentiles in Old Testament times. 2. Name five other advantages Israel had over the Gentiles. 3. What responsibility did these advantages impose upon Israel in her relation to the Gentiles? 4. By what was Israel constantly reminded that she was no better than the Gentiles? 5. For whom was the temple intended as a house of prayer? 6. What had the temple become by the time Christ appeared on earth? 7. With what brutal murders did Israel respond to her three greatest calls to repentance? 8. Explain how Israel's guilt increased progressively with these three murders. 9. How did Israel then wage actual war against God and His Anointed One? 10. Who led Israel in this war? 11. How, according to Scripture, was God to respond? 12. Did the judgment fall immediately? 13. Give Scripture to show with what great stroke God first indicated His purpose to usher in the dispensation of grace. 14. What did the risen Lord reveal to Saul about Israel when he first returned to Jerusalem after his conversion? 15. What did God now do to Israel to open the way for "the reconciling of the world"? 16. What happened to the middle wall of partition? 17. What relationship do those who are reconciled to God now hold toward each other? 18. Explain how Paul is the natural representative of the church of today. 19. In what sense is God blessing the Gentiles through Abraham's seed even now? 20. What about God's prophesied purpose to bless the world through Abraham's *multiplied* seed (Gen. 22:17, 18)?

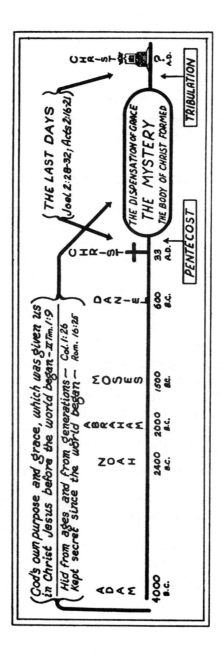

Chapter V.

THE LAST DAYS

THE GOAL OF PROPHECY

The Old Testament Scriptures have a great deal to say about the "last" or "latter" days. The phrase looks forward in a general way to *the coming of Messiah and the establishment of His kingdom* (Gen. 49:1, Num. 24:14, Deut. 4:30, Isa. 2:2, Dan. 2:28, 10:14, Hos. 3:5, Mic. 4:1). Several similar phrases are used in connection with the same events, such as: "last time," "latter time," "the days come," "His days," "those days."

The coming of Messiah and the establishment of His kingdom in the last days is the goal of prophecy. Indeed, even the New Testament Scriptures view Messiah's coming and kingdom as the great climax of the prophetic program (Mark 1:15, Luke 1:68-75, Acts 3:21-24, I Peter 1:11).

PETER AND THE LAST DAYS

When Peter stood up nineteen centuries ago and declared that the last days had come (Acts 2:16,17) he showed that he was totally ignorant of God's plan to usher in a dispensation of grace before the return of Christ.

We must not suppose, however, that this ignorance was due to some human failing in Peter himself, for on the day of Pentecost the followers of Christ "were all filled with the Holy Ghost" (Acts 2:4).

Moreover, what he said was *Scripturally correct*. In the light of all that had so far been revealed, these *were* the last days. The prophets had said nothing about the dispensation of grace or the body of Christ. There had as yet been no hint of any interruption of the prophetic program.

In Joel's prophecy concerning the last days, Pentecost is followed by the great tribulation and the return of Christ. Indeed, the prophets had "testified beforehand" only "the sufferings of Christ, and the glory that should follow" (I Pet. 1:11). Now that the sufferings were over, it seemed as though the glory would soon follow, for no one could deny that the signs of "the day of the Lord" had begun to appear.*

So Peter was *not* ignorant of the revealed program of God concerning the day in which he lived. Taught by the Lord (Acts 1:3) and filled with the Holy Spirit (Acts 2:4), he had an intelligent understanding of just where he stood in the divine plan. Hence the dynamic power of his message.

The apostles had expected the Holy Spirit to be "poured out" before the great tribulation and the return of Christ, and our Lord had promised them in commissioning them that they would then be supernaturally empowered to speak with other

*If the reader will mentally take the section entitled MYSTERY out of the foregoing chart and bring *Pentecost* and the *Tribulation* together he will have the prophetic program as Peter saw it.

tongues (Mark 16:17). Thus when the Spirit came and they began to speak in other languages Peter knew exactly what was happening and, pointing to Joel's prophecy, said without qualification: "THIS IS THAT."

"These are not drunken, as ye suppose . . . But THIS IS THAT which was spoken by the prophet Joel: And it shall come to pass in THE LAST DAYS, saith God, I will pour out of My Spirit . . . and . . . show wonders . . . and signs . . . before that great and notable day of the Lord come" (Acts 2:15-20).

All this is clear if we simply remember not to anticipate revelation; if we remember that God's purpose concerning *this present dispensation* was then still a *"mystery."* As far as God's *revealed* plan was concerned, the last days—the days so long foretold—*had* begun. Israel's long-promised Messiah had appeared, had died and risen again, had ascended to the Father's right hand and had sent the Holy Spirit to guide and empower His own. The next number on the prophetic program was the tribulation period with the judgment of the nations and Messiah's return, and the signs of these things were already beginning to appear.

THE PROPHETIC PROGRAM
INTERRUPTED

It is important to notice, however, that not *all* the signs of "the day of the Lord" appeared at Pentecost. There were the "signs in the earth beneath" but not the "wonders in the heaven above." There were the pouring out of the Holy Spirit, the tongues and visions and prophesying, but not the "blood, and fire, and vapor of smoke," nor as yet was "the sun turned into darkness and the moon into blood" (See Acts 2:17-20). Furthermore, the signs which did appear soon passed away again (I Cor. 13:8) as the prophetic program made way for the unfolding of *"the mystery,"* God's *secret,* eternal purpose.

Just before our Lord's ascension the apostles had asked: *"Lord, wilt Thou at this time restore again the kingdom to Israel?"* (Acts 1:6). Our Lord, of course, had known that Israel would reject the offer of the kingdom, but He could not tell the eleven this for they could not then have put much heart into their appeal to Israel and Israel, in turn, might have had some excuse for further rejecting Christ. Thus our Lord declined to answer their question and said:

"It is not for you to know the times or the seasons, which the Father hath put in His own power.

"But ye shall receive power after that the Holy Ghost is come upon you; and YE SHALL BE WITNESSES UNTO ME BOTH IN JERUSALEM, AND IN ALL JUDAEA, AND IN SAMARIA, AND UNTO THE UTTERMOST PART OF THE EARTH" (Acts 1:7,8).

The house of Israel, then, received a *bona fide* offer of the return of Christ and the establishment of His kingdom as Peter cried:

"Repent ye therefore, and be converted, that your sins may be blotted out, when [that so] the times of refreshing shall [may] come from the presence of the Lord:

"And He shall [may] send Jesus Christ, which before was preached unto you" (Acts 3:19,20).

This, of course, was an appeal to *the nation.* It did not mean that if *that one audience* had repented

Christ would *immediately* have returned to bring in the kingdom, for we know that several prophesied events would first have had to be fulfilled.

But the question may be asked: If the prophetic program had run its course and a repentant Israel had finally been brought to Messiah's feet, how would God have brought in the dispensation of grace? The answer is simply that He knew that they would not repent and that this was a factor in His plans to usher in the dispensation of grace.

The fact which concerned the people of Israel at that time was that a *bona fide* proposition was being made to them that if they repented the kingdom would be ushered in and Christ would return to occupy the throne of David. God was holding Israel accountable for her acceptance or rejection of Christ and His kingdom. As we know, the apostate nation did not repent but joined the Gentiles in their rebellion against God and could not have complained had the fulfillment of Joel's prophecy continued and God's wrath been poured out upon them. Indeed, those who did repent were filled with the Holy Spirit in preparation for the ordeal through which they were expected, as a result of Israel's rebellion, to pass.

Thus the world was ripe for the wrath of God more than 1900 years ago and if the prophetic program had not been graciously interrupted, the judgment would have fallen then.

"BUT WHERE SIN ABOUNDED, GRACE DID MUCH MORE ABOUND" (Rom. 5:20).

It was to Paul, that *other* apostle, that God first

made known *"the mystery [secret] of His will"* (Eph. 1:9), *"His own purpose and grace, which was given us in Christ Jesus before the world began"* (II Tim. 1:9).

In Eph. 3:1-3 the apostle says:

"For this cause I Paul, the prisoner of Jesus Christ for you Gentiles,

"If ye have heard of THE DISPENSATION OF THE GRACE OF GOD which is given me to you-ward:

"How that BY REVELATION HE MADE KNOWN UNTO ME THE MYSTERY . . ."

Paul, like the twelve, would have launched his ministry from Jerusalem, but to him our Lord revealed what He could not tell the eleven before His ascension. In Acts 22:17,18 we have Paul's own account of the incident:

"When I was come again to Jerusalem, even while I prayed in the temple, I was in a trance;

"And saw Him [Christ] saying unto me, MAKE HASTE, AND GET THEE QUICKLY OUT OF JERU-SALEM: FOR THEY WILL NOT RECEIVE THY TES-TIMONY CONCERNING ME."

At that time Paul, supposing that his reputation as a former persecutor of Christ would have induced the Jews to listen to him and doubtless feeling too that he *owed* them an explanation of his conduct, began arguing the point with the Lord. But the Lord replied simply:

"DEPART: FOR I WILL SEND THEE FAR HENCE UNTO THE GENTILES" (Verse 21).

This whole passage in Acts is most significant. Why did our Lord insist that the twelve begin their ministry at Jerusalem, yet refuse to allow Paul to begin there? Because Paul's ministry was to constitute an *interruption* of the commission and program of the twelve. The Lord said to Paul, in effect: "They did not listen to the twelve; neither will they listen to you, so leave Jerusalem and go to the Gentiles." Thus God concluded Israel in unbelief, along with the Gentiles. It is significant that after the raising up of Paul we find no further offer of the kingdom to Israel.* God had done this, however, "that He might have mercy upon all" (Rom. 11:32).

"O THE DEPTH OF THE RICHES BOTH OF THE WISDOM AND KNOWLEDGE OF GOD! HOW UN-SEARCHABLE ARE HIS JUDGMENTS, AND HIS WAYS PAST FINDING OUT!" (Rom. 11:33).

And so an interruption of the prophetic program was begun in order that God, through Paul, might offer to all men everywhere salvation by grace, solely through the merits of the crucified, risen Christ.

"And that He might reconcile BOTH [Jews and Gentiles] unto God in ONE BODY by the cross . . ." (Eph. 2:16).

During this *interruption* or *parenthesis*, then, while the establishment of Christ's kingdom is held in abeyance, God is forming *the body of Christ* from Jews and Gentiles *reconciled* to Himself by the cross (Cf. I Cor. 12:13, II Cor. 5:14-21).

The Bible student should always remember that the formation of this "one body" is not the subject of prophecy, but of the *mystery* first revealed

---

*This does not mean, however, that the offer which *had* been made was immediately withdrawn, or that God set Israel aside all at once.

through Paul. Nor is it the fulfillment of any covenant promise. It is the product of *pure grace,* through the redeeming work of Christ. This is why the unadulterated preaching of "the gospel of the grace of God" has always been the special object of Satan's wrath. In this connection Paul writes to Timothy:

"Be not thou therefore ashamed of the testimony of our Lord, nor of me his prisoner: but be thou partaker of the afflictions of the gospel according to the power of God;

"WHO HATH SAVED US, AND CALLED US WITH AN HOLY CALLING, NOT ACCORDING TO OUR WORKS, BUT ACCORDING TO HIS OWN PURPOSE AND GRACE, WHICH WAS GIVEN US IN CHRIST JESUS BEFORE THE WORLD BEGAN" (II Tim. 1:8,9).

PAUL AND THE LAST DAYS

Paul, like Peter, has much to say about "last days," but since his message concerns mainly this present dispensation of the mystery, and not the prophetic program, he generally has reference to the last days of *the dispensation of grace,* after which the prophetic program will again be resumed.

With all that was revealed to Paul about the dispensation of grace, there was one thing he never learned about it, namely, *how long it was to continue.* This *still* remains a mystery. No man knows how long it will last. God has not promised that it will continue for any specific length of time. There are no "times and seasons" for the body of Christ, nor any "signs of the times." The apostle mentions only *trends* toward the close of the age; trends which, in fact, had their beginning in his own day.

106

Paul himself had no idea that the day of grace would be extended until the present time for, writing to Timothy some nineteen hundred years ago concerning the "last days," he instructed *him* (Timothy) how to conduct himself under the circumstances (I Tim. 4:1-7, II Tim. 3:1-17). Paul must have expected the dispensation to close very shortly, for to the unsaved of *his* day (as well as of ours) he wrote:

"We then as workers together with [God], beseech you also that ye receive not the grace of God in vain.

". . . behold, NOW is the accepted time; behold, NOW is the day of salvation" (II Cor. 6:1,2).

And to the saved of *his* day (as well as of ours) he wrote:

"See then that ye walk circumspectly, not as fools, but as wise,

"REDEEMING [BUYING UP] THE TIME, BECAUSE THE DAYS ARE EVIL" (Eph. 5:15,16).

Now that God has delayed His judgment of the world for some nineteen centuries let us beware of presumption, for every moment of delay is a moment of pure grace and *at any moment* this dispensation of grace may suddenly be brought to a close. We cannot promise the lost one more hour in which to be saved, but must cry with more urgency than Paul: *"NOW is the time!"** and must ourselves buy up every opportunity to rescue the perishing, since the days are evil and the time probably very short.

*See the author's pamphlet: *Now is the time.*

107

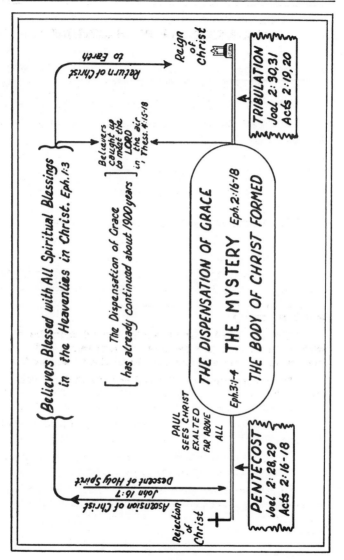

108

PAUL AND THE LORD'S RETURN

Peter's ministry in early Acts, of course, had the Lord's return *to earth* in view; His return to reign in Jerusalem over Israel and the nations.

Paul also has much to say about the Lord's return, but again there is a difference. To Paul it was revealed that the dispensation of grace would be brought to a close by the coming of Christ to catch away the members of His body, *before* the outpouring of His wrath and His return *to earth* to reign.*

That this was part of the "mystery" concerning the body, which had been revealed to Him by the glorified Lord, is clear from his own words:

"FOR THIS WE SAY UNTO YOU BY THE WORD OF THE LORD, that we which are alive and remain unto the coming of the Lord shall not prevent [precede] them which are asleep.

"For the Lord Himself shall descend from heaven with a shout, with the voice of the archangel, and with the trump of God: and the dead in Christ shall rise first:

"Then we which are alive and remain shall be caught up together with them in the clouds, to meet the Lord in the air: and so shall we ever be with the Lord.

"Wherefore comfort one another with these words" **(I Thes. 4:15-18).**

"BEHOLD, I SHOW YOU A MYSTERY; We shall not all sleep, but we shall all be changed,

"In a moment, in the twinkling of an eye, at the last trump: for the trumpet shall sound, and the dead shall be raised incorruptible, and we shall be changed" **(I Cor. 15:51-52).**

---

*See chart.

109

Note again, from these passages, that Paul could not have expected the dispensation of grace to last for many years, for he says: *"WE shall not all sleep"* and *"WE which are alive and remain shall be caught up together with them [those risen] to meet the Lord in the air."* Moreover, he consistently instructs believers from *his day* on to be *waiting* and *looking* for the Lord to come and take them to heaven (Phil. 3:20, I Thes. 1:10, Tit. 2:13).

Space does not permit a thorough study of this wonderful subject in this volume, but let us say here that God's grace and longsuffering in prolonging the present dispensation and delaying the world's judgment for nineteen hundred years should fill our hearts with wonder and gratitude, while at the same time the "blessed hope" of His coming for us should keep us continually watching and waiting, for He *may* come before the reader has finished reading this volume.

PETER AND THE MYSTERY

We have seen that Peter was not wrong when he declared at Pentecost that the last days had begun. They had indeed begun, but God had a *secret* purpose to give the world a period of grace before putting down the world's rebellion and sending Christ to reign.

But the interruption of the kingdom program by the dispensation of grace sheds light on some of Peter's last recorded words too. Writing in his second epistle concerning the delay in Christ's return to earth and the ushering in of the day of the Lord, he says:

110

**"But, beloved, be not ignorant of this one thing, that
ONE DAY IS WITH THE LORD AS A THOUSAND
YEARS, AND A THOUSAND YEARS AS ONE DAY"
(II Pet. 3:8).**

Notice, this is not *our* feeble explanation *now*
of the delay in Christ's return. This statement was
made at the *beginning* of this time of waiting; at the
dawn of the age of grace, and it indicates clearly
that Peter then recognized that an interruption in
the program had taken place. But let us go on with
his statement:

**"The Lord is NOT SLACK concerning His promise,
as some men count slackness; BUT IS LONGSUFFER-
ING to us-ward, not willing that any should perish, but
that all should come to repentance" (II Peter 3:9).**

So the delay should not be counted *slackness*
or laxness on the Lord's part, but *longsuffering*.
And now see verse 15:

**"And account that the longsuffering of our Lord is
SALVATION . . ."**

Where did Peter get all this? How did he
know about the dispensation of grace? Go on with
verse 15:

**"EVEN AS OUR BELOVED BROTHER PAUL
ALSO ACCORDING TO THE WISDOM GIVEN UNTO
HIM HATH WRITTEN UNTO YOU."**

This was written more than 30 years after
Pentecost and by that time Peter had learned from
Paul about the dispensation of grace.

Thus Peter and Paul did not work at cross
purposes or preach contradictory messages. God
simply gave Paul a further revelation of truth.

It was sometime after Paul had been sent out

111

with "the gospel of the grace of God," that he went to Jerusalem "by revelation" and communicated to Peter and the others "that gospel which [he preached] among the Gentiles" (Gal. 2:2). Peter and the rest "saw" and "perceived" that a new revelation had been committed to him and, far from disagreeing, "gave to [Paul] and Barnabas the right hands of fellowship" (Gal. 2:7-9).

Thus while the last days of prophecy had indeed begun at Pentecost Peter, in his last epistle indicates a *delay* in Christ's return to judge and reign and acknowledges this as truth revealed through Paul (II Pet. 3:3-16).

Finally, *both* Peter and Paul teach that the delay is *all of grace,* with no assurance as to how long the dispensation of God's longsuffering will be extended (II Cor. 5:20-6:2, II Pet. 3:8).

What an effect all this should have upon our conduct and service for Christ! We are living, so to speak, in the tense days between man's declaration of war on God and God's counter-declaration (Psa. 2:1-5); a few days of grace, as it were, in which the ambassadors of Christ are authorized to offer reconciliation to any individuals who will receive Him as Savior and Lord. *The next number* on the divine program is the shout with which He will recall His ambassadors and declare war on those who have spurned His grace.

QUIZ

1. What, in a general way, does the term "last days" refer to in Old Testament Scripture? 2. Was Peter right or wrong when he said at Pentecost that the "last days" had come? 3. Explain why. 4. From what famous prophecy did Peter quote in his Pentecostal address? 5. Did all the signs of that prophecy appear at Pentecost? 6. Of what was Peter ignorant when he said the "last days" had come? 7. What has happened to the fulfillment of Joel's prophecy? 8. Why did not the Lord tell His apostles when the kingdom would be restored to Israel? 9. When, according to Old Testament prophecy, would the world have been ripe for judgment? 10. Where did the twelve begin their ministry under the "great commission"? 11. Why? 12. Where did Paul hope to launch his ministry for Christ? 13. Where did the Lord send him instead, and why? 14. Between what two great prophetic periods does the dispensation of grace come? 15. What is the company of God's people in this dispensation called? 16. To what "last days" does Paul refer in his epistles? 17. Why are there no specific signs of Christ's return for the believers of this dispensation? 18. Give two Scriptures to prove that Paul did not expect the dispensation of grace to continue for 1900 years. 19. Give one Scripture each to show how Paul exhorted (a) the lost and (b) the saved, in this connection. 20. Where, in Peter's writings, does he confirm what Paul has to say about the dispensation of grace?

113

THE TWELVE APOSTLES

REPRESENTATIVES OF THE NATION ISRAEL
12 Tribes - 12 Men - 12 Thrones = Matt.19:28

CALLED BY CHRIST ON EARTH = Luke 6:13

KNEW ONLY CHRIST ON EARTH = Acts 1:9

SENT TO ISRAEL AND THE NATIONS
Matt.10:5,6   Luke 24:47, 48

SENT TO PROCLAIM GOD'S PROPHESIED PROGRAM
Salvation of Gentiles through Israel's RISE
Acts 3: 24-26

**AGREE TO CONFINE THEIR MINISTRY TO ISRAEL
AFTER RAISING UP OF PAUL** Gal. 2:1-9

THE APOSTLE PAUL

REPRESENTATIVE OF THE BODY OF CHRIST
ONE Man - both Hebrew and Roman-Reconciled=Eph.2:16

CALLED BY CHRIST IN HEAVEN = Acts 9:3-5

KNEW ONLY CHRIST IN HEAVEN = 1 Cor.15:8

SENT TO ALL MEN EVERYWHERE
Rom. 10:12 ; 11:32

SENT TO PROCLAIM GOD'S SECRET PURPOSE
Salvation of Gentiles through Israel's FALL
Rom. 11:7-33

**SUPERSEDES TWELVE AS APOSTLE OF GENTILES
AS ISRAEL REJECTS KINGDOM** Gal. 2:1-9

Chapter VI.

THE MINISTRIES OF THE TWELVE
AND PAUL COMPARED

The basic cause of the confusion which prevails in the professing Church doctrinally is the failure to recognize the distinctiveness of Paul's message and ministry from that of the twelve. The majority of even sincere believers seem not to have asked themselves the question: *Why Paul?* They seem not to have taken in the striking fact that *after* our Lord, in His so-called *great commission,* had sent the other apostles into *"all the world"* to preach "the gospel" to *"every creature"* (Mark 16:15) and make disciples of *"all nations"* (Matt. 28:19)—*after* this, He raised up *another* apostle, and the twelve through their leaders, under the guidance of the Holy Spirit, entered into a solemn agreement with this other apostle that *he* should go to the Gentiles *while they confined their ministry to Israel* (Gal. 2:7-9). Thus some years after the "great commission" to the eleven (made twelve in Acts 1:15-26), Paul could declare:

"FOR I SPEAK TO YOU GENTILES, INASMUCH AS I AM THE APOSTLE OF THE GENTILES; I MAGNIFY MINE OFFICE" (Romans 11:13).

Paul himself constantly emphasizes the distinctiveness of his apostleship and message. Three times he speaks of "my gospel" (Rom. 2:16, 16:25, II Tim. 2:8) and repeatedly he uses similar phrases, such as: "the gospel which *I* preached," "the gospel which was preached of *me*" and "that gospel which *I* preach among the Gentiles" (I Cor. 15:1, Gal. 1:11, 2:2). Again and again he makes it plain that his message was *received from the Lord* (I. Cor. 11:23, 15:1, I Thes. 4:15) *by direct revelation* (Gal. 1:12, Eph. 3:1-3). He even pronounces a curse on any who would preach to the Gentiles any other gospel than that which *he* had preached. This is why we also find him saying again and again (though in varied phraseology): *"Follow me"* (I Cor. 4:16, 11:1 Phil. 3:17, I Thes. 1:6, II Thes. 3:9).

This means, as pointed out in the preceding chapter, that the prophetic program, of which the "great commission" was a part, was interrupted by the dispensation of the grace of God through Paul. Hence the importance of distinguishing Paul's message and ministry from that of the twelve.

THE TWELVE APOSTLES

In comparing the ministries of the twelve and Paul in this chapter we will number our statements concerning the twelve apostles so that they may be compared with those concerning Paul.

1. The twelve were chosen by Christ *on earth* (Luke 6:13).

2. At the time when Paul was raised up the twelve had known only *Christ on earth.* They had not even seen Him enter heaven at His ascension, for, "a cloud received Him out of their sight" (Acts 1:9).

3. They represented *the nation Israel*—one for each tribe. This is clear from our Lord's promise to them.

"Verily I say unto you, that ye which have followed Me, in the regeneration when the Son of man shall sit in the throne of His glory, YE ALSO SHALL SIT UPON TWELVE THRONES, JUDGING THE TWELVE TRIBES OF ISRAEL" (Matt. 19:28, cf. Luke 22:29,30).

The sincere and thoughtful student of the Scriptures should take careful note of the fact that the number twelve has no connection whatever with the body of Christ, but that it is constantly found in connection with Israel. "Jacob begat the *twelve patriarchs*" (Acts 7:8). From these sprang the *twelve tribes* of Israel. These tribes had *twelve princes* over them (Num.1:16). Even when Israel was ruled by kings there were still to be princes to reign with them over each of the twelve tribes (I Chron. 27:22).

All this, of course, had been disrupted by the captivities, but now the long-promised King was in their midst—He who was to "restore again the kingdom to Israel." And as He goes forth proclaiming "the gospel of the kingdom" (Matt. 9:35), He chooses His *twelve princes* for the *twelve thrones* over Israel's *twelve tribes* (Matt. 19:28).

4. These twelve were first sent forth to proclaim the kingdom of heaven *at hand* (Matt. 10:7, cf. Dan. 2:44) and then, later, to *offer* it to Israel with a view to carrying the message to all the world (Acts 1:6-8, 3:19-26).

5. They were given power to work miracles (Matt. 10:8, cf. Mark 16:17,18).

6. Their ministry was based upon the covenants and prophecy (Isa. 60:1-3, Luke 1:70-75, Acts 3:22-26).

7. Therefore they were sent to the Jew first and looked for the salvation of the Gentiles *through regenerated Israel* (Matt. 10:5,6, Luke 24:47, Acts 3:25, 26).

8. They ministered in Palestine only (Acts 10:39, 21:17-20).*

9. In their message and ministry they anticipated Israel's *acceptance* of Christ as King and His *return to reign.* This was what they labored, hoped and prayed for (Acts 1:11, 3:19-21).

10. In the "great commission" to the twelve, water baptism was required for salvation and miraculous signs were the evidences of salvation (Mark 16:15-18, Acts 2:38).

THE APOSTLE PAUL

The reader is urged to take the time to refer to the numbered paragraphs in the preceding pages and compare Paul's ministry with that of the twelve.

1. Unlike the twelve, Paul was chosen by Christ *in heaven* (Acts 9:3-5, 26:16).

2. He knew only *Christ in heaven,* having never seen Him on earth (Acts 26:16, I Cor. 15:8).

---

*Where they *may* have gone after Acts 28 does not concern us here, for by that time the kingdom program was fully set aside. The fact is that during the Acts period they agreed with Paul to confine their ministry to Israel. Before this agreement, the one Gentile family to which Peter had ministered dwelt at Caesarea in Palestine (Acts 10:24). Peter also went to Antioch in Syria but rather than having any ministry there, was rebuked by Paul (Gal. 2:11-14).

118

3. Paul, as *one* apostle, represents the body of Christ.*

Here again the thoughtful student of Scripture will notice that whereas the number *twelve* is never associated with the body of Christ, the number *one* is consistently associated with it: *"We being many, are one body in Christ"* (Rom. 12:5), *"By one Spirit are we all baptized into one body"* (I Cor. 12:13), *"There is one body"* (Eph. 4:4), etc.

Moreover, the body is made up of *enemies, reconciled* to God through the death of His Son (Col. 1:21,22). What a perfect example Paul was of this!

Further, Paul was both a Hebrew and a Roman. He was a *born Hebrew* (Phil. 3:5) and *intensely* so (Phil. 3:5,6). But he was also a Roman, a born Roman, and intensely Roman.

When the magistrates at Philippi sent word that Paul and Silas were to be released, Paul refused to go, saying:

"THEY HAVE BEATEN US OPENLY UNCONDEMNED, BEING ROMANS, AND HAVE CAST US INTO PRISON; AND NOW DO THEY THRUST US OUT PRIVILY? NAY VERILY; BUT LET THEM COME THEMSELVES AND FETCH US OUT" (Acts 16:37).

Here they demanded an apology from the Roman magistrates and, mark well, the magistrates

---

*Other "apostles" are mentioned in connection with Paul, but always in a secondary manner. In Acts 14:14, for example, Barnabas, Paul's companion in travel, is mentioned as an apostle along with Paul, but according to Gal. 2 it is *Paul* who went up "by revelation" and communicated to the leaders there that gospel which *he* preached among the Gentiles. When "they saw" that the gospel of the uncircumcision had been committed to *Paul* and "perceived" the grace given unto *him* they gave to Paul and Barnabas the right hands of fellowship (Gal. 2:2-9). There is no basis for the statement that "there were eight apostles for the body as there were twelve for Israel." Paul is not boasting when he says, by the. Spirit, *"I am the apostle of the Gentiles, I magnify mine office"* (Rom. 11:13).

"came and besought them, and brought them out" (Verse 39).

Later, at Jerusalem, while the soldiers bound Paul for examination by scourging, Paul said to the centurion that stood by: *"Is it lawful for you to scourge a man that is a Roman, and uncondemned?"* (Acts 22:25).

When this question got back to Lysius, the chief captain who had ordered the scourging, he suddenly became friendly with Paul, explaining that it had cost him a great deal to obtain Roman citizenship.

"And the chief captain answered, With a great sum obtained I this freedom. AND PAUL SAID: BUT I WAS FREE BORN" (Acts 22:28).

At this his would-be examiners suddenly departed. They did not wish to get into trouble with the Roman government for their mistake. "The chief captain also was afraid . . . because he had bound him" (Verse 29).

Paul was a native of Tarsus, "no mean city" in the eyes of Rome (Acts 21:39). In fact, so high was his rank as a Roman, that he had the right to appeal personally to Caesar for trial. This was confirmed by Festus and the Roman council at Caesarea after conferring on the matter (Acts 25:10-12).

Why does the Holy Spirit thus stress the apostle's Roman, as well as his Hebrew, citizenship? Simply because he, a reconciled Hebrew and Roman in one person, represents the body of Christ, the Church of this dispensation, which is composed of *Jews and Gentiles* reconciled to God in *one body,* by the cross (Eph. 2:16).

4. Paul was sent out to proclaim "the gospel of the grace of God" (Acts 20:24, Eph. 3:1-3). While he *confirmed* the fact that Jesus was Israel's Messiah, he never proclaimed the kingdom at hand or offered it for Israel's acceptance. Nor had the twelve until then ever proclaimed the gospel of the grace of God.

5. While at first Paul had "the signs of an apostle," his power to work miracles was withdrawn in connection with his God-given message (Rom. 8:22, 23, I Cor. 13:8-13, II Cor. 4:16, 5:1-4, 12:7-10, Phil. 2:26,27, I Tim. 5:23, II Tim. 4:20).

6. Paul's message was not based upon covenant promises or prophecies but entirely upon the grace of God (Rom. 3:21-28, Eph. 1:7, 2:7). It was a mystery, kept secret until that time (Rom. 16:25, Eph. 3:1-3) and *gradually* revealed to and through him (Acts 26:16, 22:17,18, II Cor. 12:1-7).

7. In his message the Jew and the Gentile stood on the same footing before God (Rom. 3:22,23, 10:12,13).

8. Paul's chief ministry was among the Gentiles (Rom. 11:13, Eph. 3:1,2). When he would have ministered at Jerusalem the Lord forbade him to stay, saying: *"Depart; for I will send thee far hence unto the Gentiles"* (Acts 22:21).

9. With the raising up of Paul Israel was *concluded in unbelief.* The Lord Himself said to Paul: "THEY WILL NOT RECEIVE THY TESTIMONY CONCERNING ME" (Acts 22:18).

Hence Paul's message, unlike that of the twelve, was based upon Israel's *rejection* of Christ, and explained His *continued absence* (Eph. 1:18-2:6, Phil 2:9, Col. 3:1-3, Heb. 2:8,9).

10. Neither water baptism nor miraculous signs were included in Paul's special commission, nor did either have anything to do with salvation under his ministry. It is true that Paul *at first* did baptize some; that he circumcised at least one; that he had "the signs of an apostle," but this was the economy under which he was saved and from which he gradually emerged. Moreover, he states clearly that he *did not preach circumcision* (Gal. 5:11), *was not sent to baptize* (I Cor. 1:17) *and that the miraculous powers he himself possessed would pass away* (I Cor. 13:8-10).

PAUL NOT ONE OF THE TWELVE

Occasionally the disciples are charged with acting in the flesh in choosing Matthias to fill Judas' place as the twelfth apostle. It is said that the disciples had no business choosing a twelfth apostle in the first place. It is further argued that they *first* arbitrarily chose two candidates and *then* asked the Lord which of these two He would have to fill the vacant position. Those who make this charge generally argue that Paul, not Matthias, was God's choice for Judas' place.

This charge, however, is not based upon a careful reading of the account in Acts, nor a very thorough knowledge of the Scriptures bearing on the subject. Let us examine the record:

1. The apostles, with Peter as their chief, had

been given authority to act officially in Christ's absence (Matt. 16:19, 18:18,19).

2. It was stated in the Psalms that another should be appointed to Judas' place (Psa. 109:8, Acts 1:20).

3. The twelfth apostle had to be chosen before the kingdom could be offered at Pentecost (Matt. 19:28). Note how Peter stands up with the eleven in Acts 2:14.

4. Their action was literally bathed in prayer. They did not proceed until after *many days of united prayer* (Luke 24:49, cf. Acts 1:12-15), and when two candidates were found they *again* prayed and left the final choice to God (Acts 1:24-26).

5. It is probable that no more than two (Matthias and Joseph Barsabas) were eligible for the office, for only those could qualify who had followed with Christ *all during His earthly ministry, "beginning from the baptism of John, unto that same day that He was taken up . . ."* (Acts 1:21,22, cf. Matt. 19:28, Note: *"Ye which have followed Me"*). Surely there could not have been many such.

6. For this reason Paul would not have been eligible. He did not even see Christ until after His ascension.

7. Paul was not even saved at that time. Indeed, *after that* he "persecuted the church of God and laid it waste" (Gal. 1:13).

8. The final and conclusive proof that the eleven acted in the will of God in this matter is found in the fact that the Scripture clearly states that

Matthias *"was numbered with the eleven apostles"* (Acts 1:26) and that,

"THEY WERE ALL FILLED WITH THE HOLY GHOST" (Acts 2:4).

Most assuredly, if the disciples had been out of the will of God in so important a matter they would not have been filled with the Holy Spirit. Nor would Matthias have been filled with the Holy Spirit if he had not been divinely chosen for that particular position. A man out of the will of God is never filled with the Holy Spirit.

This, of course, indicates that Paul's apostleship was separate and distinct from that of the twelve. Paul cannot be considered as one with the twelve, for just as eleven apostles would have been too few for God's kingdom plans, so thirteen apostles would have been too many. There will be twelve thrones (besides Christ's) in the kingdom, not thirteen. Hence Paul belonged to *another program* and was sent forth to proclaim *another message*.

It is significant in this connection, that Paul also speaks of the twelve as a separate body of apostles when he says that the resurrected Christ was *"seen . . . of the twelve"* (I Cor. 15:5). This inspired reference to *twelve* apostles between the resurrection and ascension, is further proof that Matthias was, by God, considered one of the twelve from the beginning. Apparently he was with the apostles when the risen Christ appeared to them (Acts 1:21-23).

Indeed, Paul consistently speaks of his apostleship and that of the twelve as distinct from each other. In his letter to the Galatians he says:

"But I certify you, brethren, that THE GOSPEL WHICH WAS PREACHED OF ME IS NOT AFTER MAN.

"FOR I NEITHER RECEIVED IT OF MAN, NEI-THER WAS I TAUGHT IT, BUT BY THE REVELA-TION OF JESUS CHRIST" (Gal. 1:11,12).

"NEITHER WENT I UP [IMMEDIATELY] TO JERUSALEM TO THEM WHICH WERE APOSTLES BEFORE ME: BUT I WENT INTO ARABIA . . . " (Gal. 1:17).

"AND I WENT UP BY REVELATION, AND COM-MUNICATED UNTO THEM THAT GOSPEL WHICH I PREACH AMONG THE GENTILES" (Gal. 2:2).

"AND WHEN JAMES, CEPHAS, AND JOHN, WHO SEEMED TO BE PILLARS, PERCEIVED THE GRACE THAT WAS GIVEN UNTO ME, THEY GAVE TO ME AND BARNABAS THE RIGHT HANDS OF FELLOW-SHIP; THAT WE SHOULD GO UNTO THE HEATHEN, AND THEY UNTO THE CIRCUMCISION (Gal. 2:9).

QUIZ

1. What is the basic cause of the confusion which prevails in the professing Church doctrinally? 2. How do most believers view Paul in relation to the twelve? 3. What striking fact have they overlooked in this connection? 4. What solemn agreement did the leaders of the twelve make with Paul as to ministering among the Gentiles? 5. Why is it important to distinguish between Paul's ministry and that of the twelve? 6. Explain why there were twelve apostles of the kingdom and only one apostle of the grace of God. 7. Give an example to prove

that other "apostles" associated with Paul were apostles only in a secondary sense and were not considered equal as apostles with him. 8. Explain how Paul was a particularly fitting representative of the body of Christ. 9. In what land alone did the twelve minister as far as the record in Acts is concerned? 10. What relation did water baptism and miraculous signs have to salvation under the "great commission"? 11. What relation, if any, do water baptism and miraculous signs have to the gospel of the grace of God? 12. During what period of his ministry did Paul baptize and work miracles? 13. To what program did these things belong? 14. Was Paul sent to baptize? 15. What happened to Paul's miraculous powers? 16. What did Paul do about the kingdom message which the twelve had been proclaiming? 17. What charge is sometimes made against the eleven for their appointment of Matthias as the twelfth apostle? 18. Give five reasons why Matthias, not Paul, was God's choice for the apostleship left vacant by Judas. 19. How did the raising up of Paul affect the kingdom program? 20. Give three Scriptures emphasizing the distinctiveness of Paul's ministry.

Chapter VII.

PETER AND PAUL AS WITNESSES

In addition to the distinctions between the ministries of the twelve apostles and Paul, the Scriptures also clearly distinguish between the ministries of Peter (as leader of the twelve) and Paul.

VISIONS AND VOICES

A STATEMENT BY PETER

II Peter 1:16-18

"For we have not followed cunningly devised fables, when we made known unto you the power and coming of our Lord Jesus Christ, but were EYEWITNESSES of His majesty.

"For He received from God the Father honor and glory, when there came such A VOICE to Him from the excellent glory, This is My beloved Son, in whom I am well pleased.

"AND THIS VOICE . . . WE HEARD, when we were with Him in the holy mount."

A STATEMENT BY PAUL

Acts 22:7,14,15

"And I fell unto the ground, and HEARD A VOICE saying unto me, Saul, Saul, why persecutest thou Me?"

"And he [Ananias] said, The God of our fathers hath chosen thee, that thou shouldest know His will, and SEE that Just One, and shouldest HEAR the voice of His mouth.

"For thou shalt be His witness unto all men of what thou hast SEEN AND HEARD."

127

A comparison of the above passages reveals the following *similarities*.

1. Both Peter and Paul *saw* the Lord in glory.

2. Both *heard* voices from heaven.

3. Both were witnesses of what they had *seen* and *heard.**

Yet there are distinct *differences* between the circumstances and significance of their experiences.

1. Peter saw the Lord in His glory *on earth*. Paul saw Him in His glory *in heaven*.

2. Peter saw Him in His *kingdom* glory. Paul saw Him in the glory of His *grace* at the Father's right hand.

3. The voice Peter heard had the *acceptance* of Christ in view (cf. Matt. 17:5, "Hear ye Him"). The voice Paul heard had the *rejection* of Christ in view ("Why persecutest thou Me?").

4. What Peter saw was a demonstration of *"the power and coming" of Christ*. What Paul saw was a demonstration of *the grace that caused Him to delay His coming* (cf. II Peter 3:9,15).

5. Peter's experience harmonized with his position as an apostle of *the Messianic kingdom*. Paul's harmonized with his position as the apostle of *the grace of God*.

PETER ON THE MOUNTAIN TOP

In Matt. 4:17 we read:

"FROM THAT TIME JESUS BEGAN TO PREACH,

*In addition to the above passages see Acts 4:20 and 26:16.

128

AND TO SAY, REPENT: FOR THE KINGDOM OF HEAVEN IS AT HAND."

Matt. 10:5-7 tells how the Lord sent His twelve apostles forth with the same message: *"The kingdom of heaven is at hand."*

How was the message received? Matt. 16:21 answers this question:

"FROM THAT TIME FORTH BEGAN JESUS TO SHOW UNTO HIS DISCIPLES, HOW THAT HE MUST GO UNTO JERUSALEM, AND SUFFER MANY THINGS OF THE ELDERS AND CHIEF PRIESTS AND SCRIBES, AND BE KILLED, AND BE RAISED AGAIN THE THIRD DAY."

Imagine the apostles' feelings now. They were already discouraged over the poor response to their proclamation of the kingdom. And now the opposition of the rulers becomes more intense and their Lord begins to talk about being killed!

If His "defeatist" attitude bewildered them, they must have been completely at a loss to understand His reference to being raised again. Indeed, the account in Luke 18:34 states in three different ways that they did not have the slightest idea what He was talking about. Apparently they could only conclude that He was conceding defeat, for in the next verse of Matthew's account we read:

"Then Peter took Him, and began to rebuke Him, saying, Be it far from Thee, Lord: this shall not be unto Thee" (Matt. 16:22).

Undoubtedly this attitude on the part of the

129

apostles was one great reason for the transfiguration of our Lord.

While telling the apostles of His rejection by Israel and His approaching death, He nevertheless wished to reassure them as to the final outcome. Hence he took the three who were closest to Him and gave them a glimpse of the glory and majesty that would one day be His. The incident is described for us in Matt. 17:1,2:

"AFTER SIX DAYS JESUS TAKETH PETER, JAMES, AND JOHN HIS BROTHER, AND BRINGETH THEM UP INTO AN HIGH MOUNTAIN APART,

"AND WAS TRANSFIGURED BEFORE THEM: AND HIS FACE DID SHINE AS THE SUN, AND HIS RAIMENT WAS WHITE AS THE LIGHT."

That day Peter, James and John became *"eye-witnesses of His majesty"* and heard the voice of God Himself, confirming what they saw. Come what may now, they had no reason to ever doubt that Christ was God's Anointed and would eventually reign in glory.

Some thirty years after the ascension, while Christ still remained away, Peter referred back to this experience, as we have shown above, assuring his readers that he, James and John had not "followed cunningly devised fables" when they had proclaimed Christ's "power and coming," but "were eyewitnesses of His majesty," and had heard the Father's "voice from heaven" confirming what they saw.

Thus Peter saw the Lord in His glory indeed but, be it noted, in His *kingdom* glory *on earth,* and he himself associates the vision with our Lord's *"power and coming."*

SAUL ON THE ROAD TO DAMASCUS

The Lord also appeared to Paul in glory, but under very different circumstances and for a very different purpose.

As we know, Peter and the eleven did not succeed in bringing Israel to Messiah's feet. Indeed, the opposition of Israel's government to Christ became even more bitter than it had been before the cross until, finally, the blood of Stephen was shed, and then more blood and more and more.

This is where we read of Saul of Tarsus, for it was he who inspired and led the "great persecution" against the Pentecostal believers.

Concerning the murder of Stephen we read: *"And Saul was consenting unto his death,"* and in the same verse: *"And at that time there was [arose, R.V.] a great persecution against the church which was at Jerusalem"* (Acts 8:1).

That Saul was the chief persecutor is certain, for the Scripture record of the persecution places him in the foreground. Acts 8:3 says: *"As for Saul, he made havock of the church"* and the next chapter finds him *"yet breathing out threatenings and slaughter against the disciples of the Lord"* (Acts

9:1). The Damascus believers spoke of him as *"he that destroyed them which called on this name"* (Acts 9:21).

Paul himself acknowledged years later: *"I persecuted this way unto the death, binding and delivering into prisons both men and women"* (Acts 22:4), *"and many of the saints did I shut up in prison . . . and when they were put to death, I gave my voice [vote] against them. And I punished them oft in every synagogue, and compelled them to blaspheme; and being exceedingly mad against them, I persecuted them even unto strange cities"* (Acts 26:10,11). In his letter to the Galatians he sums all this up in the words: *"Beyond measure I persecuted the church of God and wasted it [laid it waste]"* (Gal. 1:13).

In all this Saul was the personification of Israel's spirit of rebellion against Messiah. But when the persecution was at its height; as Saul, breathing threatenings and slaughter against Messiah's followers, travelled toward Damascus to "destroy" still more of them, the rejected Lord Himself intervened and Saul, like Peter, saw the Lord in glory and heard a voice from heaven.

But how different the circumstances!

Peter, as the Lord's apostle, had seen, heard and proclaimed that Jesus was the Christ. Saul was Peter's bitterest enemy for proclaiming that fact. Peter was the leader of the Pentecostal church; Saul was the leader of the persecution against that church.

Moreover, Paul saw the Lord, not in His kingdom glory, as Peter had, but in the glory of His grace, exalted "far above all heavens."

There are two facts in connection with Saul's experience on the road to Damascus which deserve particular attention:

First, it should be noted that *the Lord's rejection by Israel was now assumed.* Before the ston‑ing of Stephen and the raising up of Saul, God had offered the kingdom to Israel on the assumption* that she would repent and accept her Messiah. But now, with Israel waging war against the church (of that day) and Saul of Tarsus making havock of the church, the rejected Lord calls from heaven: *"Why persecutest thou Me?" After that the kingdom was never again offered to Israel so far as the record is concerned.*

Secondly, we should notice that while Saul was Christ's bitterest enemy on earth, yet the Lord dealt with him in grace. Instead of judging him, He *saved* him!

All this is deeply significant, for, since Israel had turned to be God's enemy, God was now to conclude her, along with the Gentiles, in unbelief, *"that He might have mercy upon all"* (Rom.11:32).

---

*We realize, of course, that *God knew* Israel would reject Christ; nevertheless, *in His dealings with them* He assumed—and the assumption was legitimate—that Israel would *accept* Christ.

Looking back, years later, Paul refers to himself as one "who was before *a blasphemer,* and *a persecutor,* and *injurious,*" but he goes on to say:

"AND THE GRACE OF OUR LORD WAS EXCEEDING ABUNDANT, WITH FAITH AND LOVE WHICH IS IN CHRIST JESUS.

"THIS IS A FAITHFUL SAYING, AND WORTHY OF ALL ACCEPTATION, THAT CHRIST JESUS CAME INTO THE WORLD TO SAVE SINNERS; OF WHOM I AM CHIEF.

"HOWBEIT FOR THIS CAUSE I OBTAINED MERCY, THAT IN ME FIRST JESUS CHRIST MIGHT SHOW FORTH ALL LONGSUFFERING, FOR A PATTERN TO THEM WHICH SHOULD HEREAFTER BELIEVE ON HIM TO LIFE EVERLASTING" (I Tim. 1:14-16).

It is difficult to understand how anyone can read this portion of Scripture without seeing that God began a new dispensation with the conversion of Saul. Rather than judging Israel and the world immediately, the rejected Lord demonstrated His infinite love by saving Saul and sending him forth with *"the gospel of the grace of God"* (Acts 20:24). This *"dispensation of the grace of God"* by Paul is the dispensation under which we now live. It will not be brought to a close until the Lord Himself comes to call the members of His body to heaven. Then the prophetic program will again be resumed and the bowls of God's wrath poured out upon a Christ-rejecting world.

THE SUFFERINGS AND THE GLORY

The Lord's promise in Matt. 19:28 had left no doubt that the twelve were to occupy thrones with Christ in the kingdom, and what Peter saw and heard "in the holy mount" concerned the glory which he himself was to share at the reign of Christ.

What Paul saw and heard, however, concerned the Lord's *suffering—and his own*. The rejected Lord said to Saul: *"Why persecutest thou Me?"* but He also said to Ananias concerning Saul: *"I will show him how great things he must suffer for My name's sake"* (Acts 9:16). Christ was, in grace, to remain in exile, rejected still by the world, but Paul, the sinner saved by grace, was to bear the suffering and the rejection.

This explains Col. 1:24, where the apostle says:

"[I] now rejoice in my SUFFERINGS for you, and FILL UP THAT WHICH IS BEHIND OF THE AFFLICTIONS OF CHRIST in my flesh, for His body's sake, which is the church."

In what sense did Paul fill up that which remained of the afflictions of Christ? Surely he could add nothing to the finished work of redemption. The point is that, while Christ's *vicarious* suffering for sin was over, He was *still rejected,* and in grace chose to remain so for a time rather than proceed immediately to judge His enemies. So, putting off "the day of His wrath," He saved Saul, His chief foe, and sent him forth to proclaim grace and peace

135

to His enemies everywhere. Thus the great persecutor now became the persecuted one, bearing the afflictions of Christ's continued rejection. And as long as our Lord in grace remains away we, the members of Christ's body follow Paul in this, as it is written:

"FOR UNTO YOU IT IS GIVEN IN THE BEHALF OF CHRIST, NOT ONLY TO BELIEVE ON HIM, BUT ALSO TO SUFFER FOR HIS SAKE.

"HAVING THE SAME CONFLICT WHICH YE SAW IN ME, AND NOW HEAR TO BE IN ME" (Phil. 1:29,30).

Such suffering, however, is sweet. The apostle calls it suffering *"with Christ"* (Rom. 8:17), "the sufferings *of Christ"* (II Cor. 1:5), *"the fellowship of His sufferings,"* and longs for this fellowship (Phil. 3:10).

It may be asked: Had not the twelve suffered for Christ too? Yes, but always in the hope that Israel would yet accept Christ. When Paul, rather than Peter, takes the place of prominence in the Book of Acts it is because Israel's rejection of Christ is recognized and assumed. This is not to say, of course, that God immediately closed His dealings with Israel as a nation, for the sentence upon Israel is not officially pronounced until Acts 28:28.

Thus Paul was called to preach Christ in a Christ-rejecting world and to suffer for it. He was chosen to fill up that which still remained of the sufferings of Christ—and so are we, for He exhorts us, by the Holy Spirit: *"Brethren, be followers together of me"* (Phil. 3:17).

Christ is *still* rejected and *still* remains away and *we* bear, or should bear, in our flesh the sufferings of His rejection. In a world at enmity with God and His Christ we cry:

". . . WE ARE AMBASSADORS FOR CHRIST, AS THOUGH GOD DID BESEECH YOU BY US: WE PRAY YOU IN CHRIST'S STEAD, BE YE RECONCILED TO GOD.

"FOR HE HATH MADE HIM TO BE SIN FOR US, WHO KNEW NO SIN; THAT WE MIGHT BE MADE THE RIGHTEOUSNESS OF GOD IN HIM" (II Cor. 5:20,21).

Christ died in *our* stead, and we consider it a privilege to stand before men in *His* stead, though it frequently involves suffering. Like Paul, we plead with men and say: "Christ is not here; you did not want Him, but we are here in His stead to tell you that He loves you and died for you that you might be reconciled to God through His merits."

TWO MORE VOICES

PETER AT JOPPA

Acts 10:9-16

"On the morrow . . . Peter went up upon the housetop TO PRAY about the sixth hour.

"And he became very hungry, and would have

PAUL AT JERUSALEM

Acts 22:17-21

"And it came to pass, that when I was come again to Jerusalem, even while I PRAYED in the temple, I was in A TRANCE;

eaten: but while they made ready, he fell into A TRANCE,

"And saw heaven opened, and a certain vessel descending unto him, as it had been a great sheet, knit at the four corners, and let down to the earth:

"Wherein were all manner of four-footed beasts of the earth, and wild beasts, and creeping things, and fowls of the air.

"And THERE CAME A VOICE TO HIM, Rise, Peter; kill, and eat.

"BUT PETER SAID, Not so, Lord; for I have never eaten anything that is common or unclean.

"And the voice spake unto him again the second time, What God hath cleansed, that call not thou common.

"This was done thrice: and the vessel was received up again into heaven."

"And SAW HIM SAYING UNTO ME, Make haste, and get thee quickly out of Jerusalem: for they will not receive thy testimony concerning Me.

"AND I SAID, Lord, they know that I imprisoned and beat in every synagogue them that believed on Thee:

"And when the blood of Thy martyr Stephen was shed, I also was standing by, and consenting unto his death, and kept the raiment of them that slew him.

"And He said unto me, depart: for I will send thee far hence unto the Gentiles."

Here again Peter and Paul each heard a voice; each while in a trance and each having been engaged in prayer at the time. Peter's experience concerned God's purpose to go to the Gentiles; Paul's concerned His purpose to turn from Israel. Both talked back to God.

Peter, in his abhorrence of the unclean, objected that he had never eaten anything common or unclean. Paul, in his eagerness to minister at Jerusalem and win his kinsman to Christ, argued that they all knew him as the former persecutor of the church.

In each case, however, the Lord insisted on carrying out His purpose. To Peter He said, *"What God hath cleansed, that call not thou common,"* and bade him go to the Gentiles "nothing doubting." To Paul He replied, *"Depart: for I will send thee far hence unto the Gentiles."*

We are well aware of the fact that Peter did not proclaim the mystery of God's purpose and grace to these Gentiles. He did not even know it. He did not even know why God was sending him and, when called to account, explained simply: *"What was I that I could withstand God?"* (Acts 11:17). Furthermore, his ministry to Cornelius' household was accompanied by water baptism and miraculous signs.

Nevertheless Peter's mission was *one of the first steps in the unfolding of the mystery, God's plan to bless the nations in spite of Israel's rejection of Christ.*

While recognizing fully the kingdom aspect of Peter's message and Cornelius' conversion, we should not forget the following facts:

1. The incident took place after *the conversion of Saul,* which was the *first* step in the introduction of the new dispensation (I Tim. 1:13-16).

2. Peter was not sent to Cornelius under the so-called "great commission" but by a special commission; not because Israel had *accepted* Messiah but in view of the fact that she was *rejecting* Him. It was *not* the next step in the carrying out of the "great commission," for according to that commission Israel must first be brought to Messiah's feet (see Luke 24:47, Acts 1:8, 3:25,26) and it had become increasingly evident that Israel would not accept Messiah.

3. Here for the first time we learn that God has put *"no difference"* between Jew and Gentile (Acts 15:9). This, as we have seen, was not so under the "great commission," nor will it be so in the day of the Lord, when that commission is carried out (Matt. 24:14 cf. Isa. 60:1-3). But before the Acts period closes it is fully demonstrated that *"There is no difference,"* either as to man's sin (Rom. 3:22,23) or as to God's grace (Rom. 10:12).

4. *It was on the basis of Peter's experience that Paul's ministry to the Gentiles was recognized by the church at Jerusalem* (Read carefully Acts 15:7-35).

As to Paul's experience in the temple on that first return to Jerusalem after his conversion, it indicates clearly that Israel's rejection of Christ had now been assumed. The message of the twelve having been spurned, Paul now supposed that they would listen to *him,* seeing he had once led them in their persecution of Christ. But the Lord knew better and said: *"They will not receive thy testimony concerning Me."*

Again, let us remember why God thus broke off dealings with Israel *as a nation."*

"FOR GOD HATH CONCLUDED THEM ALL IN UNBELIEF, THAT HE MIGHT HAVE MERCY UPON ALL.

"O THE DEPTH OF THE RICHES BOTH OF THE WISDOM AND KNOWLEDGE OF GOD! HOW UN-SEARCHABLE ARE HIS JUDGMENTS, AND HIS WAYS PAST FINDING OUT!" (Romans 11:32,33).

QUIZ

1. Where did the "transfiguration" of our Lord take place? 2. In what greater glory did Paul later see Christ? 3. What did the voice from heaven say at the "transfiguration"? 4. What was the significance of the "transfiguration"? 5. What did the voice from heaven say to Paul when he *first* saw the glorified Lord? 6. In what way was this significant? 7. How did the details of the "transfiguration" harmonize with Peter's ministry? 8. How did the details of the revelation of Christ to Paul harmonize with his ministry? 9. What had been the apostles' reaction to Christ's prediction of His death and resurrection? 10. How had Peter responded? 11. How should the "transfiguration" have affected this situation? 12. Give three Scriptures describing Saul's role as persecutor of Christ. 13. How did God reply to Saul's (and Israel's) rebellion against Christ? 14. Give one Scripture indicating that God began a new dispensation with the conver-

sion of Saul. 15. Give one Scripture indicating the relation between Christ's rejection and Paul's suffering for Christ. 16. Give one Scripture indicating that we too are to suffer for Christ's rejection. 17. Give three indications that Peter's mission to Cornelius was one of the first steps in the unfolding of the mystery. 18. What was Peter's vision on Joppa's housetop intended to teach him? 19. What was Paul's vision in the temple intended to teach him? 20. What relation was there between Peter's visit to Cornelius and Paul's subsequent ministry among the Gentiles?

Chapter VIII.

PETER AND PAUL AS BUILDERS

PETER'S CONFESSION

Matt. 16:13-19

"When Jesus came into the coasts of Caesarea Philippi, He asked His disciples, saying, Whom do men say that I, the Son of man, am?

"And they said, Some say that thou art John the Baptist: some, Elias; and others, Jeremias, or one of the prophets.

"He saith unto them, but whom say ye that I am?

"And Simon Peter answered and said, THOU ART THE CHRIST, THE SON OF THE LIVING GOD.

"And Jesus answered and said unto him, Blessed art thou, Simon Barjona: for flesh and blood hath not revealed it unto thee, but My Father which is in heaven.

"And I say also unto thee, that thou art Peter, and UPON THIS ROCK I WILL

PAUL'S CLAIM

I Cor. 3:10-15

"ACCORDING TO THE GRACE OF GOD WHICH IS GIVEN UNTO ME, AS A WISE MASTER-BUILDER, I HAVE LAID THE FOUNDATION, AND ANOTHER BUILDETH THEREON. BUT LET EVERY MAN TAKE HEED HOW HE BUILDETH THEREUPON.

"FOR OTHER FOUNDATION CAN NO MAN LAY THAN THAT IS LAID, WHICH IS JESUS CHRIST.

"NOW IF ANY MAN BUILD UPON THIS FOUNDATION GOLD, SILVER, PRECIOUS STONES, WOOD, HAY, STUBBLE;

"EVERY MAN'S WORK SHALL BE MADE MANIFEST: FOR THE DAY SHALL DECLARE IT, BECAUSE IT SHALL BE REVEALED BY FIRE;

143

BUILD MY CHURCH; AND THE GATES OF HELL SHALL NOT PREVAIL AGAINST IT.

"AND I WILL GIVE UNTO THEE THE KEYS OF THE KINGDOM OF HEAVEN: AND WHATSO-EVER THOU SHALT BIND ON EARTH SHALL BE BOUND IN HEAVEN: AND WHATSOEVER THOU SHALT LOOSE ON EARTH SHALL BE LOOSED IN HEAVEN."

AND THE FIRE SHALL TRY EVERY MAN'S WORK OF WHAT SORT IT IS.

"IF ANY MAN'S WORK ABIDE WHICH HE HATH BUILT THEREUPON, HE SHALL RECEIVE A RE-WARD.

"IF ANY MAN'S WORK SHALL BE BURNED, HE SHALL SUFFER LOSS: BUT HE HIMSELF SHALL BE SAVED; YET SO AS BY FIRE."

PETER AND THE MESSIANIC CHURCH

It should be carefully noted that it was Peter's *confession* that won for him the name *Petros, A Stone,* and it was upon this confession (*"this rock"*, Gr. *Petra*) that Christ was to build His church. In claiming that the church is founded upon Peter himself, Rome utterly disregards the context, exalts Peter above Christ and flatly contradicts the Word of God which says:

"OTHER FOUNDATION CAN NO MAN LAY THAN THAT IS LAID, WHICH IS JESUS CHRIST" (I Cor. 3:11).

But it should be noticed particularly that Peter confessed Jesus as *"the Christ* (Heb. *Messiah, Anointed One), the Son of the living God."*

The twelve, remember, had been sent out to preach: *"The kingdom of heaven is at hand"* (Matt. 10:5-7). Christ Himself, of course, was

God's Anointed Son, chosen to occupy the throne in this kingdom.

As the Lord, more and more rejected in Israel, now asks His disciples: "Whom say *ye* that I am," it is thrilling to hear Peter reply instantly and without qualification: *"Thou art the Christ, the Son of the living God."*

This truth: Jesus as rightful King and Son of God, was to be the very foundation of the Messianic church* and this is how true believers recognized the Lord at that time.

On another occasion Peter reaffirmed his faith in Jesus as the Messiah when he said:

"We believe and are sure that Thou art that CHRIST, THE SON OF THE LIVING GOD" (John 6:69).

Nathanael recognized Him in the same way, and said:

"Rabbi, Thou art THE SON OF GOD; Thou art THE KING OF ISRAEL" (John 1:49).

Martha said:

"Yea Lord: I believe that Thou art THE CHRIST, the Son of God, which should come into the world" (John 11:27).

John, writing about our Lord's earthly life, closes his gospel record:

"And many other signs truly did Jesus in the presence of His disciples, which are not written in this book:

---

*i.e., the *kingdom* church, not the church of *this* dispensation. This is clear from the fact that in the next verse Peter is given the keys of "the kingdom of heaven" and also from the fact that "the church which is His body" was then still a mystery "hid in God" (Eph. 3:1-11).

145

"But these are written, that ye might believe that JESUS IS THE CHRIST, THE SON OF GOD; and that believing ye might have life through His name" (John 20:30,31).*

PAUL AND THE BODY OF CHRIST

We know, however, that Israel as a nation rejected Christ and the building of the Messianic church could not go on to completion. Messiah, the Foundation and Corner Stone was rejected and the building, even today, lies in ruins. Thus God is showing Israel that her house will not stand unless she recognizes Jesus as His Son and her King.

Meanwhile God is building *another* house, or at least another part of the great compound structure referred to in Eph. 2:21,22. The building of *this* house, the church of this age, was a secret which Peter and the eleven knew nothing about when they followed Christ as king and offered His kingdom to Israel at Pentecost.

The plans and specifications for the building of this church were committed to Paul by the glorified Lord Himself. He says, by the Spirit:

"ACCORDING TO THE GRACE OF GOD WHICH IS GIVEN UNTO ME, AS A WISE MASTER-BUILDER,° I HAVE LAID THE FOUNDATION AND ANOTHER BUILDETH THEREON" (I Cor. 3:10).

When Paul says: *"I have laid the foundation,"* he does not mean that the church of this dispensation is not also to be founded upon Christ, for in the

---

*Though "the *grace* of our Lord Jesus Christ," rather than His *kingdom*, is God's message for today, we too must, of course, believe that He is the rightful King and the Son of God.

°Gr. *chief architect*; however, the chief architects of those days were apparently also in charge of the building, so that *Master-builder* is a fair translation.

next verse he states clearly that no other foundation can be laid than Jesus Christ. This is why it is so important that "every man take heed how he buildeth thereupon" (3:10). Indeed, in Eph. 2:20 he also says that we are *"built upon the foundation of [laid down by] the apostles and prophets."* That is, we are *"built upon Jesus Christ."*

The point in Paul's claim is that we now know Christ *in a different way*. Whereas Peter and the eleven knew Him as the King to reign on earth, we know Him (the same Person) as the glorified Head of the body (Eph. 1:19-23).

Paul, by the Spirit, indicates that a dispensational change has taken place, when he says:

"Wherefore HENCEFORTH know we no man after the flesh: yea, THOUGH WE HAVE KNOWN CHRIST AFTER THE FLESH, YET NOW HENCEFORTH KNOW WE HIM NO MORE" (II Cor. 5:16).

Before that time men were expected to trust in Jesus as *"the Christ, the Son of the living God,"* the King to reign as God on David's throne. But with the raising up of Paul Israel's rejection of Christ was assumed and *we* trust the rejected King as *our glorified Lord and Savior*. Hence Paul declares:

"If thou shalt confess with thy mouth JESUS AS LORD, and shalt believe in thy heart that God RAISED Him from the dead, thou shalt be saved" (Rom. 10:9, R.V.).

THE TWO NOT TO BE CONFUSED

We must be careful not to confuse this church described in Ephesians with that of which our Lord spoke to Peter. *That* was a prophesied church.

147

This was a mystery. The plans and specifications for *that* church are found in the Old Testament Scriptures. The plans and specifications for *this* church were *"kept secret since the world began"* (Rom. 16:25), *"hid from ages and from generations'* (Col. 1:26), *"in other ages . . . not made known"* (Eph. 3:5), but now revealed to and through the Apostle Paul.

Peter and Paul, then, both built upon the same foundation, but whereas the millennial church will be built upon our Lord as *Israel's Messiah,* the church of the present dispensation is built upon Him as *the glorified Head of the body,* rejected on earth, but exalted far above all, at God's right hand in heaven.

This distinction is clearly brought out by a comparison of Acts 2 with II Tim. 2.

In the former passage *Peter* declares that God has raised Christ from the dead *to sit on the throne of David* (Acts 2:29-36). In the latter passage *Paul* exhorts Timothy:

"Consider what I say; and the Lord give thee understanding in all things.

"REMEMBER THAT JESUS CHRIST OF THE SEED OF DAVID WAS RAISED FROM THE DEAD ACCORDING TO MY GOSPEL:

"Wherein I suffer trouble, as an evil doer, even unto bonds: but the Word of God is not bound" (II Tim. 2:7-9).

To understand what the apostle means when he says that Jesus Christ, of the seed of David, was (also) raised from the dead according to *his* gospel, we must turn to Eph. 1 and 2, where we find him praying that believers might be given the spiritual perception to see

". . . what is the hope of His calling, and what the riches of the glory of His inheritance in the saints,

"AND WHAT IS THE EXCEEDING GREATNESS OF HIS POWER TO US-WARD WHO BELIEVE, ACCORDING TO THE WORKING OF HIS MIGHTY POWER,

"WHICH HE WROUGHT IN CHRIST, WHEN HE RAISED HIM FROM THE DEAD, AND SET HIM AT HIS OWN RIGHT HAND IN THE HEAVENLY PLACES" (Eph. 1:18-20).

"BUT GOD, WHO IS RICH IN MERCY, FOR HIS GREAT LOVE WHEREWITH HE LOVED US,

"EVEN WHEN WE WERE DEAD IN SINS, HATH QUICKENED US TOGETHER WITH CHRIST, (BY GRACE YE ARE SAVED;)

"AND HATH RAISED US UP TOGETHER, AND MADE US SIT TOGETHER IN HEAVENLY PLACES IN CHRIST JESUS" (Eph. 2:4-6).

Surely Peter would have preached such a message at Pentecost, had he known it. But he did not know it. At Pentecost he proclaimed Christ only as the Savior-King whom God had raised from the dead to sit on David's throne. He called upon Israel to repent and be baptized for the remission of sins so that the times of refreshing might come and God might send back Jesus, whom they had rejected and crucified (Acts 3:19-21).

Peter's ministry, indeed, was accompanied by miraculous signs which "vanished away" during Paul's ministry, but who would sigh for "Pentecostal power" when he has come to know the power of Christ's resurrection? (Eph. 1:19,20, Phil. 3:10).

149

It is this message which Satan hates so bitterly and opposes so viciously that Paul suffered trouble for it as an evil doer, even unto bonds. And little wonder! It had seemed that with Israel's rejection of Christ all hope for the world was gone; that man had made his own salvation impossible; that God's promises had failed. *And then came the revelation of the mystery!* The chief of sinners was saved and sent forth to proclaim *"the gospel of the grace of God."* The very cross which had spelled man's condemnation was now revealed as the effective means of his salvation, and those trusting in Christ's shed blood were freely granted the remission of their sins and given a position in Christ at God's right hand in the heavenlies!

PAUL THE MASTER-BUILDER

Paul was not self-important in calling himself the "master-builder" of the church of this dispensation. He makes it clear that this position was given to him *"according to the grace of God."* Indeed, he always associates his unique position with the grace of God, for his conversion and commission was the supreme demonstration of that grace (See Rom. 1:5, 12:3, 15:15,16, I Cor. 15:9,10, Gal. 1:15,16, 2:9, Eph. 3:7,8 and I Tim. 1:12-16).

Moses was the master-builder of the tabernacle. God gave him the plans and specifications for it, and said: *"See . . . that thou make all things according to the pattern showed to thee in the mount"* (Heb. 8:5).

As Moses represents the law, Paul represents grace. Paul too was a master-builder, for to him God committed the plans and specifications for a greater building, "an holy temple," the church which is Christ's body. Step by step the details were made known to him by direct revelation so that, as "a wise [intelligent] master-builder," he had the right and responsibility to outline them to us, the builders.

THE BUILDERS' RESPONSIBILITY

Why are God's builders failing so utterly to build according to the plans and specifications set forth in Paul's epistles? Why do they ignore the warning:

"I HAVE LAID THE FOUNDATION . . . LET EVERY MAN TAKE HEED HOW HE BUILDETH THEREUPON."

They have taken Petrine material and built it upon the Pauline foundation. They have talked about "building the kingdom" and have tried vainly to carry out the so-called "great commission." They have taken water baptism, tongues, healings and signs of the times from another dispensation and have brought them into the dispensation of the grace of God after God has caused them to "vanish away," until the church is so confused and divided that few know what to believe.

This comes from taking too lightly the apostolic anathema of Gal. 1:8:

"BUT THOUGH WE, OR AN ANGEL FROM HEAVEN, PREACH ANY OTHER GOSPEL UNTO YOU THAN THAT WHICH WE HAVE PREACHED UNTO YOU, LET HIM BE ACCURSED."

Are our spiritual leaders unaware of the condition of the church or have they forgotten that they will give an account to God for their workmanship when the building is inspected?

Surely God is not to blame for the present condition of the church. *The builders are to blame.* Instead of preaching the Word rightly divided, they have fed their congregations with milk and music. Some catchy phrase, some striking verse from here or there or anywhere, regardless of its context; this, along with some sort of entertainment, is made to do for what should be intelligent and spiritually powerful preaching of the Word. And the majority of Christians have been fed on this sort of diet for so long that they are spiritually sick—so sick that their leaders feel justified in continuing the light diet indefinitely.

It is often argued that souls are being saved, but will the builders of the church never awaken to the fact that hands raised or people coming forward do not measure the success of their work? *Will their work abide?* That is the question. Not does it receive public approval, but *will it abide the divine inspection?*

Too often spiritual leaders have applied Paul's warning in I Cor. 3:10-17 to Christian conduct in general, while the passage deals specifically with the *builders* and their *workmanship* in the erection of the church. The result: look at the church—yes, even the Fundamental, Bible-believing church. Examine it carefully and see whether the building is in sound condition. See whether it is composed mostly of *"gold, silver, precious stones,"* or of *"wood, hay and stubble."* And then ask yourself what the great divine Inspector will say to the builders when He examines their workmanship.

Many an evangelist, many a preacher, who enjoys prominence and popularity today will weep in *that* day, to see his work go up in flames. Even though "he himself shall be saved" it will be a dreadful thing to "suffer loss" when the rewards are given out.

How may God's workmen overcome faulty building and escape disapproval of their work by the great Building Inspector? *There is only one way*:

"STUDY TO SHOW THYSELF APPROVED UNTO GOD, A WORKMAN THAT NEEDETH NOT TO BE ASHAMED, RIGHTLY DIVIDING THE WORD OF TRUTH" (II Tim. 2:15).

QUIZ

1. How did Simon win for himself the name *Petros, A Stone*? 2. On what *Petra,* or *rock,* then, was Christ to build "His church"? 3. Give Scripture to prove that this church was *not* to be built upon Peter himself. 4. To what church did our Lord refer in Matt. 16:18? 5. To what did our Lord promise to give Peter the keys? 6. Give proof that the Lord could not have referred to "the church which is His body." 7. Give two other Scriptural examples indicating that believers at that time looked to Jesus as *Messiah* and *Son of God.* 8. How must men confess Jesus today to be saved? Give Scripture. 9. What is the relation between our Lord and the church of this present dispensation? 10. At Pentecost Peter declared that

God had raised Christ from the dead for what purpose? 11. What further revelation did *Paul* receive and make known about the resurrection of Christ? 12. Paul later reminded Timothy that Jesus Christ, of the seed of David, had been raised from the dead according to what? 13. What relation does Paul sustain to the building of the church of this dispensation? Give Scripture. 14. How does he admonish the builders in this connection? 15. Of what different types of materials may God's building be composed? 16. By what means will the workmanship of the builders be tried, and what will be the one great test of satisfactory workmanship? 17. How will the results affect the builders? 18. Give Scripture to prove that the *salvation* of the workmen will not be affected by the quality of their workmanship. 19. According to I Cor. 3:10-15, who is to blame for the condition of the church today? 20. What Scripture indicates how we may be sure to be approved as God's workmen?

Chapter IX.

PETRINE AND PAULINE AUTHORITY

PETER AND HIS KEYS

In connection with the building of the Messianic church our Lord said to Peter:

"AND I WILL GIVE UNTO THEE THE KEYS OF THE KINGDOM OF HEAVEN: AND WHATSOEVER THOU SHALT BIND ON EARTH SHALL BE BOUND IN HEAVEN: AND WHATSOEVER THOU SHALT LOOSE ON EARTH SHALL BE LOOSED IN HEAVEN" (Matt. 16:19).

On this verse, mainly, Rome bases her claims for papal authority. She argues that our Lord conferred upon a called-out group (Gr. *ekklesia*: *church*) full authority to act officially in His name, even to the remission of sins, and that such official acts were to be bound in heaven. She argues, further, that the authority of this church was centralized in the twelve apostles, over whom Christ placed one of themselves, St. Peter, as chief.

These claims are based upon the fact that while John 20:23 may have been spoken by Jesus to many of His disciples, Matt. 18:18 was apparently addressed to the twelve apostles, and Matt. 16:19 certainly to Peter alone. Thus it is claimed that authority in spiritual matters was given to the church, represented by the twelve apostles and personified in the Apostle Peter.

155

Rome's conclusion is that since the church of today is (according to Catholic doctrine) a perpetuation of the organization which Christ instituted and vested with divine authority, there must of necessity be apostolic succession. She contends that the apostolic body is perpetuated in her Sacred College of Cardinals with its twelve congregations, and that one of their number, the Pope or Bishop of Rome, succeeds Peter as their chief and the supreme head of the church on earth—that spiritual authority today is still vested in the church, represented by the College of Cardinals and personified in the Pope himself.

PROTESTANT INTERPRETATIONS

Protestants may lift their hands in horror at such claims, but their own interpretations of these passages are as weak as cotton thread. We list some of them:

1. The Catholic interpretation in modified form is found in the ritualistic creeds of many Protestant denominations. They make Rome's claims, with reservations and apologies.

2. Some Protestants argue that in these words our Lord merely gave the apostles authority to *state the terms* of salvation.

3. Others contend that the apostles were given the ability to *discern and declare* whose sins were forgiven and whose were not. That is, they could pronounce sins forgiven, not by any *authority* given to them, but because of God-given powers to *discern* the true spiritual state of those to whom they ministered.

4. Still others claim that our Lord meant to impress upon His followers their great responsibility and to warn them that through *their* behavior some would accept Him while others would reject Him; some would have their sins remitted, while others would have their sins retained.

But all of these arguments can be placed in one category: they wrest the natural meaning of Scripture and are easily answered by Rome as she points to the Book itself and insists: *"But this is what it says."*

THE SOLUTION

The solution to this problem and the answer to Rome's pretentions is again a dispensational one. It lies in the fact that from time to time God changes His dealings with men—a premise which must be granted by Romanists if indeed our Lord did confer such powers upon His disciples after several thousand years of human history had elapsed—and that the church of today is *not* a perpetuation of the organization which Christ founded while on earth.

Our Lord did in fact give to the twelve, with Peter as their chief, authority to act officially in His absence.

Let us consider John 20:23 in the light of its context, beginning at verse 21:

"Then said Jesus to them again, Peace be unto you: AS MY FATHER HATH SENT ME, EVEN SO SEND I YOU.

"And when He had said this, He breathed on them, and saith unto them, RECEIVE YE THE HOLY GHOST:

157

"WHOSE SOEVER SINS YE REMIT, THEY ARE REMITTED UNTO THEM; AND WHOSE SOEVER SINS YE RETAIN, THEY ARE RETAINED" (John 20:21-23).

"As My Father hath sent Me, even so send I you." In the light of these words is it strange to find our Lord granting official powers? These words should be compared with the Lord's words to the twelve in Luke 22:28-30:

"Ye are they which have continued with Me in My temptations.

"AND I APPOINT UNTO YOU A KINGDOM, AS MY FATHER HATH APPOINTED UNTO ME;

"That ye may eat and drink at My table in My kingdom, and sit on thrones judging the twelve tribes of Israel."

Does this mean, then, that our Lord committed even the forgiveness of sins into the hands of failing men? No, not *failing* men, for at Pentecost the Holy Spirit took supernatural control of them. In that foretaste of the millennium the believers lived together in a way that even the most spiritual believers cannot, or do not, live today. Indeed, we do not find the apostles charged with one single mistake until after the conversion of Saul. Moreover God gave them supernatural *gifts* to qualify them for their work.

It is understood, of course, that the apostles possessed no essential power in themselves to remit sins. It was *delegated* power exercised, as we say, under the control of God the Holy Spirit.

In Mark 2:7 the scribes find fault with Christ, saying: *"Why doth this man thus speak blasphemies? Who can forgive sins but God only?"*

Are we, perhaps, prone to agree too readily with these scribes? We must not forget that our Lord Himself said:

"The Father judgeth no man, but hath committed all judgment unto the Son."

"And hath given Him authority to execute judgment also, BECAUSE HE IS THE SON OF MAN." (John 5:22,27).

The Lord Jesus certainly had authority to admit men into the kingdom or shut them out from it. Surely He, as the Son of *Man,* could remit sins, and what He bound on earth was surely bound in heaven.

And now He gives these powers to His followers as officials in the kingdom:

"AS MY FATHER HATH SENT ME, EVEN SO SEND I YOU."

"AND I APPOINT UNTO YOU A KINGDOM, AS MY FATHER HATH APPOINTED UNTO ME."

Matt. 21:43 makes it clear that the kingdom was to be TAKEN FROM the chief priests and elders in Israel and Luke 12:32 makes it equally clear that the kingdom was to be GIVEN TO the "little flock" of Christ's followers. We quote these passages here:

Matt. 21:43: "Therefore say I unto you, THE KINGDOM OF GOD SHALL BE TAKEN FROM YOU, AND GIVEN TO A NATION* BRINGING FORTH THE FRUITS THEREOF."

Luke 12:32: "FEAR NOT, LITTLE FLOCK; FOR

---

*Note carefully that the kingdom was to be given to *"a nation,"* not *"the nations."* Moreover, this nation was to bring forth the fruits which Israel, under her leaders of that day had failed to produce. This *"nation"* was the believing remnant in Israel, composed of Messiah's followers.

IT IS YOUR FATHER'S GOOD PLEASURE TO GIVE YOU THE KINGDOM."

Matt. 19:28 makes it further clear that authority in this kingdom* was to be centralized in the twelve apostles:

"AND JESUS SAID UNTO THEM, VERILY I SAY UNTO YOU, THAT YE WHICH HAVE FOLLOWED ME, IN THE REGENERATION WHEN THE SON OF MAN SHALL SIT IN THE THRONE OF HIS GLORY, YE ALSO SHALL SIT UPON TWELVE THRONES, JUDGING THE TWELVE TRIBES OF ISRAEL."

Finally, in Matt. 16:19 Peter is singled out as chief of the twelve when our Lord says:

"AND I WILL GIVE UNTO THEE THE KEYS OF THE KINGDOM OF HEAVEN."

Peter is consistently singled out as the leader of the twelve in this way:

"Acts 1:15: ". . . PETER stood up in the midst of the disciples . . . ."

Acts 2:14: ". . . PETER, standing up with the eleven . . . ."

"Acts 2:37: ". . . PETER and . . . the rest of the apostles . . . ."

Acts 5:29: ". . . PETER and the other apostles . . . ."*

It is regretable that Protestants, instead of proving from the Scriptures the fact that the church of today is *not* a perpetuation of the organization our Lord founded while on earth, try in vain to *disprove* what Matt. 16:19 plainly states! Obviously, one who has the keys to a building has the power to admit others or to shut them out. A similar pas-

---

*Under Christ.

*References in the epistles also single Peter out in this way.

sage (Isa. 22:20-23) describes Eliakim as about to be given the key to the house of David; i.e., it was to be in his power to admit men to, or exclude them from, the government of Israel.

THE OFFICIAL ACTS OF THE TWELVE

The first official act of the "little flock" was to appoint a successor to Judas as a twelfth apostle and, as we have seen, what they bound on earth was bound in heaven, for *"Matthias . . . was numbered with the eleven apostles . . . And they were all filled with the Holy Ghost"* (Acts 1:26, 2:4).

At Pentecost again we find the apostles fully exercising their authority. When those present were convicted and asked Peter and the rest of the apostles what they should do, Peter replied:

"REPENT, AND BE BAPTIZED EVERY ONE OF YOU IN THE NAME OF JESUS CHRIST FOR THE REMISSION OF SINS, AND YE SHALL RECEIVE THE GIFT OF THE HOLY GHOST" (Acts 2:38).

And then the apostles (and perhaps others of the disciples) baptized them "FOR THE REMISSION OF SINS." Compare this with the words of our Lord: *"Whosoever sins ye remit they are remitted unto them"* and *"whatsoever ye shall bind on earth shall be bound in heaven."* There is perfect harmony here.

But could not some shrewd person have deceived them? Did Ananias deceive them? He was carried out dead! As we have pointed out, "they were all filled with the Holy Ghost" (Acts 2:4) and endued with special miraculous powers (Acts 1:8), including "the gift of knowledge."

161

In Acts 3:19-21 we find Peter actually offering Israel "the times of refreshing" and the return of Christ. He did this with full official authority and there is every evidence that this offer was bound (accepted as binding) in heaven.

There are numerous such cases in the record of the apostles' ministry, but one of particular significance is found in Acts 10, just after the conversion of Saul:

Peter was not out of the will of God when he hesitated to go to the Gentiles. He well knew the prophetic program, that the nations were to be blessed through the rise and salvation of Israel (Isa. 60:1-3). Filled with the Holy Spirit, he had declared that God had raised up His Son Jesus to bless Israel first, in turning them away from their iniquities, so that the Abrahamic Covenant might be fulfilled and the nations might be blessed *through them* (See Acts 3:25,26 and cf. Mark 7:27, Luke 24:47 and Acts 1:8). Israel must *first* be brought to Messiah's feet.

But here Peter was sent by a *special commission* to go to the Gentile house of Cornelius, *"nothing doubting."* The others at Jerusalem later called him to account for his action, but after he had *"rehearsed the matter from the beginning, and expounded it by order unto them"* they, in turn, *"glorified God, saying, Then hath God also to the Gentiles granted repentance unto life"* (Acts 11:4,18).

Without in the least detracting from the kingdom aspect of this scene, it should be clearly borne in mind that when Peter went to Cornelius' household it was *not* according to the prophetic program or the so-called "great commission." He was *not* sent to these Gentiles because Israel had received Christ, but in spite of the fact that Israel was rejecting Christ. *But what Peter had done on earth was bound in heaven* and Paul's subsequent ministry was later recognized and endorsed by the Jerusalem church on the basis of Peter's action here (See Acts 15:1-18).

Still another, perhaps the final, official act of the apostles is referred to in Gal. 2, where they, through their leaders,* recognized Paul as "the apostle of the Gentiles."

We quote:

"AND I WENT UP BY REVELATION [TO JERU-SALEM] AND COMMUNICATED UNTO THEM THAT GOSPEL WHICH I PREACH AMONG THE GENTILES, BUT PRIVATELY TO THEM WHICH WERE OF REPU-TATION, LEST BY ANY MEANS I SHOULD RUN, OR HAD RUN, IN VAIN."

"AND WHEN JAMES, CEPHAS, AND JOHN, WHO SEEMED TO BE PILLARS, PERCEIVED THE GRACE THAT WAS GIVEN UNTO ME, THEY GAVE TO ME AND BARNABAS THE RIGHT HANDS OF FELLOW-SHIP; THAT WE SHOULD GO UNTO THE HEATHEN, AND THEY UNTO THE CIRCUMCISION" (Gal. 2:2,9).

Here by a solemn agreement they, who had originally been sent into "all the world" and to "every creature," now promised to confine their ministry to Israel while Paul went to the Gentiles.

Were these leaders of the twelve out of the will of God in making this agreement? By no means!

---

*Though the James of this passage was probably not one of the twelve.

163

Subsequent revelation proves that they were very much *in* the will of God, both in loosing themselves from their commission to evangelize the world and in agreeing that Paul should go to the Gentiles, for Israel's rejection of Christ had brought about a change in the divine program.

Here alone is the answer to Catholicism.* Here alone is the axe laid to the *root* of the tree, for in the light of these Scriptures it is impossible to maintain that the church of today is a perpetuation of the organization our Lord established while on earth. There is a vast difference between *the kingdom of heaven,* proclaimed by the twelve, and *the body of Christ,* revealed through Paul.

Thus *by Rome's own argument* there can be no apostolic succession, for by the authority given the twelve (an authority which Rome vigorously insists they had) they loosed themselves from their obligation to carry out the "great commission" to its completion, and recognized *Paul* as the apostle of the new dispensation. And mark well: *what they bound on earth was bound in heaven, and what they loosed on earth was loosed in heaven.*

The prophetic program had been interrupted. The kingdom was to be held in abeyance while the King remained a royal Exile. Prophecy had given way to "the mystery" of God's purpose and grace.

PAULINE AUTHORITY

Paul too was given great authority. Again and again we are reminded that he speaks by divine

*See the author's booklet: *The Answer to Catholicism*: *Do the Protestants Have It?*

revelation, as the mouth-piece of Christ Himself. He makes it clear, too, that he did *not* receive this authority from men:

"BUT I CERTIFY YOU, BRETHREN, THAT THE GOSPEL WHICH WAS PREACHED OF ME IS NOT AFTER MAN.

"FOR I NEITHER RECEIVED IT OF MAN, NEITHER WAS I TAUGHT IT, BUT BY THE REVELATION OF JESUS CHRIST" (Gal. 1:11,12, cf. I Cor. 11:23, 15:3, Eph. 3:2,3, I Thes. 4:15, etc.).

He reminds the Romans and the Colossians of his special authority as the apostle of the Gentiles and the minister of the body:

"FOR I SPEAK TO YOU GENTILES, INASMUCH AS I AM THE APOSTLE OF THE GENTILES, I MAGNIFY MINE OFFICE" (Rom. 11:13).

"Who now rejoice in my sufferings for you, and fill up that which is behind of the afflictions of Christ in my flesh FOR HIS BODY'S SAKE, WHICH IS THE CHURCH:

"WHEREOF I AM MADE A* MINISTER, according to the dispensation of God which is given to me for you, to fulfill the Word of God" (Col. 1:24,25).

To the unruly Corinthians he writes:

". . . IF I COME AGAIN I WILL NOT SPARE, SINCE YE SEEK A PROOF OF CHRIST SPEAKING IN ME . . ." (II Cor. 13:2,3).

It should be noted, however, that Paul's authority was not of a political nature; it was entirely *spiritual* and *doctrinal*. This is evident from such passages as the following:

"BUT THOUGH WE, OR AN ANGEL FROM HEAVEN, PREACH ANY OTHER GOSPEL UNTO YOU THAN

---

*No article in the original. He was pre-eminently *the* minister of the body.

THAT WHICH WE HAVE PREACHED UNTO YOU, LET HIM BE ACCURSED.

"AS WE SAID BEFORE, SO SAY I NOW AGAIN, IF ANY MAN PREACH ANY OTHER GOSPEL UNTO YOU THAN THAT YE HAVE RECEIVED, LET HIM BE ACCURSED" (Gal. 1:8,9).

"IF ANY MAN TEACH OTHERWISE, AND CON-SENT NOT TO WHOLESOME WORDS, EVEN THE WORDS OF OUR LORD JESUS CHRIST, AND TO THE DOCTRINE WHICH IS ACCORDING TO GODLINESS:

"HE IS PROUD . . ." etc. (I Tim. 6:3,4).

"The signs of an apostle" were wrought by Paul, but he did not have the "keys" to the body as Peter did to the kingdom, nor was he given authority to remit sins. Indeed, since baptism "for the remission of sins" had been set aside in favor of justification by grace, through faith, without works, he could have no part in remitting sins except indirectly by proclaiming the glad news. This will be considered more fully in another chapter.

QUIZ

1. On what Scripture passage, mainly, does Rome base her claims for papal authority? 2. Give two other passages on which she bases her claims for the authority of the (Roman) Church? 3. By what reasoning does she apply these passages to the (Roman) Church of *today*? 4. What basic weakness is there in most Protestant interpretations of these verses? 5. Give two verses (apart from those already given) indicating that our Lord was to confer authority upon His apostles to act officially in His name? 6. Was their authority to remit sins their

own or was it delegated? 7. Why has the Father committed the future judgment of men to His Son? 8. Show from Scripture whom the kingdom of Israel was to be *taken from.* 9. Show from Scripture whom it was to be *given to.* 10. How can you tell from early Acts that Peter was the leader of the twelve? 11. What basic error do most Protestants hold along with Rome, which hinders them from answering Rome's claims? 12. What was the first official act of the apostles? 13. Give Scripture to show in what sense the apostles remitted sins. 14. How were they protected against deception by false "converts"? 15. What example do we have as evidence that they were not thus deceived? 16. Give an example of the apostles binding something which was also bound in heaven. 17. Give an example of the apostles loosing something which was also loosed in heaven. 18. What is the basic answer to Roman Catholicism? 19. How do Rome's own claims settle this matter? 20. Give three Scriptures indicating the nature of Paul's authority with respect to God's program for the present dispensation.

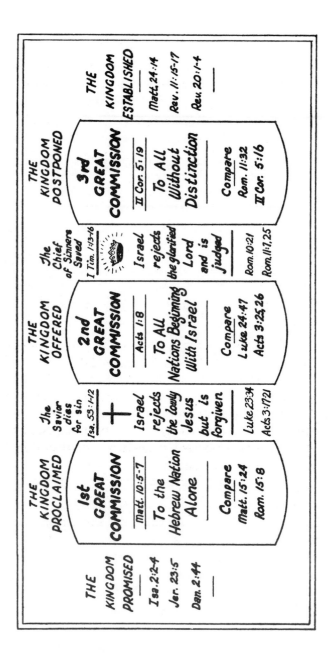

Chapter X.

THE SO-CALLED GREAT COMMISSION

How familiar has the term *"the great commission"* become! It is mostly used in a general way of our Lord's parting instructions to the eleven as recorded in the four Gospels and the Acts (Matt. 28:18-20, Mark 16:15-18, Luke 24:46-48, John 20:21-23, Acts 1:7,8).

This so-called "great commission" is generally supposed to embody our Lord's "marching orders" to His church today. This has come about, however, because ministers of the Word, rather than *expounding* these instructions with a view to having them faithfully carried out, have been satisfied to pick out certain phrases from them for devotional sermons.

All that most church members hear of the so-called "great commission," is Matthew's *"Go"* and *"Lo, I am with you,"* Mark's *"All the world"* and *"every creature,"* Luke's *"Ye are witnesses,"* John's *"As My Father hath sent Me, even so send I you"* and Acts' *"Ye shall receive power after that the Holy Ghost is come upon you."*

CHOOSING COMMISSIONS

To those who go beyond these picked phrases to examine the record in its entirety, however, the acceptance of the "great commission" as *our* marching orders has presented great difficulties. The *legalism* of Matt. 28:20 (cf. 23:1-3), the *baptismal salvation* and *miraculous signs* of Mark 16:16-18, the *"Jerusalem first"* of Luke 24:47 and Acts 1:8, and the *authority to remit sins* in John 20:22,23, are all so obviously incompatible with the gospel of the grace of God, that Fundamentalist 'Bible teachers have been forced to choose individual records of the commission as binding in this dispensation, in accordance with the amount of difficulty they have experienced harmonizing the various commands with the present truth. This has naturally contributed much to the confusion prevailing among Fundamentalists today.

Comparatively few Christian people are aware of the fact that our spiritual leaders have never agreed as to which of the five passages referred to above embodies *our* commission for today, but the disagreement has been sharp.

Dr. A. C. Gaebelein, for example, believed that the Matthew commission is *not* our commission. He chose Luke 24:46-48 as *"the Gentile commission."* The late Dr. H. A. Ironside, however, *did* hold to the record in Matthew as *"our marching orders,"* while Dr. I. M. Haldeman, on the other hand, stressed the commission in Mark. Dr. Wm. L. Pettingill disagreed with them all and wrote: *"The commission under which the Church is supposed to work is that of Acts 1:8."*

From the writings of Dr. Ironside, the so-called "Arch-bishop of Fundamentalism,"* it might be assumed that nearly all Fundamentalists agree that the Matthew 28 commission is ours. In his writings he seems astonished at any other conclusion and implies that only Bullingerites would question the matter. Referring to the Matthew commission, he says:

"People who have never investigated Bullingerism and its kindred systems will hardly believe me when I say that even the Great Commission upon which the church has acted for 1900 years, and which is still our authority for worldwide missions, is, according to these teachers, a commission with which we have nothing whatever to do, that it has no reference to the Church at all . . . Yet such is actually their teaching" (Wrongly Dividing the Word of Truth, p. 17).

Later on in the same book he calls this interpretation *"absurd,"* *"grotesque"* and *"wicked"!* (Wrongly Dividing, pp. 17,18).

Apparently the "Archbishop of Fundamentalism" was so intent on going after the "Bullingerites" that he forgot that many of his colleagues, plus Mr. J. N. Darby, the founder of the Brethren (with whom Dr. Ironside was for years associated), emphatically denied that the Matthew commission is ours. We quote from a few of their writings:

Dr. James M. Gray: "This is the Kingdom Commission, as another expresses it, not the Christian Commission . . . Its accomplishment has been inter-

*And doubtless the most popular Fundamentalist leader of the past quarter century.

171

rupted, but will be taken up before the Lord comes to deliver Israel at the last" (*Christian Worker's Commentary,* p. 313).

Dr. Wm. L. Pettingill: "Mark's Gospel, like Matthew's and Luke's, is primarily a Kingdom book, and I am satisfied that none of them contains the Church's marching orders—not even the so-called 'Great Commission' of Matt. 28:18-20" (*Bible Questions Answered,* p. 100).

Dr. Arno C. Gaebelein: "This is the Kingdom Commission . . . A time is coming when this great commission here will be carried out by a remnant of Jewish disciples" (*Gospel of Matthew,* Vol. 2, p. 323).

Mr. J. N. Darby: "The accomplishment of the commission here in Matthew has been interrupted . . . we find no accomplishment of it . . . for the present it has, in fact, given place to a heavenly commission, and the Church of God" (*Collected Writings,* p. 327).

So it has *not* been generally agreed that the Matthew commission is for our obedience. But the sad fact is that while many of Dr. Ironside's colleagues disagreed with him as to the Matthew commission, they also disagreed with each other as to which "great commission," or which record of the so-called "great commission," embodies *our* marching orders. They did, however, seem to agree to keep far away from the commission in John 20:21-23 while Rome, on the basis of this passage, boldly claims the authority to remit sins. The Fundamentalist church has not yet succeeded in clearing up these difficulties.

172

Think of it! At this late date, more than nineteen hundred years after our Lord gave these commands, the church is not even agreed as to exactly what God would have His people do and teach! Let us not close our eyes to this fact, but let us face it so that it may be remedied, for how can we obey our "marching orders" if we do not know what they are? *"For if the trumpet shall give an uncertain sound, who shall prepare himself to battle?"*

Even among those who have come to see the mystery we still see the effects of this mistake of supposing that our Lord, in the short interval between His resurrection and ascension, gave the *same* men *different* commissions, intending that *others* should commence carrying out one or more of these commissions *at a future date*—and all without any explanation of this in the record itself!

Noting that the apostles never got farther than their own nation, as far as Scripture is concerned, they conclude that "the uttermost part of the earth" in Acts 1:8 should have been rendered "the uttermost part of the land [i.e., Palestine]" and that "all nations" in Matt. 28:19 means *only* the *Gentile* nations. Hence, of these two commissions (as they see it), *both* given by the Lord to the eleven before His ascension, the one in Acts 1:8 is presumed to have been for their obedience, while they are supposed to have understood that the one in Matt. 28:19 was not to be carried out by them, but by others of a future day. It is further argued that, according to Luke's record (24:47), "repentance and remission of sins" was to be preached among all the *Gentile* nations, *"having begun"* at Jerusalem.

173

But all this is making a complex problem out of a simple one.

It is true that the Greek word *ge* in Acts 1:8 *may* sometimes be rendered *land*, but in the great *majority* of cases it *must* be rendered *earth, not land*. Furthermore, similar phraseology is found, for example, in Matt. 12:42 where we read that the Queen of Sheba came from "the uttermost parts of the *earth* [*ge*]" to hear the wisdom of Solomon, and in Mark 13:27, where we are told that angels are to be sent to gather God's elect "from *the four winds,* from the uttermost part of the *earth* [*ge*]." Surely the Queen of Sheba did not journey to Jerusalem merely from the uttermost part of the land of Palestine, nor can "the four winds" possibly designate that one land alone.

It is also true that the phrase "the nations" frequently refers to the *Gentile* nations, especially when the one nation, Israel, is being separately discussed. This is so in the nature of the case. But it is a mistake to suppose that the phrase "the nations" always refers to the *Gentile* nations and a greater mistake to suppose that the phrase "*all* nations" must necessarily refer to the *Gentile* nations.

When we read, for example, that *"the Lord is high above all nations"* (Psa. 113:4), that God *"hath made of one blood all nations"* (Acts 17:26) and that *"all nations shall come and worship"* before Christ (Rev. 15:4), can Israel possibly be excluded?

Israel most assuredly is included in the "all nations" of Matt. 28:19 for the simple reason that she had not yet been brought to Messiah's feet. She is also included in the "all nations" of Luke 24:47

174

for, mark well, the record there reads: *"beginning* [or having begun] at JERUSALEM," not: "having covered the land of Palestine."

Perhaps the most important point of all to observe in this connection is that in the Matthew commission our Lord said to the eleven apostles: "GO YE," just as He did in Mark 16:15 and Acts 1:8. By what rule of hermeneutics or logic have we the right to exclude from the interpretation of this command the very ones to whom He gave it?

THE INCONSISTENCY OF CHOOSING
COMMISSIONS

In solving this difficulty (which men have made for themselves) it should be noted first that *all of the instructions referred to were given to the same men within a period of forty days,* with no hint either of a change in program or that certain of the instructions were to be carried out then and others later. The contention that certain of these records contain the *kingdom* commission and other, or others, the *Gentile* commission is therefore strained and unnatural.

To argue that one or more of these records apply *only* to a *future* generation is, as we have said, also strained and unnatural, for it is not logically possible to exclude from the direct interpretation of these passages the very persons to whom He gave the instructions. While, to be sure, they may not have *completed* their mission, nevertheless when He said, "Go *ye*," He evidently meant *they* should proceed to obey His orders. It would be strange

175

indeed if *they understood* His *"Go* ye" to mean that others later on should go.

It should next be noted that the legalism of Matthew 28:20, the baptismal salvation and miraculous signs of Mark 16:16-18, the "Jerusalem first" of Luke 24:47 and Acts 1:8 and the instructions to remit sins in John 20:22,23 *all* agree with what the apostles actually *did* as recorded in the book of Acts.

There is no indication of any revelation to them that the death of Christ had freed them from observance of the Mosaic law. They continued daily with one accord in the temple (Acts 2:46) and took part in its worship (Acts 3:1), careful not to start a new sect separate from Judaism, for *they,* who had accepted Messiah, were the true Israel.

The person who baptized Saul of Tarsus was *"a devout man according to the law"* (Acts 22:12) and as late as Acts 21:20 we find James pointing out *"how many thousands of Jews there are which believe; AND THEY ARE ALL ZEALOUS OF THE LAW."*

Not until the great council at Jerusalem (Acts 15) did the Jewish believers even agree that the *Gentiles* were not to be under the law. Whether or not the Jewish church at Jerusalem was to remain under the law did not even come up for discussion. It was clearly assumed they were so to remain. This is because the twelve had been commissioned to teach law observance, as we have seen.

Indeed, in the Millennium, of which Pentecost was a foretaste, the law will be taught at Jerusalem and Israel will be zealous to hear and obey.

The apostles also taught the baptismal salvation of Mark 16:16, for Peter demanded repentance and baptism *for the remission of sins* (Acts 2:38). As to the miraculous signs of Mark 16:17,18, the most casual reading of early Acts will show that these abounded. The "Jerusalem first" of Luke 24:47 and Acts 1:8 was also carefully adhered to and sins were remitted by men (instrumentally) as they baptized those who believed (Acts 2:38, 22:16).

All the records of the so-called "great commission," then, agree with what the apostles actually *did,* as recorded in the Acts, so that there is no reason to suppose that certain of these commands were for their obedience while others were not.

The contention that the "formula" for baptism in the Matthew commission differs from that used by the apostles in Acts presents no difficulty here, for it is not stated that they were to use any *formula,* or form of words, when baptizing. It is simply stated in Matt. 28:19 that they were to baptize *in the name of* (i.e., *by the authority of*) the triune God, while in Acts we read that they did baptize in the name of the Lord Jesus. Those who believe that *"in Him dwelleth all the fulness of the Godhead bodily"* will find no difficulty here. The difficulty arises only when it is supposed that the apostles were to repeat certain words in baptizing. This whole idea of a baptismal *formula* is a deep-rooted but wholly unscriptural tradition.

Neither does the promise: *"Lo, I am with you, even unto the end of the age,"* present any difficulty for, remember, this *present dispensation* is a paren-

thetical period of grace which was then still a secret
"hid in God" (Eph. 3:9).

THREE GREAT COMMISSIONS

In order to obtain a clear understanding of *our*
great commission, let us now consider *three* great
commissions given in succession by the Lord Himself; one before His crucifixion, another after His
resurrection and a third after His ascension.

A GREAT COMMISSION

Much stress has been laid on the "Go" of the
so-called "great commission," but this was not the
first time our Lord had commanded His apostles
to "go." His *first* great commission to the apostles
is found in Matt. 10:5-10:

**"These twelve Jesus sent forth, and commanded
them, saying, GO NOT into the way of the Gentiles, and
into any city of the Samaritans enter ye not:**

**"But GO RATHER to the lost sheep of the house of
Israel.**

**"And AS YE GO, preach, saying, The Kingdom of
heaven is at hand.**

**"Heal the sick, cleanse the lepers, raise the dead, cast
out devils [demons]: freely ye have received, freely give.**

**"Provide neither gold, nor silver, nor brass in your
purses.**

**"Nor scrip [bag or satchel] for your journey, neither
two coats, neither shoes, nor yet staves: for the workman
is worthy of his meat."**

To this our Lord added further instructions re-
garding their conduct among friends and enemies,
and predicted some of the afflictions they would be
called upon to endure. The whole of this commission actually covers all of Matt. 10 (See 11:1).

Surely this commission is not *our* "great commission," but if we had been among the twelve apostles when these directions were given we would certainly have considered them a "great commission."

The command to confine their ministry exclusively to Israel would not have seemed strange to them, for this was based on the well known Abrahamic Covenant that through Abraham's multiplied seed the nations should be blessed (Gen.22:17,18 cf. Acts 3:25,26). Moreover, the prophets had repeatedly predicted that the nations would find blessing and salvation through *redeemed* Israel. Not until Israel was *saved* could blessing flow through her to the Gentiles (Isa. 59:20—60:3, Zech. 8:13).

It was perfectly normal, then, that our Lord should send the apostles first to the house of Israel exclusively. Indeed, He had emphatically declared concerning His own ministry:

"... I AM NOT SENT BUT UNTO THE LOST SHEEP OF THE HOUSE OF ISRAEL" (Matt. 15:24).

This doubtless was taken for granted by those who recognized Israel as the chosen nation. The apostle Paul, looking back some years later, wrote:

"Now I say that JESUS CHRIST WAS A MINISTER OF THE CIRCUMCISION for the truth of God, TO CONFIRM THE PROMISES MADE UNTO THE FATHERS:

"AND THAT THE GENTILES MIGHT GLORIFY GOD FOR HIS MERCY; as it is written, For this cause I will confess to Thee among the Gentiles, and sing unto Thy name.

"And again He saith, Rejoice, ye Gentiles, with His people" (Rom. 15:8-10).

179

Mark well the details of this millennial promise. It is *mercy* to the Gentiles but the fulfillment of *promises* to Israel. The Gentiles will indeed rejoice *"with His people,"* but not until *His people* themselves have come to rejoice in Him. Thus the Lord had come, first of all, "to save HIS PEOPLE from their sins" (Matt. 1:21), and He was now sending the twelve apostles forth as His co-workers.

In harmony with all this the twelve were commissioned to proclaim the kingdom of heaven "at hand" and were given power to work miracles as the signs of the long-promised blessing (cf. Isa. 35:5,6). Surely *they* must have considered this a *great commission.*

In order to facilitate a comparison of this commission with the two to be considered later on, we will list the outstanding details by number:

1. Under this commission the apostles were sent to the nation Israel *exclusively* (Matt. 10:5,6, cf. 15:24 and Rom. 15:8).

2. Under this commission the kingdom was to be proclaimed *"at hand"* (Matt. 10:7).

3. Under this commission the apostles were given *miraculous powers* (Matt. 10:8).

4. Under this commission they were *not to lay up provisions* for the future (Matt. 10:8-10, cf. 5:42, Luke 12:32,33).

5. Under this commission *repentance and baptism were required for the remission of sins.* While water baptism is not mentioned in this particular passage, it is clear from the whole record that our Lord and His apostles, like John the Baptist, pro-

180

claimed the kingdom and required repentance and baptism for the remission of sins (See Mark 1:4 and cf. John 4:1,2).

A GREATER COMMISSION

After our Lord's death and resurrection He gave the apostles (excepting Judas Iscariot) a *greater commission*. This has come to be called, erroneously, "the great commission," "our Lord's last commands" and "our marching orders." From this error has sprung much of the prevailing discord over water baptism, physical and political signs, etc.

This new commission was in fact no departure from the prophetic program; it was a *further development* of it.

In the records of our Lord's command to go and preach "the gospel," there is no indication that He meant a different gospel from that which they had been preaching. And, remember, *their* gospel (good news) concerned Messiah and His kingdom. It is specifically and repeatedly called *"the gospel of the kingdom"* (Matt. 4:23, 9:35, 24:14, Mark 1:14, Luke 9:2,6, etc.).

To *assume* that our Lord now sends these apostles to proclaim *"the gospel of the grace of God"* is wholly unwarranted. In fact, *"the gospel of the grace of God"* is not preached nor even mentioned until Paul is raised up and sent forth to declare it (See Acts 20:24, cf. Rom. 3:21-28, Eph. 3:1-3).

Let us now compare the pre- and post-resurrection commissions of our Lord, remembering that both were given to the same group of men:

181

1. As the apostles had been sent to one nation alone, they were now sent to *all nations, beginning at Jerusalem* (Luke 24:47, Acts 1:8). This was no departure from the former program, but a further development of it, for our Lord had dealt with Israel so that they might become a blessing to all nations.

Now it was assumed that Israel would accept her risen Messiah and that the program would go on.

2. Under this commission the kingdom, formerly proclaimed "at hand," was actually *offered* for Israel's acceptance (Acts 2:36-39, 3:19-26). Here again is a further development of the *same* program.

3. Under this commission Christ's disciples were given *greater* miraculous powers than before (Mark 16:17,18, John 14:12, cf. early Acts). Again a further development of the *same* program.

4. Under this commission the *whole* Pentecostal church actually had *all things common.* Read carefully, Acts 2:44,45, 4:32-37 and see how this too is a further development of the *same* program.

5. Under this commission repentance and baptism were required for the remission of sins *and* the Holy Spirit thereupon bestowed (Mark 16:16-18, cf. Acts 2:38). Once more, a further development of the *same* program.

What a mistake to call this *"the great commission"* and *"our marching orders"!* How pathetic to see sincere believers vainly trying to carry out this commission and these orders! Worst of all, what confusion, division and heartache this blunder has brought into the church, not to mention the effects upon the unsaved who stand by and wonder.

If this commission embodies God's program for today, how shall we answer the Seventh Day Adventist when he teaches legalism from Matt. 28:20 and Matt. 23:2,3, or the so-called "Disciples of Christ" when they teach baptismal salvation from Mark 16:16, or the Pentecostalists when they insist from Mark 16:17,18 that miraculous powers are the signs of true faith, or Rome when she quotes John 20:22,23 and insists on the right to remit sins?

THE GREATEST COMMISSION

"Wherefore henceforth know we no man after the flesh: Yea, though we have known Christ after the flesh, yet now henceforth know we Him no more.

"Therefore if any man be in Christ, he is a new creature [creation]: old things are passed away; behold, all things are become new.

"And all things are of God, who hath reconciled us to Himself by Jesus Christ, AND HATH GIVEN TO US THE MINISTRY OF RECONCILIATION;

"To wit, that God was in Christ, reconciling the world unto Himself, not imputing their trespasses unto them; AND HATH COMMITTED UNTO US THE WORD OF RECONCILIATION" (II Cor. 5:16-19).

If the records of the so-called "great commission" did contain our Lord's "last commands" they would indeed be "our marching orders," for the latest orders of the commanding officer are the ones to be obeyed, but it is *not a fact* that the "great commission" embodies our Lord's "last commands." After His ascension the rejected Christ spoke again from His exile in heaven and gave another and greater commission to Paul and to us. Again and again the apostle speaks of the dispensation of grace committed to him by the glorified Lord Himself.

In determining which of our Lord's commissions is for *our* obedience, we should ask ourselves two questions:

1. Why did God raise up Paul, *another* apostle, some time after Matthias had been chosen, according to Scripture, to make up the number of the twelve?

2. Why, after having been commanded to go into "all the world" (Mark 16:15) to make disciples of "all nations" (Matt. 28:19), did the twelve apostles remain at Jerusalem (Acts 8:1) and why did they, through their leaders, later agree to confine their ministry to Israel, while Paul went to the Gentiles (Gal. 2:9)? Were they all out of the will of God or was a change in dispensation taking place? The answer can only be that a change in dispensation was taking place.

At the very heart of the great revelation to Paul lies God's gracious offer of *reconciliation,* made to a world at enmity with His Son and Himself. The proclamation of this glorious message is *our great commission* for, as we have seen above, the apostle says: "God . . . hath *committed* unto us the word of reconciliation" (II Cor. 5:19).

This offer of reconciliation by grace through faith is the heart of "the gospel of the grace of God." After the nations, and even *the* nation, had turned against God, He did something remarkable. He replied to the brutal murder of Stephen by *saving* Saul, the leader of the persecution against the

Pentecostal church and the personification of Israel's (and the world's) spirit of rebellion. Thus *"Where sin abounded, grace did much more abound, THAT . . . GRACE MIGHT REIGN"* (Rom. 5:20, 21).

Saul's conversion was the first step in the ushering in of *the reign of grace*, for he writes by inspiration:

"And I thank Christ Jesus our Lord, who hath enabled me, for that He counted me faithful, putting me into the ministry:

"Who was before a blasphemer, and a persecutor, and injurious; but I OBTAINED MERCY, because I did it ignorantly in unbelief.

"And THE GRACE OF OUR LORD WAS EXCEEDING ABUNDANT, with faith and love which is in Christ Jesus.

"This is a faithful saying, and worthy of all acceptation, that Christ Jesus came into the world to save sinners; of whom I am chief.

"HOWBEIT FOR THIS CAUSE I OBTAINED MERCY, THAT IN ME FIRST [CHIEFLY] JESUS CHRIST MIGHT SHOW FORTH ALL LONGSUFFERING, FOR A PATTERN TO THEM WHICH SHOULD HEREAFTER BELIEVE ON HIM TO LIFE EVERLASTING" (I Tim. 1:12-16).

Thus, as it became necessary to set Israel aside, God demonstrated the riches of His grace by saving her leader in the rebellion and sending him forth with an offer of grace to all men everywhere. *"The casting away of them [Israel]"* and *"the reconciling of the world"* go together (Rom. 11:15).

"For God hath concluded them all in unbelief, THAT HE MIGHT HAVE MERCY UPON ALL" (Rom. 11:32).

The message of reconciliation also lies at the

very root of the truth concerning the body of Christ. Indeed, it is by the reconciliation of Jews and Gentiles to God that the body is formed:

"That He might RECONCILE both unto God in ONE BODY by the cross, having slain the enmity thereby" (Eph. 2:16).

From this it follows that the message of reconciliation is a vital part of the mystery, for the formation of the body was a mystery until revealed to and through Paul.

It was God's *revealed* purpose to bless the world through the *rise* of Israel (Isa. 60:1-3) and this purpose will yet be accomplished. But it was God's *hidden* purpose to bless the world through the *fall* of Israel, and this is *now* being accomplished (Rom. 11:11,12,15).

The glorious truth that God would usher in a reign of grace (Rom. 5:21), casting aside all distinctions to save believing Jews and Gentiles (Rom. 11:32), and to reconcile them to God in one body (Eph. 2:16), in Christ (Eph. 2:15), seated in the heavenlies (Eph. 2:6), was never once prophesied since the world began, though it was purposed by God *before* the world began (Eph. 1:4-9).

The proclamation of the glorious message of reconciliation, by which the body is formed, is *our great commission.* In comparing it with the two earlier commissions to the twelve, we should note the following:

1. Under this commission we, with Paul, are sent to *all* men, *without distinction* (11 Cor. 5:14-21).

186

2. Under this commission Christ's return to judge and reign is held in abeyance, and reconciliation is offered to God's enemies everywhere (II Cor. 5:16, 19, cf. Rom. 11:25, Heb. 2:8,9).

3. Under this commission miraculous powers have been withdrawn (Rom. 8:23, II Cor. 4:16, 5:1, 2, 12:7-10, I Tim. 5:23, II Tim. 4:20).

4. Under this commission the "sell all" and "lay not up" order has been rescinded (II Cor. 12:14, I Tim. 5:8). Indeed, the apostle even had to take up offerings for those at Jerusalem who had sold all and were *now* beginning to lack (See Acts 4:34 and cf. Acts 11:27-30, Rom. 15:26, I Cor. 16:1-3).

5. Under this commission *faith alone* is required for salvation (II Cor. 5:18-21, Rom. 3:21,24-28, 4:5, Eph. 2:8-10, etc.).

6: Besides all this, particular attention should be given to the words:

"Wherefore HENCEFORTH KNOW WE NO MAN AFTER THE FLESH: YEA, THOUGH WE HAVE KNOWN CHRIST AFTER THE FLESH, YET NOW HENCEFORTH KNOW WE HIM NO MORE" (II Cor. 5:16).

The word "henceforth," or *from now on,* is most significant here. It cannot be denied that prior to this men had been known or recognized after the flesh. Our Lord had originally instructed His apostles *not* to go to the Gentiles or the Samaritans, but to go only to "the lost sheep of the house of Israel," and had insisted that He Himself had been sent to none but "the lost sheep of the house of Israel" (Matt. 10:6, 15:24). Even under His second great commission, after His resurrection, our Lord had instructed the apostles to minister first to the people of the favored nation and Peter was called to account for ministering to the Gentile household of Cornelius.

As to knowing Christ after the flesh: had they not known Him after the flesh as they thronged Him (Mark 5:31), as He ate with them (Luke 15:2), as He touched them and made them whole? (Luke 4:40). Did they not know Him after the flesh when they nailed Him to the tree? (John 19:16-18). Did they not know Him after the flesh when Thomas was invited to feel the wounds in His hands and His side? (John 20:27). Does not John testify that they had "seen" Him with their eyes, had "looked upon" Him and had "handled" Him? (I John 1:1). Did they not still know Him after the flesh even after the ascension, when Peter declared to the house of Israel that God had raised Him from the dead to sit upon the throne of David? (Acts 2:30,31).

But now Paul declares by revelation: *"Though we have known Christ after the flesh, yet now henceforth know we Him no more."* Does this not indicate a change in dispensation?

We now know Christ as the One in whom all fullness dwells (Col. 1:19), even all the fullness of the Godhead (Col. 2:9). We know Him as the One who has been exalted far above all (Eph. 1:20,21, Phil. 2:9-11) and now sends forth His ambassadors to offer the riches of His grace to all who will receive.

The first two great commissions were originally given to twelve men because the promises to Israel, with her twelve tribes, were in view. The third great commission was originally given to *one* man because there was *one* God, *one* lost world, *one* Mediator and *one* body in view.

What a high and glorious mission is ours to proclaim the gospel of the grace of God and the offer of reconciliation! How we should hasten to carry it out! How the love of Christ for His enemies should constrain us to plead with men to be reconciled while it is still "the accepted time"! (II Cor. 5:20,21).

QUIZ

1. What is the term "great commission" generally understood to mean? 2. What bearing is this commission supposed to have on us today? 3. How are the *records* of the "great commission" generally dealt with from the pulpit? 4. What happens when these records are *studied* with a view to carrying out the "great commission"? 5. Name three outstanding Christian leaders of the past generation who did *not* believe that the commission recorded in Matthew is our commission? 6. Name three such leaders who held to different records of the "great commission" as for our obedience, and state which record each chose. 7. What is strained and unnatural about the view that certain of these records contain our commission, while others do not? 8. How would you prove that *all* the records of the "great commission" applied directly to those living then? 9. Explain how *all* the records of our Lord's commission harmonize with what the apostles actually did as

recorded in early Acts. 10. To whom did our Lord command the apostles *not* to go in His *first* great commission? 11. To whom, exclusively, did our Lord say He Himself was sent at that time? 12. Why was this? 13. What gospel were the twelve to preach under this first commission? 14. Name two other details of Christ's first great commission to the twelve. 15. When was the next great commission given to the apostles? 16. Explain how this commission was not a departure from, but rather a further development of, the first great commission. 17. Give Scripture to show what *our* great commission is. 18. When and to whom was this commission first given? 19. What gospel are we to proclaim under this commission? 20. Name three points of contrast between *our* great commission and the so-called "great commission."

Chapter XI.

GOOD NEWS

THE "FOUR GOSPELS"

It has often been stated that the so-called Four Gospels are actually four accounts of our Lord's earthly ministry as recorded by four different writers. These four accounts are given to us in the Scripture, not as different gospels but as portrayals of our blessed Lord Himself in four different aspects. Matthew portrays Him as *King,* Mark as *Servant,* Luke as *Man* and John as *God;* and each writer, while acknowledging the other aspects of Christ's person and place, keeps consistently to the particular aspect which he was inspired to portray.

Some have suggested that one biography; one composite picture, so to speak, would have been better, but one might as well try to depict a house by one composite picture. It would seem rather odd to have the mop, the refuse can, the milk box and the connection for the hose all showing up on the front porch! And where in the picture would there be room for all the doors and windows on all four sides? Similarly four separate accounts of our Lord's ministry were necessary to set forth the four aspects of His person, position and work.

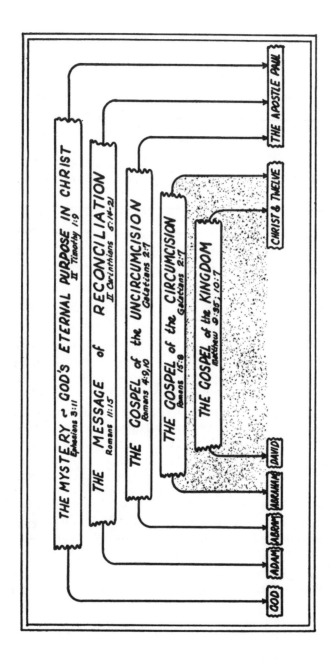

IS THERE ONLY ONE GOSPEL?

But while it is technically incorrect to call these four records four *gospels,* it is equally incorrect to say, as many have said, that the Scriptures present only one gospel.

First, the word *gospel* (Gr. *evangelion*) means simply *good news* and to say that the Bible presents only one gospel is like saying that God has sent man only one item of good news down through the ages.

Second, God uses *distinctive* terms to designate the various items of good news: e.g., "the gospel [good news] of the kingdom" (Matt. 9:35), "the gospel of the grace of God" (Acts 20:24), "the gospel of the uncircumcision" (Gal. 2:7), etc. Surely if God distinguishes between these gospels they cannot be exactly the same.

Next, it should be noted that God has revealed His good news to man *progressively.* To Adam and Eve He proclaimed the gospel, or good news, that the woman's seed should some day crush the head of the Serpent (Gen. 3:15). To Abraham He preached the gospel, or good news, that in him all nations should be blessed (Gal. 3:8). And all down through the Old Testament Scriptures we find God proclaiming more and more good news to man. Finally the Lord sent His apostles to proclaim "the gospel of the kingdom" (See Luke 9:1-6), but mark well: at that time *they did not even know that Christ was to die.* In this connection read carefully, Luke 18:31-34:

"Then He took unto Him the twelve, and said unto them, Behold, we go up to Jerusalem, and all things that

193

are written by the prophets concerning the Son of man shall be accomplished.

"For He shall be delivered unto the Gentiles, and shall be mocked, and spitefully entreated, and spitted on:

"And they shall scourge Him, and put Him to death: and the third day He shall rise again.

"AND THEY UNDERSTOOD NONE OF THESE THINGS: AND THIS SAYING WAS HID FROM THEM, NEITHER KNEW THEY THE THINGS WHICH WERE SPOKEN (Luke 18:31-34).

Note carefully that after the apostles had been preaching "the gospel" for some time (perhaps two or more years) they did not have the slightest idea what the Lord was talking about when He predicted His death.* Obviously, then, "the gospel" which they preached was not "the gospel" which Paul later preached or "the gospel" by which we are saved (See I Cor. 15:1-4). "The gospel" which they preached was "the gospel of the *kingdom*" (Matt. 9:35 cf. Luke 9:2), not "the preaching of the cross" (I Cor. 1:18).

This leads us to still another matter of vital importance in any consideration of God's good news to man: If a friend should come to the reader and say: "Did you hear the good news?" the reader would naturally inquire: *"What good news?"* We must always be sure to make this inquiry in our study of the Scriptures too when we come upon the term "the gospel," for *this term alone in no way indicates what the good news might be.*

This is illustrated by the passage referred to above. Luke 9:6 says that the apostles "departed,

---

*Even though the prophets had long predicted it and the apostles should have believed them (Luke 24:25).

and went through the towns, preaching *the gospel.*"
From this it has frequently been assumed that they
went forth preaching salvation through the cross,
as we do. Yet Luke 18:31-34 makes it clear that
they had no idea Christ would even die. A glance
at the context in Luke 9, however, makes it all
plain, for in verse 2 we read: *"And He sent them
to preach THE KINGDOM OF GOD,"* not His death
for sin.

From what has thus far been pointed out, it is
evident that *many* gospels could be discussed in this
chapter. We will, however, limit ourselves to the
five indicated on the foregoing chart, because in
them we find something of the philosophy of God's
dealings with men.

Before dealing separately with each of these
gospels, the reader should turn to the chart and
carefully note the following:

1. *The gospel of the kingdom* takes us back to
David, with whom the covenant of the kingdom
was made.

2. *The gospel of the circumcision* takes us back
before David to *Abraham,* with whom the covenant
of circumcision was made.

3. *The gospel of the uncircumcision* takes us
back before David and Abraham to *Abram* who, as
an *un*circumcised heathen, was justified by faith.

4. *The message of reconciliation** takes us back
before David, Abraham and Abram to Adam, the
"one man" by whom the world was *alienated* from
God.

*See footnote on next page.

5. *The mystery** takes us back before David, before Abraham, before Abram, before Adam to *God Himself* and "the good pleasure of His will."

THE GOSPEL OF THE KINGDOM

The gospel of the kingdom, as we have seen, takes us back to *David.* This good news was based on a promise made to King David:

"AND THINE HOUSE AND THY KINGDOM SHALL BE ESTABLISHED FOR EVER" (II Sam. 7:16. See also verses 4-17, I Chron. 17:4-15 and Psa. 89:34-37).

David's kingdom was to be established forever, of course, because Christ, the Son of David, was to occupy the throne and make it truly the seat of God's rule over the earth. For this reason we read that it "shall never be destroyed" or "left to other people," but "shall stand forever" (Dan. 2:44).

This glorious kingdom, which "the God of heaven" was—and is—to establish on earth is, as we have seen, the goal of God's great prophetic plan. This plan is comprehensively outlined in Jer. 23:5,6:

"BEHOLD, THE DAYS COME, SAITH THE LORD, THAT I WILL RAISE UNTO DAVID A RIGHTEOUS BRANCH, AND A KING SHALL REIGN AND PROS-PER, AND SHALL EXECUTE JUDGMENT AND JUS-TICE IN THE EARTH.

"IN HIS DAYS JUDAH SHALL BE SAVED, AND ISRAEL SHALL DWELL SAFELY: AND THIS IS HIS NAME WHEREBY HE SHALL BE CALLED, THE LORD OUR RIGHTEOUSNESS."

---

*While we do not find such phrases as "the gospel of reconcilia-tion" or "the gospel of the mystery" in Scripture, both of these great messages are nevertheless presented as *good news* and are even *designated* as *gospels.* See Col. 1:21-23, Romans 16:25.

This is why, when our Lord arrives on the scene, we find Him preaching *"the gospel* [or *good news*] *of the kingdom"* (Matt. 4:23, 9:35, etc.).

THE KINGDOM AT HAND

The difference between the *prophecies* concerning the kingdom and *"the gospel* of the kingdom" was that the kingdom once predicted was *now* proclaimed *"at hand."*

John the Baptist, our Lord and the twelve, of course, preached many things, but the *theme*, the *subject* of their message, during our Lord's earthly ministry, was: "THE KINGDOM OF HEAVEN IS AT HAND." There can be no question as to this, for the record is most explicit here:

Matt. 3:1,2: "In those days came JOHN THE BAPTIST, preaching in the wilderness of Judaea,

"And saying, Repent ye: for THE KINGDOM OF HEAVEN IS AT HAND."

Nothing else? This is all that is said here because this was the *subject* of his message. We read elsewhere (Luke 3:18) that "many other things in his exhortation preached he unto the people," but *this* is given as the *theme* of his message.

Matt. 4:17: "From that time JESUS began to preach and to say, Repent: for THE KINGDOM OF HEAVEN IS AT HAND."

Nothing else? Again this is all that is said here because this was the *theme* of His message, though, indeed, He said many other things in connection with this theme.

Matt. 10:5-7: "THESE TWELVE Jesus sent forth, and commanded them, saying, Go not into the way of the

Gentiles, and into any city of the Samaritans enter ye not:
   "But go rather to the lost sheep of the house of Israel.
   "And as ye go, preach, saying, THE KINGDOM OF HEAVEN IS AT HAND."

But were they to preach nothing else? Once more this is all that we are told here because this was to be the *theme* of their message.

Thus the *gospel,* or *good news* which John the Baptist, our Lord and the twelve proclaimed before Christ's death and resurrection was not "the preaching of the cross" but the good news that the long-promised kingdom was now "at hand."

THE TRANSFER OF AUTHORITY
IN ISRAEL

It should be carefully noted that we do not have an actual *offer* of the kingdom until after the resurrection of Christ (See Acts 3:19,20), for the prophets had consistently testified of *"the sufferings of Christ, and the glory that should FOLLOW"* (I Pet. 1:11). The order had always been the same in prophecy: first the shame, then the glory; first the cross, then the crown. From Joel 2:28-32 alone it is clear that there could be no *offer* of the kingdom until the Spirit had been "poured out." Moreover, the circumstances confirm this for, suppose the kingdom had been offered and accepted before the cross, would Judas have occupied one of the twelve thrones in the kingdom? Furthermore, the offer of the kingdom could be made only on the basis of the New Covenant, which was not made until the death of Christ (Matt. 26:28).

The Apostle John informs us that when some would have made Jesus king by force, He hid away from them (John 6:15) and that when a multitude from Jerusalem came acclaiming Him as king, He responded by riding to meet them on "a young ass" —not a very royal figure, to say the least (John 12:13,14, cf. Zech. 9:9).

Thus while the kingdom is *proclaimed "at hand"* during the period covered by the "four gospels," we find no offer of it until the early part of the book of Acts.

It was already evident when our Lord was on earth, however, that the *leaders* in Israel would not inherit the kingdom. John had called upon them to "bring forth . . . fruits meet for repentance"; so had Christ and the twelve, but instead they plotted to kill Christ (Matt. 21:33-39). Hence our Lord said to them:

"Therefore say I unto you, THE KINGDOM OF GOD SHALL BE TAKEN FROM YOU, AND GIVEN TO A NATION* BRINGING FORTH THE FRUITS THEREOF" (Matt. 21:43).

Who was to constitute the "nation" to which the Lord would give the kingdom? This is answered for us in Luke 12:32:

"FEAR NOT, LITTLE FLOCK; FOR IT IS YOUR FATHER'S GOOD PLEASURE TO GIVE YOU THE KINGDOM."

And the princes in this kingdom were to be none other than the twelve apostles,° for in Matt. 19:28 it is written:

---

*Not "the nations".
°With Matthias replacing Judas (Acts 1:20).

"And Jesus said unto them, Verily I say unto you, That ye which have followed me, in the regeneration when the Son of man shall sit in the throne of his glory, YE ALSO SHALL SIT UPON TWELVE THRONES, JUDGING THE TWELVE TRIBES OF ISRAEL."

The twelve apostles, then, and the "little flock" of Christ's followers, were to replace the chief priests and elders of that day as Israel's rulers in the kingdom. If we would gain a clear understanding of the gospel of the grace of God, it is essential that we understand these truths associated with "the gospel of the kingdom."

THE GOSPEL OF THE CIRCUMCISION

Such terms as "the gospel of the kingdom" and "the gospel of the grace of God" are relatively easy to understand but it is doubtful whether one believer in a thousand has any idea of the meaning of the term *"the gospel* [or *good news*] *of the circumcision"* (Gal 2:7).

This gospel takes us back before David to the great Abrahamic Covenant, for the "sign" of circumcision was given to Abraham, not only to separate him and his seed from the ungodly and licentious Gentiles, and as a "seal" of the righteousness of faith (Rom. 4:11), but also, and mainly, as *a token of God's covenant with him* (Gen. 17:11).

According to this covenant, Abraham's multiplied seed (later called *"the Circumcision"*) was to become a blessing to all nations. There was much more than this, but this is the particular part of the covenant which concerns us here. It was after

200

Abraham had offered to God his beloved son Isaac, that God promised:

"That in blessing I will bless thee, and in multiplying I WILL MULTIPLY THY SEED AS THE STARS OF THE HEAVEN, AND AS THE SAND WHICH IS UPON THE SEA SHORE; and thy seed shall possess the gate of his enemies;

"AND IN THY SEED SHALL ALL THE NATIONS OF THE EARTH BE BLESSED; because thou hast obeyed my voice" (Gen. 22:17,18).

The "gospel of the circumcision," then, was *the good news based on this covenant.* We read in Gal. 2:7 that "the gospel of the circumcision,* was [committed] unto Peter" and we find him preaching it in Acts 3:25,26:

"YE ARE THE CHILDREN OF THE PROPHETS, AND OF THE COVENANT WHICH GOD MADE WITH OUR FATHERS, SAYING UNTO ABRAHAM, AND IN THY SEED SHALL ALL THE KINDREDS OF THE EARTH BE BLESSED.

"UNTO YOU FIRST GOD, HAVING RAISED UP HIS SON JESUS, SENT HIM TO BLESS YOU, IN TURNING AWAY EVERY ONE OF YOU FROM HIS INIQUITIES."

This, in a nutshell, is "the gospel of the circumcision" and those of the Circumcision who heard should certainly have considered it good news that the blessing of all nations through them was now imminent.

But the fact that the gospel of the circumcision was committed to Peter does not mean that it was not also committed to the rest of the twelve, or that

---

*There is no warrant for making this read: "the gospel *to* the circumcision," although even this would not alter the essential meaning of Gal. 2:7.

he did not at the same time preach the gospel of the kingdom, or that our Lord had not also preached the gospel of the circumcision.

The "gospel of the kingdom" and "the gospel of the circumcision" are very closely related, as are the Abrahamic and Davidic Covenants. Whereas the former concerned the *nation,* the latter concerned that nation's *government* and *throne.*

It is significant that the New Testament Scriptures open with the words:

"The book of the generation of JESUS CHRIST, THE SON OF DAVID, THE SON OF ABRAHAM" (Matt. 1:1).

Both before and after Pentecost God's great program to bless the nations through Israel with Christ as King was recognized, but before Pentecost the emphasis had been on the kingdom while after Pentecost the emphasis was on the fact that Israel was to be the channel of blessing to the world. Hence in the gospel records we read of "the gospel of the kingdom," while in Gal. 2:7 we read that "the gospel of the circumcision" had been committed to Peter (as distinct from Paul). This matter will be discussed more fully at the end of this chapter.

THE GOSPEL OF THE UNCIRCUMCISION

Whereas the gospels of the kingdom and of the circumcision were proclaimed by our Lord on earth and the twelve apostles, *the gospel of the uncircumcision* was committed to Paul—and the twelve recognized this, for in Gal. 2:7 Paul says of their leaders that *"they saw that the gospel of the uncircumcision was committed unto me."*

202

In the gospel of the uncircumcision all is by grace and through faith. This good news is not based on any covenant,* for the Apostle Paul in proclaiming it takes us back beyond David and Abraham to *Abram,* the ungodly heathen who received full justification by faith alone long before he was circumcised.

Proving from the case of Abraham himself that God was not obliged to justify the circumcised alone, or to send salvation to the heathen through them, he points out that God had justified the very father of the Hebrew nation by grace, through faith, entirely apart from circumcision, and that he had received circumcision years later as a sign of the righteousness which he had already received by faith:

"Cometh this blessedness then upon the circumcision only, or upon the uncircumcision also? for we say that faith was reckoned to Abraham for righteousness.

"HOW WAS IT THEN RECKONED? WHEN HE WAS IN CIRCUMCISION, OR IN UNCIRCUMCISION? NOT IN CIRCUMCISION, BUT IN UNCIRCUMCISION.

"AND HE RECEIVED THE SIGN OF CIRCUMCISION, A SEAL OF THE RIGHTEOUSNESS OF THE FAITH WHICH HE HAD YET BEING UNCIRCUMCISED: THAT HE MIGHT BE THE FATHER OF ALL THEM THAT BELIEVE, THOUGH THEY BE NOT CIRCUMCISED; THAT RIGHTEOUSNESS MIGHT BE IMPUTED UNTO THEM ALSO" (Rom. 4:9-11).

The apostle thus demonstrated that simply because God had chosen Abraham's seed as the channel through which to bless all nations, they must

---

*Though the blessing of Abraham now comes on the Gentiles *through Christ* (Gal. 3:14,16).

not presume that He could not bless them in any other way; much less that He meant to bless and save Israel *alone,* for God had justified their own father Abraham through faith, entirely apart from circumcision. Why could He not now do the same?

We must not overlook the fact that whereas "the gospel of the circumcision" is *ex*clusive, "the gospel of the uncircumcision" is *in*clusive, taking in *all believers,* whether Jews or Gentiles, for Paul's whole point in Romans 4 is that faith was reckoned to Abraham for righteousness *before* he was circumcised *"that he might be the father of all them that believe, though they be not circumcised."* Thus "the gospel of the *un*circumcision" takes in *both* Jew and Gentile. Indeed, it is most significant that in view of Israel's rejection of Christ, God should now send forth Paul to point this out and to offer salvation by faith alone to Jew and Gentile alike.

Under "the gospel of the kingdom" the twelve were explicitly commanded *not* to go to the Gentiles or the Samaritans, but only to the lost sheep of the house of Israel (Matt. 10:5,6). Under "the gospel of the circumcision" these same apostles were ex-plicity instructed to go to Israel *first* (Luke 24:47, Acts 1:8). In both cases the reason was that God had *promised* to bless the nations *through Israel.*

But now, with Israel refusing to become the channel of blessing, God temporarily suspends the fulfillment of the covenants, raises up *another* apos-tle, and sends him forth with the glorious "gospel of the uncircumcision," in which:

"THERE IS NO DIFFERENCE* BETWEEN THE JEW AND THE GREEK: FOR THE SAME LORD OVER ALL IS RICH UNTO ALL THAT CALL UPON HIM.

"FOR WHOSOEVER SHALL CALL UPON THE NAME OF THE LORD SHALL BE SAVED" (Rom. 10:12,13).

It should be clearly noted that Paul's ministry to the Gentiles with "the gospel of the uncircumcision" superseded our Lord's earthly ministry and the Pentecostal ministry of the twelve. This is emphatically stated in two passages in Romans and Galatians. The first, in Romans 15, shows how Paul's ministry superseded that of Christ *on earth*:

"Now I say that Jesus Christ WAS a minister of the circumcision [the Hebrew nation] for the truth of God, to confirm the promises made unto the fathers:

"And that the Gentiles might glorify God for His mercy; as it is written . . ." (Rom. 15:8,9).

This was in line with the prophetic program. Christ *confirmed* the promises made unto the fathers. Had Israel, at Pentecost, accepted Christ, these promises (of her future blessing) would have been *fulfilled* and the Gentiles would have (as they some day will) glorified God for His mercy.

But though these promises had been so conclusively confirmed, Israel rejected Christ and now Paul, by inspiration, writes to the Roman believers:

"Nevertheless, brethren, I have written the more boldly unto you in some sort [in a sense], as putting you in mind, because of the grace that is given to me of God,

---

*Rom. 1:16 by no means contradicts this. The difficulty is that some, taking this verse out of its context, suppose that Paul here teaches that the gospel *should still* go to the Jew first, whereas the whole passage (Rom. 1:13-16) is a defense of his going to the *Gentiles*, the gospel *having first gone* to the Jew. Since God's good news is now all of grace, no one is first. This will be further discussed in a later chapter.

"THAT I SHOULD BE THE MINISTER OF JESUS CHRIST TO THE GENTILES, MINISTERING THE GOSPEL OF GOD, THAT THE OFFERING UP OF THE GENTILES MIGHT BE ACCEPTABLE, BEING SANCTIFIED BY THE HOLY GHOST" (Rom. 15:15,16).

The second passage, in Galatians 2, shows how Paul's ministry superseded that of the twelve:

"And I went up by revelation, and communicated unto them that gospel which I preach among the Gentiles, but privately to them which were of reputation, lest by any means I should run, or had run, in vain."

"BUT ... WHEN THEY SAW THAT THE GOSPEL OF THE UNCIRCUMCISION WAS COMMITTED UNTO ME, AS THE GOSPEL OF THE CIRCUMCISION WAS UNTO PETER;"

"AND WHEN JAMES, CEPHAS, AND JOHN, WHO SEEMED TO BE PILLARS, PERCEIVED THE GRACE THAT WAS GIVEN UNTO ME, THEY GAVE TO ME AND BARNABAS THE RIGHT HANDS OF FELLOWSHIP; THAT WE SHOULD GO UNTO THE HEATHEN, AND THEY UNTO THE CIRCUMCISION" (Gal. 2:2,7,9).

Mark well: the twelve, who had *first* been sent into "all the world" to preach "the gospel" to "every creature," "beginning at Jerusalem," now recognized that the present fulfillment of this great commission had been interrupted through Israel's unbelief and, acknowledging the new commission given to Paul, their leaders shook hands with Paul and Barnabas in a solemn agreement that Paul, with Barnabas, should now go to the Gentiles, while they confined their ministry to Israel. This is how it came that Paul could write in Rom. 11:13:

"FOR I SPEAK TO YOU GENTILES, INASMUCH AS I AM THE APOSTLE OF THE GENTILES, I MAGNIFY MINE OFFICE."

206

THE GOSPEL OF RECONCILIATION

The message of reconciliation, like that of the uncircumcision, was first committed to the Apostle Paul. The message takes us back before David, before Abraham, before Abram, to *Adam,* the father of the human race, the "one man" by whom "sin entered into the world," and explains *why* God was now to deal with Jew and Gentile on the same basis.

The Lord Jesus, while on earth, did not proclaim the message of reconciliation. Only once, so far as the record goes, did He even use the word *reconcile,* and then only in reference to the reconciliation of two brothers. Neither did the apostles at Pentecost proclaim reconciliation, much less the reconciliation of Jew and Gentile to God in one body.

Likewise, we do not find our Lord on earth or the twelve at Pentecost going back to Adam in their preaching. They speak again and again of the promises made to David and Abraham, but never even mention the name *Adam.* Our Lord did once *refer* to Adam, without mentioning his name, but in this case He was dealing with the matter of marriage and divorce and stated simply: "He which made them at the beginning made them male and female."

The message of reconciliation could not be preached to all the world until the casting away of Israel, for the simple reason that friends need not be reconciled, and Israel, in early Acts, was still God's favored people. Therefore we read:

207

"FOR IF THE CASTING AWAY OF THEM [IS-RAEL] BE THE RECONCILING OF THE WORLD, what shall the receiving of them be but life from the dead?" (Rom. 11:15).

Reconciliation postulates *alienation;* hence it was not until God had begun to set aside Israel that He began to offer reconciliation through Paul. Moreover, it was when Israel joined the Gentiles in rebellion against God and His Christ that man's *natural* alienation from God was fully *demonstrated.* This is why Paul, in the message of reconciliation, takes us back, not to David and Abraham, with whom the covenants had been made, but to *Adam,* by whom all mankind had been alienated from God.

". . . BY ONE MAN SIN ENTERED INTO THE WORLD, AND DEATH BY SIN; AND SO DEATH PASSED UPON ALL MEN, FOR THAT ALL HAVE SINNED" (Rom. 5:12).

Israel's fall was natural, for *the children of Israel were the children of fallen Adam too.* God had put a difference between Israel and the Gentiles, among other reasons, simply to show that *basically, essentially, "there is no difference."*

This was what God was now to teach by setting Israel aside and offering *reconciliation* to Jew and

---

*Some years ago there was a Jewish paper dealer from whom we bought paper in lots for the publication of the *Berean Search-light.* One day as we were "discussing" the price of a case of paper, he exclaimed: "If you get me down any lower I'll go bankrupt!" I replied, humorously, that if the time ever came that I could get the better of a son of Abraham in business I would consider myself a good businessman, adding: *"Say, Sam, are you and I blood relatives?"* He seemed rather startled at this question, but replied with a twinkle in his eye: *"No, I am a son of Abraham."* I pressed him further, and said: *"I know, but tell me, are you at all related to Adam?"* At this he scratched his head and hesitated a few moments. He knew the Old Testament quite well. Finally he replied: *"You got me that time!"* He knew we *both* were sons of Adam.

208

Gentile on an equal basis. This gracious offer is not based on covenant promises, but on the *facts* of man's alienation from God, his desperate need and God's infinite love and mercy.

Thank God, the message of reconciliation is not concerned exclusively with the "one man" by whom sin entered into the world. Indeed, it is *chiefly* concerned with *"the second Man," "the last Adam,"* the *"one Mediator between God and men, the Man Christ Jesus"* (I Cor. 15:45,47, I Tim. 2:5).

"THEREFORE AS BY THE OFFENCE OF ONE [or, ONE TRESPASS] JUDGMENT CAME UPON ALL MEN TO CONDEMNATION; EVEN SO BY THE RIGHTEOUSNESS OF ONE [or, ONE RIGHTEOUS ACT] THE FREE GIFT CAME UPON ALL MEN UNTO JUSTIFICATION OF LIFE.

"FOR AS BY ONE MAN'S DISOBEDIENCE MANY WERE MADE SINNERS, SO BY THE OBEDIENCE OF ONE SHALL MANY BE MADE RIGHTEOUS" (Rom. 5:18,19).

It is by this other "one Man" and His death on Calvary, that sinners—Jewish and Gentile alike—may be reconciled to a holy God. In Col. 1:21,22 the apostle of reconciliation declares:

"And you, that were sometime ALIENATED AND ENEMIES in your mind by wicked works, yet now hath He RECONCILED

"IN THE BODY OF HIS FLESH THROUGH DEATH, TO PRESENT YOU HOLY AND UNBLAMEABLE AND UNREPROVEABLE IN HIS SIGHT."

Thus, *"when we were enemies, we were reconciled to God by the death of His Son"* (Rom. 5:10 and cf. Eph. 2:11-18).

As we have seen, the proclamation of this

glorious message is *our* great commission, as we are distinctly told in II Cor. 5:18,19. We quote the passage here with more of its context, so that the reader may understand and appreciate it more fully:

"WHEREFORE HENCEFORTH KNOW WE NO MAN AFTER THE FLESH: YEA, THOUGH WE HAVE KNOWN CHRIST AFTER THE FLESH, YET NOW HENCEFORTH KNOW WE HIM NO MORE.

"THEREFORE IF ANY MAN BE IN CHRIST, HE IS A NEW CREATURE: OLD THINGS ARE PASSED AWAY; BEHOLD, ALL THINGS ARE BECOME NEW.

"AND ALL THINGS ARE OF GOD, WHO HATH RECONCILED US TO HIMSELF BY JESUS CHRIST, AND HATH GIVEN TO US THE MINISTRY OF RECONCILIATION;

"TO WIT, THAT GOD WAS IN CHRIST, RECONCILING THE WORLD UNTO HIMSELF, NOT IMPUTING THEIR TRESPASSES UNTO THEM; AND HATH COMMITTED UNTO US THE WORD OF RECONCILIATION.

"NOW THEN WE ARE AMBASSADORS FOR CHRIST, AS THOUGH GOD DID BESEECH YOU BY US: WE PRAY YOU IN CHRIST'S STEAD, BE YE RECONCILED TO GOD.

"FOR HE HATH MADE HIM TO BE SIN FOR US, WHO KNEW NO SIN; THAT WE MIGHT BE MADE THE RIGHTEOUSNESS OF GOD IN HIM" (II. Cor. 5:16-21).

This is *our* great commission; may we discharge it faithfully!

We insist that it is an *offer,* however, not a promise of universal reconciliation. The apostle does not beseech men to be reconciled in this life, merely, so as to escape a short period of discipline. There is no hint in his plea that all will eventually be reconciled regardless of their response to his

210

offer. On the contrary, he pleads with them to be reconciled *now*, since *"now* is the accepted time"; he begs them to be reconciled before it is *too late,* so that they may not have received the gracious offer "in vain" (Read carefully the verses which follow: II Cor. 6:1,2). It is true, indeed, that at the name of Jesus every knee shall one day bow, of things in heaven, and things in earth and things under the earth, and that every tongue shall eventually confess Him as Lord (Phil. 2:10,11), but this is universal *subjugation,* not *reconciliation.* This final subjugation of all beings, celestial, terrestrial and infernal, to Christ will not be the result of the *present offer*:

"THAT IF THOU SHALT CONFESS WITH THY MOUTH THE LORD JESUS [JESUS AS LORD], AND SHALT BELIEVE IN THINE HEART THAT GOD HATH RAISED HIM FROM THE DEAD, THOU SHALT BE SAVED" (Rom. 10:9).

Nor must we confuse the prediction of universal subjugation with God's purpose to *"reconcile all things unto Himself . . . whether they be things IN EARTH, or things IN HEAVEN"** (Col. 1:20).

Concerning our responsibility to proclaim God's offer of reconciliation to the lost, one thing is certain: If we would faithfully discharge our great commission, we must be so constrained by the love of Christ (II Cor. 5:14) that, though men may consider us "beside ourselves" (Ver. 13), we will *live* for Him who *died* for us (Ver. 15), *"beseeching"* men and *"praying"* them, in Christ's stead, to be reconciled to God (Ver. 20), knowing that *"NOW is*

*Note: "Things *under* the earth" are excluded here.

211

the accepted time" and *"NOW is the day of salvation"* (6:2).

THE MYSTERY

We have already discussed "the mystery" at some length, but must consider it here in connection with the various gospels.

Just as the kingdom of Christ is the subject of the prophetic Scriptures, so *the body of Christ* is the subject of the great mystery revealed to and through the Apostle Paul.

The apostle defines this "mystery," made known to him by revelation (Eph. 3:3), as follows:

"That they who are of the nations should be joint heirs, and a joint body, and joint partakers of His promise in Jesus Christ by the glad tidings" (Eph. 3:6, New Tr.).*

There are, as we have seen, many aspects of the mystery, but the great central truth is that God was to form of believing Jews and Gentiles one joint body in Christ.

It will be readily seen that this glorious truth concerning the body naturally follows the revelation concerning the gospels of the uncircumcision and of reconciliation. Indeed the apostle himself points out that the joint body is the *product* of the reconciliation of Jews and Gentiles to God. Explaining how God *"hath broken down the middle wall of partition between us,"* he goes on to say that this was done

". . . FOR TO MAKE IN HIMSELF OF TWAIN ONE NEW MAN, SO MAKING PEACE;

---

*The Authorized Version unfortunately renders the prefix *su* (*co-* or *joint*) in three different ways in this one verse.

"AND THAT HE MIGHT RECONCILE BOTH UNTO GOD IN ONE BODY BY THE CROSS, HAVING SLAIN THE ENMITY THEREBY:

"AND CAME AND PREACHED PEACE TO YOU WHICH WERE AFAR OFF, AND TO THEM THAT WERE* NIGH.

"FOR THROUGH HIM WE BOTH HAVE ACCESS BY ONE SPIRIT UNTO THE FATHER" (Eph. 2:14-18).

We have already pointed out that until we come to the writings of Paul we do not find one single word as to this great mystery or any of its associated mysteries. But this does not mean that it was an afterthought on God's part, for in proclaiming the mystery the apostle takes us back before David and Abraham, before Abram and Adam, to God, who planned it all.

Though the most spiritual believer at Jerusalem could not have known what God would do when Israel rejected His risen, glorified Son, God had a gracious, glorious plan in mind from the beginning. He simply says that it was *"KEPT SECRET since the world began"* (Rom. 16:25), that *"in other ages [it] was NOT MADE KNOWN"* (Eph. 3:5), that *"from the beginning of the world [it] had been HID in God"* (Eph. 3:9), that it had been *"HID from ages and from generations"* (Col. 1:26), but in all this He makes it most clear that the whole plan was

"ACCORDING TO THE ETERNAL PURPOSE WHICH HE PURPOSED IN CHRIST JESUS OUR LORD" (Eph. 3:11).

How we should rejoice that the (temporary) casting away of Israel, the offer of justification to

---

*Note: Here Israel is no longer considered "nigh" to God.

Jew and Gentile alike, and the reconciliation of *both* Jews and Gentiles to Himself in one body, was God's wonderful plan from the beginning; the surprise of His grace, to be revealed when sin had risen to its height! How we should worship Him

"Who hath saved us, and called us with an holy calling, NOT ACCORDING TO OUR WORKS, BUT ACCORDING TO HIS OWN PURPOSE AND GRACE, WHICH WAS GIVEN US IN CHRIST JESUS BEFORE THE WORLD BEGAN" (II Tim. 1:9).

BASIC CONNECTIONS AND DISTINCTIONS
BETWEEN THESE GOSPELS

It will be noticed on the foregoing chart that the two portions covering the gospel of the kingdom and the gospel of the circumcision are shaded. This is because these two gospels are intimately linked together.

1. Both were based on *covenants* and did not reveal "the exceeding riches of God's grace" as Paul's good news did.

2. Both were related to *prophecy,* not to the mystery.

3. Both were bound up with ordinances and signs. *Circumcision* was the sign of the Abrahamic Covenant (Gen. 17:11). *Water baptism* was the sign of the Davidic Covenant (Ex. 29:4, cf. Ex. 19:5,6, Isa. 61:6, Matt. 3:1-6).

4. These two gospels were proclaimed by John the Baptist, Christ and the twelve.

5. Matt. 1:1 introduces Christ as "the Son of David, the Son of Abraham," and the Abrahamic

214

Covenant, concerning the nation is, of course, intimately bound up with the Davidic Covenant, concerning the King to reign over that nation.

The remaining three messages (the outer three on the chart) are also closely linked together.

1. These three are based on *grace alone,* not on covenants or promises.

2. All three were previously *kept secret,* not foretold.*

3. None had any relation to ordinances or signs.° We are circumcized and baptized *in Christ* (I Cor. 6:11, Phil. 3:3, Col. 2:9-12).

4. All three of these messages were first committed to Paul.

5. These gospels are inseparably linked as *one progressive revelation.* This is why the Apostle Paul speaks of *"my gospel"* (Rom. 2:16, 16:25, II Tim. 2:8) and uses the general term *"the gospel of the grace of God,"* when referring to his *whole* Christian ministry (Acts 20:24).

It may be further noted that John the Baptist, Christ and the twelve, in their proclamations, went from the particular to the general, while Paul went from the general to the particular. This is because the prophesied program was passing off the scene at the same time when the program of the mystery was appearing on the scene.

Thus, *Christ Himself* is first announced in the gospels; then *His Messiahship* is proclaimed in "the gospel of the kingdom" and after His crucifixion

---

*Gal. 3 :8 says : "And the Scripture *foreseeing,*" not *foretelling.*
°Although ordinances and signs were at first *recognized* as part of the program which was then passing away.

215

Israel's opportunity to become a blessing to the world is stressed in "the gospel of the circumcision." Or, to put it another way: Christ, the Son of David is first presented; then the Davidic Covenant of the kingdom is recalled and, after the cross, the broader Abrahamic Covenant.

Conversely, as Israel persisted in her rejection of Christ, the Apostle Paul began with the broad *"gospel of the uncircumcision"* as a basis for the *message of reconciliation,* by which both Jews and Gentiles were to become *one body in Christ.* So he began with what the Scriptures had clearly foreseen (though not foretold) and ended with the mystery itself, which was *"KEPT SECRET since the world began."*

The above may be illustrated by the following outline:

John the Baptist, Christ & the Twelve					~The Apostle Paul~
Prophecy					**The Mystery**
Matt. 1:21-23					Eph. 1:22,23
Rom. 15:8					Col. 1:15-27
Christ as King of Israel	Gospel of the Kingdom Matt. 9:35 Matt. 10:5-7	Gospel of the Circumcision Acts 3:25,26 Gal. 2:7	Gospel of the Uncircumcision Rom. 4:9,10 Gal. 2:7	Gospel of Reconciliation II Cor. 5:19 Eph. 2:16	Christ as Head of Body
From the Particular to the General					From the General to the Particular

216

QUIZ

1. What is misleading about the term: "The Four Gospels"? 2. Why was it necessary to have four separate accounts of our Lord's earthly ministry? 3. What is wrong with the contention that the Bible presents only *one* gospel? 4. Why is it particularly necessary to bear the context in mind when we read the simple phrase "the gospel"? 5. Draw from memory the chart on the five gospels discussed in this chapter. 6. How was the kingdom proclaimed before the cross? 7. What two Scripture passages tell us that the kingdom was to be "taken from" Israel's rulers and "given to" the "little flock" of Christ's followers? 8. What passage contains our Lord's promise that the twelve will occupy twelve thrones in the kingdom? 9. When was the kingdom first *offered* to Israel? 10. The "gospel of the circumcision" was based on what great covenant? 11. Explain how the gospels of the kingdom and of the circumcision were related. 12. On what great *facts* was "the gospel of the *un*circumcision" based? 13. Where do we read that "the gospel of the uncircumcision" was particularly committed to Paul? 14. What does reconciliation postulate, or presuppose? 15. Where do we find that the message of reconciliation is related to the casting away of Israel? 16. The message of reconciliation revolves mainly around what two men? 17. Explain the significance of the fact that according to II Cor. 5, the proclamation of reconciliation is *not a promise, but a plea.* 18. Explain how the formation of the body is related to the proclamation of reconciliation. 19. Give three Scriptures proving that "the mystery" was not revealed until Paul. 20. Show how the gospels of the uncircumcision, reconciliation and the mystery are related.

Chapter XII.

THE DISPENSATIONAL PLACE OF MIRACULOUS SIGNS AND WATER BAPTISM

The truths which we have been considering vitally affect our *practice* as members of the body of Christ and our *service* for Him, for if we do not clearly understand God's message and program for the present dispensation, how can we serve Him effectively?

The prevailing confusion in the church is largely due to ignorance and even indifference as to these matters. How many of God's people today are trying zealously to serve Him, without first finding out exactly what it is He wishes them to do! Hence, even among those who sincerely trust in Christ as Savior, many are still striving vainly to establish His kingdom on earth, while others seek for some or all of the miraculous powers of Pentecost and all together insist on practicing the ordinance of water baptism, though unable to agree as to *who* should be baptized, or *how,* or *why.*

Miraculous signs and baptism deserve exhaustive treatment in separate volumes, but we must deal with them briefly here because of their relation to the whole dispensational problem.

MIRACULOUS SIGNS

It cannot be denied that miraculous demonstrations abounded during our Lord's earthly ministry and the period covered by the book of Acts. Neither can it be denied that such demonstrations abounded among *Gentile members of the body of Christ* before the close of the Acts period.

Some hold that *all true* believers today *do* possess the miraculous powers of Pentecost, since our Lord, in His "great commission," explicitly said: *"And these signs shall follow them that believe . . ."* (Mark 16:17,18). Others believe that *certain* people are granted the power to work miracles, especialy miracles of healing. Notwithstanding these claims, however, *God* is *not* bestowing miraculous powers upon men today. If the "great commission" with its Pentecostal signs were indeed being carried out today there would be no question about miracles, for saved and unsaved alike were compelled to acknowledge the mighty miracles of the Pentecostal era* (Acts 3:11, 4:14,16, etc.). As to alleged evidence of the supernatural powers of present day Pentecostalist "healers": the Roman Church, the Unity movement, Christian Scientists, and others who claim healing powers can present "evidences" fully as convincing. Are their powers, then, also God-given?

---

*Note: we refer to supernatural *gifts* and *demonstrations*. We recognize, of course, that miracles are being performed all about us constantly, but while God, for example, may miraculously heal the sick, according to His will, He does not use "divine healers" to accomplish this, nor have we the right to *claim* physical health in the present dispensation. As one has said: "Despite the 'divine healers,' the death rate is still one apiece!"

219

MIRACLES AND SPIRITUALITY

The usual reason given for the absence of these powers is lack of faith and spirituality. If only we had the faith of the early believers, we are told; if only we were as spiritual as they, we too would possess these miraculous powers.

It is not denied that even the most consecrated believer falls far short of God's standards of spirituality, nor that there is a particular lack of true spirituality among Christians today, but this does not explain their inability to perform miracles. Such an argument would be answered by the case of the Corinthians alone. Paul called them *un*spiritual babes (I Cor. 3:1) and sternly rebuked them for their carnality, for their "envying, and strife, and divisions" (I Cor. 3:3), for their immorality (I Cor. 5:1), for their dishonesty and oppression of each other (I Cor. 6:7, 8), for their unfaithfulness in giving (I Cor. 9:11-14), for their selfishness and pride (I Cor. 11:21,22) and exclaimed to them: "And *ye* are puffed up, and have not rather mourned!" (I Cor. 5:2, cf. 4:18).

Yet this *same* Corinthian church, at this *same* time, *abounded* in miraculous gifts (I Cor. 1:7, 12:8-11, 14:12,18,26). The absence of these miraculous powers in the church today must, therefore, have another explanation.

THE SIGNIFICANCE OF THE SIGNS

First the general fact should be noted that in Old Testament history miraculous demonstrations prevailed in times of great crisis as, for example, in the cases of Moses and Aaron and of Elijah and Elisha.

Doubtless the call to Israel to repent, from the time of John the Baptist to Pentecost, and the presentation of Christ to Israel for her acceptance, was the greatest crisis in Israel's history up to that time.

Secondly, it had been predicted by the prophets that miracles would abound at Messiah's coming (Isa. 35:5,6, etc.). This is why we read in Matt. 8:16,17:

"When the even was come, they brought unto Him many that were possessed with devils: and He cast out the spirits with His word, and healed all that were sick:

"THAT IT MIGHT BE FULFILLED WHICH WAS SPOKEN BY ESAIAS THE PROPHET, SAYING, HIMSELF TOOK OUR INFIRMITIES, AND BARE OUR SICKNESSES."

This, also, is why Peter declared at Pentecost:

"Ye men of Israel, hear these words; Jesus of Nazareth, a man APPROVED OF GOD AMONG YOU BY MIRACLES AND WONDERS AND SIGNS, which God did by Him in the midst of you, as ye yourselves also know" (Acts 2:22).

Thus Paul writes to the Romans that "Jesus Christ was a minister of the circumcision . . . to *confirm* the promises made unto the fathers" (Rom. 15:8).

In the third place, we should remember that these miracles had a special significance in connection with the casting out of Satan, so long the prince of this world (John 12:31), and the establishment of Christ's kingdom, for we read in I John 3:8:

". . . FOR THIS PURPOSE THE SON OF GOD WAS MANIFESTED, THAT HE MIGHT DESTROY THE WORKS OF THE DEVIL."

Thus, in His attack on the kingdom of Satan, our Lord said:

"And if Satan cast out Satan, he is divided against himself; how shall then his kingdom stand?"

"BUT IF I CAST OUT DEVILS BY THE SPIRIT OF GOD, THEN THE KINGDOM OF GOD IS COME UNTO YOU" (Matt. 12:26,28).

In accordance with this the Lord also commanded the seventy to declare in each city the significance of the miracles they wrought there:

"AND HEAL THE SICK THAT ARE THEREIN, AND SAY UNTO THEM, THE KINGDOM OF GOD IS COME NIGH UNTO YOU" (Luke 10:9).

In Acts it is the same for, remember, Acts is the record of what the Lord Jesus *continued* to do and to teach after His resurrection (Acts 1:1,2). The miracles of the Pentecostal era were wrought by *the risen Christ,* so that Peter, referring to one case, declared:

"And His name through faith in His name hath made this man strong, whom ye see and know: yea, the faith which is by Him hath given him this perfect soundness in the presence of you all" (Acts 3:16).

"BE IT KNOWN UNTO YOU ALL, AND TO ALL THE PEOPLE OF ISRAEL, THAT BY THE NAME OF JESUS CHRIST OF NAZARETH, WHOM YE CRUCIFIED, WHOM GOD RAISED FROM THE DEAD, EVEN BY HIM DOTH THIS MAN STAND HERE BEFORE YOU WHOLE" (Acts 4:10).

And as Christ had been "approved of God" by miraculous signs, so we are told in Heb. 2:3,4, of the "great salvation"

". . . which at the first began to be spoken by the Lord, and was confirmed unto us by them that heard Him;

222

"GOD ALSO BEARING THEM WITNESS, BOTH WITH SIGNS AND WONDERS, AND WITH DIVERS MIRACLES, AND GIFTS OF THE HOLY GHOST, ACCORDING TO HIS OWN WILL."

This "great salvation," which "began to be spoken by the Lord," was, of course, that of Matt. 1:21 and Luke 1:67-77, and concerned the reign of Christ on earth. And now this message was "confirmed . . . by them that heard Him," so that Peter offered to Israel the times of refreshing and the return of Christ, upon condition that they repent and turn to Him (Acts 3:19,20).

And so God confirmed our Lord's Messiahship with mighty signs and wonders, both during His earthly ministry and after His ascension into heaven.

MIRACLES AMONG THE GENTILES

What, then, was the reason for the miraculous gifts among the Gentiles, especially under Paul's ministry? Even these were associated indirectly with the Messianic kingdom.

We must not forget that Paul, though entrusted with *another* commission and "the gospel of the grace of God," nevertheless *confirmed* Peter's message and proclaimed and proved to the Jews everywhere that "Jesus is the Christ," for the offer of the kingdom, made at Pentecost, was not officially withdrawn until Acts 28:28. Hence it is not strange to find these miraculous confirmations of Christ's kingdom rights continued until that time.

We must also remember the inspired declaration that "the Jews require a sign" (I Cor. 1:22).

The way *they* could tell that the new program was of God was that Paul had all "the signs of an apostle" (II Cor. 12:11,12) and that the Gentile believers also possessed miraculous powers. Even before Paul went to the Gentiles, Peter was sent to the first Gentile household to be thus convinced. Note the record concerning this:

"And they of the circumcision which believed were astonished, as many as came with Peter, because that on the Gentiles also was poured out the gift of the Holy Ghost.

"FOR THEY HEARD THEM SPEAK WITH TONGUES, AND MAGNIFY GOD . . ." (Acts 10:45,46).

MIRACULOUS GIFTS WITHDRAWN

But with the setting aside of Israel there was no longer any need of this, and the later epistles of Paul do not even recognize such gifts as being in order.

Indeed, in his first letter to the Corinthians, the apostle made it clear that their miraculous powers were to be withdrawn:

"CHARITY [LOVE] NEVER FAILETH: BUT WHETHER THERE BE PROPHECIES, THEY SHALL FAIL; WHETHER THERE BE TONGUES, THEY SHALL CEASE; WHETHER THERE BE KNOWLEDGE, IT SHALL VANISH AWAY" (I Cor. 13:8).

Certainly Paul did not mean that supernatural *predictions* would fail to come true, nor that men would stop *talking* or *knowing*. He referred to the miraculous *gifts* of prophecy, tongues and knowledge. These were to be "done away."

"AND NOW ABIDETH FAITH, HOPE, CHARITY [LOVE], THESE THREE; BUT THE GREATEST OF THESE IS CHARITY [LOVE]" (I Cor. 13:13).

As to the healing miracles: those who were healed by the Lord and His followers would doubtless have entered into the kingdom and have gone on living, had the kingdom been established, but now that Israel rejected Christ and His reign all these healed ones died. So it was not because our Lord had failed that those He healed did not remain alive and well; it was because the kingdom was refused and "this present evil age" settled down upon the world.

In Paul's early letters there is abundant proof that the gift of healing was already being withdrawn, for there he says:

"FOR WE KNOW THAT THE WHOLE CREATION GROANETH AND TRAVAILETH IN PAIN TOGETHER UNTIL NOW.

"AND NOT ONLY THEY, BUT OURSELVES ALSO, WHICH HAVE THE FIRSTFRUITS OF THE SPIRIT, EVEN WE OURSELVES GROAN WITHIN OURSELVES, WAITING FOR THE ADOPTION, TO WIT, THE REDEMPTION OF OUR BODY" (Rom. 8:22,23).

"FOR IN THIS [TABERNACLE] WE GROAN, EARNESTLY DESIRING TO BE CLOTHED UPON WITH OUR HOUSE WHICH IS FROM HEAVEN" (II Cor. 5:2).

Add to these passages such statements as the following: *"Though our outward man perish, yet the inward man is renewed day by day"* (II Cor. 4:16), *"There was given to me a thorn in the flesh . . . lest I should be exalted above measure"* (II Cor. 12:7), *"And I was with you in weakness, and in fear, and in much trembling"* (I Cor. 2:3), *"Through infirmity of the flesh I preached the gospel unto you at the first"* (Gal. 4:13), *"Who is weak, and I am not*

225

weak?" (II Cor. 11:29), *"Epaphroditus . . . was sick nigh unto death: but God had mercy on him"* (Phil. 2:25-27), *"Trophimus have I left at Miletum sick"* (II Tim. 4:20), *"Use a little wine for thy stomach's sake and thine often infirmities"* (I Tim. 5:23).

TAKING PLEASURE IN INFIRMITIES

The gift of healing, then, was being withdrawn as Paul wrote his early epistles. God, however, was replacing it with something better, for we are *"blessed with all spiritual blessings in heavenly places"* (Eph. 1:3). Indeed, our high and holy calling, our perfect position in Christ, our spiritual wealth, might well puff us up did not God allow us to be visited with bodily affliction (II Cor. 12:7). Meantime He assures us: *"My grace is sufficient for thee: for My strength is made perfect in weakness* (II. Cor. 12:9). Thus these afflictions become blessings in disguise and serve to draw us closer to God. This is why the Apostle Paul goes on to say:

". . . MOST GLADLY THEREFORE WILL I RATHER GLORY IN MY INFIRMITIES, THAT THE POWER OF CHRIST MAY REST UPON ME.

"THEREFORE I TAKE PLEASURE IN INFIRMITIES, IN REPROACHES, IN NECESSITIES, IN PERSECUTIONS, IN DISTRESSES FOR CHRIST'S SAKE: FOR WHEN I AM WEAK, THEN AM I STRONG" (II Cor. 12: 9, 10).

WATER BAPTISM

Water baptism and miraculous signs both belong to the so-called "great commission" (Matt. 28:19, Mark 16:16-18, Acts 1:8), yet, strangely, many pastors who would excommunicate any of their members for speaking in tongues or seeking to perform miracles, nevertheless cling tenaciously to the practice of water baptism. Surely it would seem that if the "great commission" is for our obedience today, the Pentecostalists are more consistent than the great majority of their Fundamentalist brethren in this matter. Here, then, let us point out briefly the dispensational significance of water baptism and the glory of the "one baptism" of the present dispensation.

In all the division and confusion which has prevailed in the church over the subject of baptism, the primary question at issue has been almost completely overlooked. That question is not whether water baptism is found in the Scriptures, nor *who* should be baptized, nor *how*. The *first* question which concerns us is: should we practice water baptism now? Is it included in God's program for *the present dispensation?**

If, instead of becoming wrought up over secondary questions, the spiritual leaders of the past centuries had first asked themselves this basic question, much discord and heartache could have been avoided.

WATER BAPTISM AND THE
MESSIANIC KINGDOM

We have already seen that the opening message of the New Testament Scriptures is *"Repent ye: for the kingdom of heaven is at hand"* (Matt. 3:2). This message was first proclaimed to Israel

*See the author's booklet entitled: "Water Baptism: Is It Included In God's Program For Today?"

by John the Baptist and was later taken up by our Lord (Matt. 4:17) and His twelve apostles (Matt. 10:5-7). The proclamation of this message and its results are what the "Four Gospels" record.

The fact that this kingdom was now proclaimed "at hand" indicates that it had been predicted and expected, and so it had.

Under the Old Covenant God had promised:

"Now therefore, if ye will obey My voice indeed, and keep My covenant, then ye shall be a peculiar treasure unto Me above all people: for all the earth is Mine:

"And ye shall be unto Me A KINGDOM OF PRIESTS, and AN HOLY NATION. These are the words which thou shalt speak unto the children of Israel (Ex. 19:5,6).

Until they did obey God's voice indeed, only certain people *in* Israel were set apart as priests, but in connection with the coming of Messiah and the conversion of all Israel, God later promised that they would indeed become a whole nation of priests through whom the Gentiles should approach God:

"BUT YE SHALL BE NAMED THE PRIESTS OF THE LORD: MEN SHALL CALL YOU THE MINISTERS OF OUR GOD . . . (Isa. 61:6).

The first rite to be performed at the induction of the priest into his office was his washing with water (Ex. 29:4). This spoke of his need of cleansing before approaching the presence of God. Hence, as John proclaimed the kingdom at hand, in which *all* Israel should stand before God as priests, he demanded repentance and water baptism for the remission of sins (Mark 1:4).*

---

*Under the Mosaic law the priests and those ceremonially "unclean" were both washed, or baptized. Thus under the kingdom program the Jews and the "unclean" Gentiles alike had to be baptized (Matt. 28:19).

That John's baptism was associated with the manifestation of Christ to Israel cannot be denied, for John himself said:

"AND I KNEW HIM NOT: BUT THAT HE SHOULD BE MADE MANIFEST TO ISRAEL, THEREFORE AM I COME BAPTIZING WITH WATER" (John 1:31).

Mark well, John baptized the people *"for the remission of sins."* Nor was this changed after the resurrection of Christ, for at Pentecost Peter offered Christ's return and the times of refreshing to Israel, again calling upon them to *"repent and be baptized . . . for the remission of sins"* (Acts 2:38)* This was in strict obedience to the commission given to him by the risen Lord, in which it was expressly stated that *"He that believeth and is baptized shall be saved"* (Mark 16:16).*

As with miraculous signs, the departure from this program came with Israel's rejection of her risen Messiah and the raising up of Paul to proclaim the gospel of the grace of God. And, like miraculous signs, this part of the program was not discontinued all at once. Even after the raising up of Paul God still continued for some time to stretch forth His hands to a disobedient and gainsaying people (Rom. 10:21). The departure, however, did not begin until after Saul's conversion. Then Peter was sent

---

*Those who speak of "Christian baptism" beginning at Pentecost under the "great commission," should carefully note this fact. At a public debate on this subject we once produced six books and booklets by prominent Fundamentalists, upholding their baptism theories, in which they had quoted Acts 2:38, but had omitted the words *"for the remission of sins."*

*Fundamentalists who claim to be carrying out the "great commission" generally interpret this to mean: *"He that believeth and is saved ought to be baptized."* It can only be said in this connection that those who thus handle so plain a statement from God's Word may also "interpret" other passages to mean what they do not say. Modernism and the cults have already gone down this road.

to the first Gentile family only to have his sermon interrupted while, to the astonishment of His companions, these Gentiles were saved and received the Holy Spirit apart from water baptism (Acts 10:44-46). True Peter *then* baptized them (Acts 10:47) to keep the books straight, as it were, but the departure from the program of the "great commission" is clear. The practice of water baptism continued for some time after this, while Christ was still being made manifest to Israel.

PAUL AND THE "ONE BAPTISM"

But in the ministry of Paul, with which the rest of Acts is concerned, water baptism is *never* required for the remission of sins. Obviously, then, another commission was replacing that given to the eleven before our Lord's ascension.

It is significant that while Paul did baptize some,* and mentions this in his first letter to the Corinthians, he states that he is glad he has baptized so few of them, adding:

"FOR CHRIST SENT ME NOT TO BAPTIZE, BUT TO PREACH THE GOSPEL: NOT WITH WISDOM OF WORDS, LEST THE CROSS OF CHRIST SHOULD BE MADE OF NONE EFFECT.

"FOR THE PREACHING OF THE CROSS IS TO THEM THAT PERISH FOOLISHNESS; BUT UNTO US WHICH ARE SAVED IT IS THE POWER OF GOD" (I Cor. 1:17,18).

It is also significant that *Paul, the apostle of the Gentiles and minister of the body of Christ NEVER ONCE, IN ANY OF HIS LETTERS, COMMANDS*

*He also circumcised Timothy, spoke with tongues, healed the sick, etc.

OR EVEN EXHORTS US TO BE BAPTIZED
WITH WATER.

In his later letters, written after the setting
aside of Israel, he states emphatically that there is
now but "ONE BAPTISM" (Eph. 4:5). This baptism is the operation of the Holy Spirit whereby
believers are made one with Christ in His death,
burial and resurrection (Rom. 6:3-4, Gal. 3:26,27,
Col. 2:9-12), and so are also made members of "one
body," the "body of Christ" (I Cor. 12:13,27, Gal.
3:26-28).

If believers, especially spiritual leaders, better
understood the "one baptism" by which the "one
Spirit" baptizes us into "one body," our unity in
Christ would be more fully enjoyed. Indeed, we
are exhorted to endeavor to "keep" or *observe* the
unity that the Spirit has made, remembering that
there is but *"one body . . . one Spirit . . . one hope
. . . one Lord, one faith, one baptism, one God and
Father . . ."* (Eph. 4:3-6).

One thing is certain: the student who is willing
to put aside preconceived notions and human tradi-
tions, and search the Scriptures concerning this
"one baptism" with an open mind, sits down to a
veritable feast of spiritual good things.

QUIZ

1. Explain how it was that Gentile members of the
body of Christ once possessed miraculous powers. 2.
Prove from Scripture that lack of faith or spirituality is
not the reason for the absence of the Pentecostal gifts
today. 3. Give Scripture to show how Christ was "ap-

proved of God" among His people. 4. What relation was there between the miracles of Christ's day and the kingdom of Satan? 5. Give Scripture showing how God bore witness to the Pentecostal ministry of the twelve. 6. How did Peter and his companions know that those of Cornelius' household had received the Holy Spirit? 7. What did the Apostle Paul write in I Cor. 13 about the gifts of prophecy, tongues and knowledge? 8. What eventually happened to all those who were healed by our Lord and His followers? 9. Why? 10. Give five Scriptures indicating that healing powers were already being withdrawn in Paul's day. 11. What greater blessings do we have than physical and material wellbeing? 12. How do physical infirmities often prove to be blessings? 13. What was Paul's attitude with respect to infirmities? 14. What is the *first* question which concerns us with respect to the ceremony of water baptism? 15. Give Scripture showing how John the Baptist associated water baptism with Israel and the kingdom. 16 Give three Scriptures proving that water baptism was required for salvation under John the Baptist, under the "great commission" and at Pentecost. 17. Where, in Scripture, do we find the first departures from the Pentecostal program? 18. Prove from Scripture that the Pentecostal program did not cease all at once. 19. Was Paul *sent* to baptize; was it part of his special commission? 20. What is accomplished by the "one baptism" of this dispensation?

Chapter XIII.

PAUL'S EARLY MINISTRY

A DISPENSATIONAL PROBLEM

The early ministry of Paul has puzzled many earnest and diligent Bible students.

They see quite clearly what his ministry *led up to.* They rejoice in his pure message of grace. They understand fully that water baptism and the Pentecostal signs have no more place in the body of Christ than circumcision and the law, but they are perplexed, not to say somewhat disappointed, to find circumcision, baptism and miraculous signs all practiced by Paul during his early ministry as recorded in the book of Acts.

A FAULTY EXPLANATION

This problem has led some to suppose that the mystery was not revealed to Paul until his Roman imprisonment and that "the body of Christ," the church of this age, only began, historically, after Acts 28:28.

But this extreme conclusion is as unscriptural as that which marks Pentecost as the historical beginning of the body, for we read distinctly of the mystery and of the body of Christ in Paul's *earlier* epistles, written before Acts 28, as well as in those written after (Rom. 16:25, I Cor. 2:7, Rom. 12:5, I Cor. 12:12,13,27, etc.). Indeed, this fact has driven those who date the body from Acts 28 to the conclusion that there must be *two bodies*,—that "the body of Christ" of which Paul speaks in Romans and I Corinthians is a different body from "the body of Christ" to which his later epistles refer.

They have been *driven* to this conclusion, we say, for such an explanation is, to say the least, forced and unnatural. We cannot help feeling that such theories must sound shabby even to those who present them, and should cause them to re-examine the foundation of their structure, for a wrong premise will surely lead to wrong conclusions. Certainly the theory of the "two bodies" leads to most extreme and unscriptural conclusions.

One who resorts to this theory writes that *"since Paul's ministry was primarily to the Jews during the Acts, his epistles written during that same time could not be otherwise."*

Such statements are as thoroughly unscriptural as they are extravagant, for the record makes it crystal clear that his early ministry and his early epistles were *primarily to the Gentiles,* not the Jews.

PAUL'S ACTS MINISTRY

In Acts 22:18 and 21 Paul relates how, upon first returning to Jerusalem after his conversion, the Lord had revealed to him that his testimony would not be received there and that he was to be sent to the Gentiles:

"**And [I] saw Him saying unto me, Make haste, and get thee quickly out of Jerusalem: for THEY WILL NOT RECEIVE THY TESTIMONY CONCERNING ME.**"

"And He said unto me, Depart: for I WILL SEND THEE FAR HENCE UNTO THE GENTILES."

And the story of his ministry from then on is in perfect harmony with this.

Acts 13:46,47: "LO, WE TURN TO THE GENTILES. FOR SO HATH THE LORD COMMANDED US . . ."

Acts 15:3: "And being brought on their way by the church, they passed through Phenice and Samaria, DECLARING THE CONVERSION OF THE GENTILES . . ."

Acts 18:6: "FROM HENCEFORTH I WILL GO UNTO THE GENTILES."

"Acts 21:18,19: "And the day following Paul went in with us unto James; and all the elders were present.

"And when he had saluted them, HE DECLARED PARTICULARLY WHAT THINGS GOD HAD WROUGHT AMONG THE GENTILES BY HIS MINISTRY."

PAUL'S EARLY EPISTLES

When we compare Paul's early epistles with the latter part of the book of Acts (the period during which they were written) the picture remains the same:

Rom. 11:13, "I SPEAK TO YOU GENTILES, INASMUCH AS I AM THE APOSTLE OF THE GENTILES, I MAGNIFY MINE OFFICE."

I Cor. 12:2, "YE KNOW THAT YE WERE GENTILES, CARRIED AWAY UNTO THESE DUMB IDOLS . . ."

Gal. 1:15,16, ". . . it pleased God . . . to reveal His Son in me, THAT I MIGHT PREACH HIM AMONG THE HEATHEN [GENTILES] . . ."

Gal. 4:8, "Howbeit then, when ye knew not God, YE DID SERVICE UNTO THEM WHICH BY NATURE ARE NO GODS."

I Thes. 2:14, "For ye, brethren, became followers of the churches of God which in Judaea are in Christ Jesus: for YE ALSO HAVE SUFFERED LIKE THINGS OF YOUR OWN COUNTRYMEN, EVEN AS THEY HAVE OF THE JEWS."

Imagine contending, in the light of such Scriptures as these, that Paul's early epistles were written primarily to the Jews! Surely these quotations from Acts and the early epistles prove conclusively that Paul's early ministry was primarily to the Gentiles and not primarily to the Jews. It is true that he went to the Jew first, but that is a very different matter. And herein lies the solution to the problem of Paul's early ministry.

THE SOLUTION

There is an important fact which we fear our "two body" brethren have overlooked.

Paul went to the Jew first, *not* because it seemed that Israel might yet accept Christ as her King, but simply because God would not leave her with any excuse for rejecting Messiah.

Paul confirmed Peter's message and mightily contended with the Jews everywhere that *"Jesus is the Christ."* Miracles also accompanied this confirmation ministry—greater miracles, indeed, than Peter himself had wrought but, unlike Peter, *Paul never offered the kingdom to Israel.*

As we have seen, Paul, like the twelve, would have launched his ministry from Jerusalem, Israel's capital city, but the Lord Himself appeared to him, and insisted upon his leaving Jerusalem immediately. At this time the Lord made two very important statements to Paul:

1. "THEY WILL NOT RECEIVE THY TESTI-MONY CONCERNING ME."

2. "I WILL SEND THEE FAR HENCE UNTO THE GENTILES."

What was God doing here? He was concluding Israel in unbelief and disobedience and, even at that early date, calling Paul to minister to the Gentiles.

The national rebellion had grown to such proportions that *"a great persecution"* was being waged against the church at Jerusalem. Paul, who but lately had been the leading persecutor, now thinks that perhaps *his* testimony might turn the tide (Acts 22:19-21). But God knows better. He knows that the crisis in Israel's history has been reached. Persuasion will be useless. Salvation now will be sent to the Gentiles, not *through Israel,* but *in spite of her,* and Paul himself is chosen for this purpose.

This incident in Paul's early Christian experience should be viewed in the light of three important verses of Scripture:

Rom. 11:15: ". . . IF THE CASTING AWAY OF THEM [ISRAEL] BE THE RECONCILING OF THE WORLD . . ."

Rom. 11:32: "GOD HATH CONCLUDED THEM ALL IN UNBELIEF THAT HE MIGHT HAVE MERCY UPON ALL."

Eph. 2:16: "AND THAT HE MIGHT RECONCILE BOTH UNTO GOD IN ONE BODY BY THE CROSS . . ."

Of course, God's gracious *purpose* in the casting away of Israel was only in *process* of being revealed as God *gradually* set her aside. The *fulness* of it is not unfolded until the later epistles, where Paul prays that believers may be given wisdom

237

and spiritual understanding to comprehend it. But the reconciling of believing Jews and Gentiles unto God in one body, the blessing of the Gentiles through the *fall* of Israel, most assuredly began considerably before the close of the book of Acts.

PETER, PAUL AND ISRAEL

One fact should be apparent even to the casual observer: Peter's ministry very definitely anticipated Israel's *acceptance* of Messiah (Acts 1:6, 2:30, 38,39, 3:17-26), but Paul's just as definitely assumed Israel's continued *rejection* of Messiah. In fact, he was raised up by God *in view of Israel's rejection of Christ,* for God's answer to the stoning of Stephen and the dreadful persecution of Acts 8:1-3 was the salvation of Saul, the chief persecutor and the leader of the rebellion. *Matchless grace!*

Those who hold the extreme views above referred to, argue further that "the blessing of the Gentiles [in Acts] is dependent upon the realization of the blessing promised to the Jew."

This was true of Peter's ministry, as Acts 3:25, 26 indicates, but the very opposite was true of Paul's ministry. Acts 13:46 alone should settle this. Here, by no stretch of imagination can we conclude that the Gentiles were being blessed through Israel's realization of her blessings. The Gentiles, on the contrary, were being blessed because the Jews had put the Word of God from them.

". . . SEEING YE PUT IT FROM YOU . . . LO, WE TURN TO THE GENTILES."

All this substantiates our basic contention that

238

while Peter's ministry had to do with the blessing of the Gentiles through the *rise* of Israel, Paul's had to do with the blessing of the Gentiles through the *fall* of Israel. The former is the subject of *prophecy,* the latter of the *mystery.*

Is it correct to speak of Israel's "primacy" during the later Acts period? Romans 11 makes it clear that Israel's fate was already settled before Acts 28,* even though the sentence had not yet been officially pronounced.

"ISRAEL HATH NOT OBTAINED THAT WHICH HE SEEKETH FOR . . . THE ELECTION HATH OBTAINED IT, AND THE REST WERE BLINDED . . . THEIR FALL . . . THE FALL OF THEM . . . THE DIMINISHING OF THEM . . . IF BY ANY MEANS I . . . MIGHT SAVE SOME OF THEM . . . THE CASTING AWAY OF THEM . . . BLINDNESS [or DULLED PERCEPTION] IN PART IS HAPPENED TO ISRAEL, UNTIL THE FULNESS OF THE GENTILES BE COME IN . . . THEY ARE ENEMIES . . . GOD HATH CONCLUDED THEM ALL IN UNBELIEF . . ." (Rom. 11:7-32).

Before the martyrdom of Stephen, Peter promised the return of Christ to earth upon condition of Israel's repentance. After Stephen, God raised up Paul *who never made such an offer.* Acts is the story of the fall of Israel, and the stoning of Stephen marks the crisis.

THE JEW FIRST

But what about Paul's famous statement in Rom. 1:16:

"FOR I AM NOT ASHAMED OF THE GOSPEL OF CHRIST: FOR IT IS THE POWER OF GOD UNTO

---
*Romans was written *before* Paul's journey to Rome (Rom. 1:10-15).

SALVATION TO EVERY ONE THAT BELIEVETH; TO THE JEW FIRST AND ALSO TO THE GREEK."

Many have missed the very point of this passage by taking this one verse out of its context. They have made it Paul's defense for going to the Jew first, when in reality he defends his ministry among the *Gentiles* in this passage. Let us see:

In accordance with the prophetic plan our Lord had instructed the apostles to make disciples of all nations *"beginning at Jerusalem"* (Matt. 28:19, cf. Luke 24:47).

The twelve apostles began their work there. Peter declared to the "men of Israel" in Jerusalem's temple:

"Ye are the children of the prophets and of the covenant which God made with our fathers, saying unto Abraham, AND IN THY SEED SHALL ALL THE KINDREDS OF THE EARTH BE BLESSED.

"Unto YOU FIRST God, having raised up His Son Jesus, sent Him to bless you, in turning away every one of you from his iniquities" (Acts 3:25,26).

Acts 11:19 further makes it clear that, until Peter was sent to Cornelius, even the scattered disciples had preached the Word *"to none but unto the Jews only."* Israel was to be the channel of blessing to the world.

The apostles sought earnestly to bring the favored nation to Messiah's feet, but—

"BUT TO ISRAEL HE SAITH, ALL DAY LONG HAVE I STRETCHED FORTH MY HANDS UNTO A DISOBEDIENT AND GAINSAYING PEOPLE" (Rom. 10:21).

The gospel had gone to the Jew first and had been rejected, but God would not allow Israel to stand in the way of Gentile blessing, so He began to set Israel aside, raising up Paul to bring good news to the Gentiles notwithstanding.

Contrast Peter's "you first" at Jerusalem, with Paul's "you first" at Antioch, where he says to the Jews:

"IT WAS NECESSARY THAT THE WORD OF GOD SHOULD FIRST HAVE BEEN SPOKEN TO YOU, —BUT—SEEING YE PUT IT FROM YOU AND JUDGE YOURSELVES UNWORTHY OF EVERLASTING LIFE, LO, WE TURN TO THE GENTILES" (Acts 13:46).

All this throws clear light on Romans 1:16.

Paul by no means contends here that the gospel should *continue* to be sent to the Jew first, otherwise Rom. 1:16 would most assuredly contradict Rom. 10:12,13, which says:

"FOR THERE IS NO DIFFERENCE BETWEEN THE JEW AND THE GREEK: FOR THE SAME LORD OVER ALL IS RICH UNTO ALL THAT CALL UPON HIM.

"FOR WHOSOEVER SHALL CALL UPON THE NAME OF THE LORD SHALL BE SAVED."

Rom. 11:7 and 25 should be enough to convince us that Paul at that time understood that God had given the nation up and that a judicial blindness was already settling upon it.

As he opens his Roman epistle, therefore, he argues for his responsibility to go to *the Gentiles also*. Note carefully the emphasis in the whole passage:

"... THAT I MIGHT HAVE SOME FRUIT AMONG YOU ALSO, EVEN AS AMONG OTHER GENTILES.

"I AM DEBTOR BOTH TO THE GREEKS, AND

241

TO THE BARBARIANS: BOTH TO THE WISE AND
TO THE UNWISE [He does not even mention the Jew
here].

"SO, AS MUCH AS IN ME IS, I AM READY TO
PREACH THE GOSPEL TO YOU THAT ARE AT
ROME ALSO.

"FOR I AM NOT ASHAMED OF THE GOSPEL
OF CHRIST: FOR IT IS THE POWER OF GOD UNTO
SALVATION TO EVERY ONE THAT BELIEVETH; TO
THE JEW FIRST, AND ALSO TO THE GREEK" (Rom.
1:13-16).

His argument here is clearly that he is not
ashamed to go to the *Gentiles at Rome* with the gospel, since it is the power of God unto salvation *to
every one that believeth.*

God's good news concerning Christ *had been*
sent to the Jew first, but now, through Paul, was
being sent to the Gentile also, and Paul was ready,
as much as in him was, to preach it to those *"at
Rome also."*

Rom. 1:16, when thus considered in the light
of its context, by no means conflicts with the rest of
Romans. Those who use this passage to teach
Jewish precedence today, miss one of the basic
lessons of the book of Romans: that there is no
longer any difference, in the sight of God, between
the Jew and the Gentile and that both alike must
now approach God as the fallen sons of Adam.

The great motive for Jewish missionary work
in this age of grace is given to us, not in Rom. 1:16,
but in Rom. 11:30-33:

"FOR AS YE [GENTILES] IN TIMES PAST HAVE
NOT BELIEVED GOD, YET HAVE NOW OBTAINED
MERCY THROUGH THEIR [ISRAEL'S] UNBELIEF:

242

"EVEN SO HAVE THESE ALSO NOW NOT BE-LIEVED, THAT THROUGH YOUR MERCY THEY ALSO MAY OBTAIN MERCY.

"FOR GOD HATH CONCLUDED THEM ALL IN UNBELIEF THAT HE MIGHT HAVE MERCY UPON ALL.

"O THE DEPTH OF THE RICHES BOTH OF THE WISDOM AND KNOWLEDGE OF GOD! HOW UN-SEARCHABLE ARE HIS JUDGMENTS AND HIS WAYS PAST FINDING OUT!"

THE GRADUAL UNFOLDING OF
THE MYSTERY

The question of Paul's early ministry is impor-tant to the understanding of the mystery. There are some who see distinctions everywhere, but they fail to see the sweep, the progress, the development in the unfolding of God's wonderful plan. They do not see how, when it seemed that the prophetic purpose had failed and the Gentiles would be de-prived of blessing because of Israel's unbelief, God overruled and unfolded His secret, eternal purpose of grace, which at the same time explained how, and how alone, the prophetic purpose could and would after all be fulfilled; indeed, how alone any sinner ever had been, or could be saved. This is the difference between "the gospel" and "the mys-tery [or secret] of the gospel." When we see it we cry with the Psalmist, *"Surely the wrath of man shall praise Thee; and the remainder of wrath shalt Thou restrain!"*

Was the mystery communicated to Paul in one single revelation or in a series of revelations? Let us see what the Scriptures have to say as to this:

Acts 26:16: "But rise, and stand upon thy feet: for I have appeared unto thee for this purpose, to make thee a minister and a witness BOTH OF THESE THINGS WHICH THOU HAST SEEN, AND OF THOSE THINGS IN THE WHICH I WILL APPEAR UNTO THEE."

Acts 22:17,18: "And it came to pass, that, when I was come again to Jerusalem, even while I prayed in the temple, I was in a trance; AND SAW HIM SAYING UNTO ME . . ."

II Cor. 12:1: ". . . I WILL COME TO VISIONS AND REVELATIONS OF THE LORD."

II Cor. 12:7: "And lest I should be exalted above measure through THE ABUNDANCE OF THE REVELATIONS, there was given to me a thorn in the flesh . . ."

Undoubtedly Paul both received and communicated *one* great body of truth *gradually*, otherwise *his* term, "my gospel"* and *our* term, "the distinctive ministry of Paul" are wholly misleading, but all was made known by "the revelation of Jesus Christ" to Paul. In each case Paul saw the Lord Himself.

Thus the old program gradually passed away as the new one took its place. There was development in the revelation given to Paul as well as in the historical unfolding of God's secret purpose. God raised up Paul for ONE great purpose, to declare ONE great new message progressively, though his message confirmed and in no way contradicted the message of Peter and the eleven concerning Christ.

There was a time when the writer viewed the mystery as a particular point in Paul's preaching,

---

*This term indicates the vital connection between the gospel of the uncircumcision, the message of reconciliation, etc. Probably the most comprehensive term for the good news which Paul proclaimed is that found in Acts 20:24: *"the gospel of the grace of God."*

but now, thank God, he sees it as one great, grand message, the comprehension of which is unspeakably precious.

We would ask our "two body" brethren to consider the following proposition:

We agree that God had a *revealed, prophesied* purpose. We agree that He also had a *secret, eternal purpose* which was the key to the *fulfillment* of the prophesied purpose. Did He have still another purpose—a sort of *buffer* between the two? Or did He have several unrelated purposes? What was Paul's message during his early ministry? Was it the gospel of the kingdom? Most certainly it was not. Was it the gospel of the circumcision? This would contradict Gal. 2:7. What was it then? It was *"the gospel of the UNcircumcision," "the gospel of the grace of God,"* and these cannot be dissociated from the mystery.

Eph. 3:1-3, "For this cause I Paul, the prisoner of Jesus Christ for you Gentiles,

"IF YE HAVE HEARD OF THE DISPENSATION OF THE GRACE OF GOD WHICH IS GIVEN ME TO YOU-WARD:

"HOW THAT BY REVELATION HE MADE KNOWN UNTO ME THE MYSTERY . . ."

Surely it is altogether gratuitous to suppose that Paul had "a special temporary ministry" during the Acts period, for it is *during* the Acts period that he expresses the desire

"THAT I MIGHT FINISH MY COURSE WITH JOY [Here he looks ahead to the close of his ministry], AND THE MINISTRY WHICH I HAVE RECEIVED OF THE LORD JESUS [Here he looks back to the begin-

245

ning], TO TESTIFY THE GOSPEL OF THE GRACE OF GOD" (Acts 20:24).

What we must recognize is simply that the old economy was that under which Paul was saved and from which he gradually emerged. Therefore it was right and consistent for him to do certain things before Acts 28 which would have been contrary to the will of God after Acts 28.

But it is more than gratuitous—it is a flat contradiction of Scripture—to teach that Paul received the revelation of the mystery in prison at Rome and that this supposed revelation superseded his other revelations and marked the historical beginning of the body of Christ of which we are members. The facts which we have already considered, that both "the mystery" and "the body of Christ" are referred to and dealt with at length in Paul's early epistles, stamps this teaching as wholly unscriptural, as does also the fact that the apostle emphatically states in his *later* epistles that he is in prison FOR the mystery (Eph. 6:20, Col. 4:3).

It has been observed by one extreme dispensationalist that in Acts 21 there are two distinct groups—*"the Jews which believe"* and *"the Gentiles which believe,"* while in the body of Christ this distinction disappears.

This is a good point, for it shows that God had not yet concluded his dealings with Israel. But it must be noticed that even while God was *permitting* this distinction to remain *outwardly,* He was already saying, through Paul, that IN CHRIST *there was neither Jew nor Gentile* (See I Cor. 12:13 and Gal. 3:27,28).

246

Some have supposed that Paul meant, in Gal. 3:27,28, that in *the body* of Christ there was neither Jew nor Greek and that this did not apply to the Jews under Peter and the twelve. This, of course, does violence to the wording of the passage which clearly states that it was *in Christ* that the distinction had disappeared. The Jewish believers at Jerusalem were certainly in Christ. Some had even been "in Christ" before Paul (Rom. 16:7). But *now* all in Christ became members of *one body*. That Gal. 3:27, 28 included the Jewish believers at Jerusalem as well as those saved through Paul's ministry is further confirmed by II Cor. 5:16,17: *"HENCEFORTH know we NO MAN after the flesh ... Therefore if ANY MAN be in Christ, he is a new creature."* Even Peter knew this and was rebuked when later he went back on the light he had received (Acts 15:9, cf. Gal. 2:11,12).

QUIZ

1. What problem perplexes many Bible students with respect to Paul's early ministry? 2. This difficulty has led some to conclude that the mystery was not revealed and the body of Christ, the church of this dispensation, did not begin until when? 3. How do the early epistles of Paul disprove this contention? 4. Give three Scriptures from Acts proving that Paul's early (Acts) ministry was primarily to the Gentiles. 5. Why did Paul generally go to the Jew *first* during his early ministry? 6. Give three Scriptures from Paul's *early* epistles, proving that these were written primarily to Gentiles. 7. Did Paul ever *offer* the kingdom to Israel, so far as the record is con-

cerned? 8. Explain how Paul *confirmed* Peter's message to the Jews. 9. Give Scripture to prove that Israel, as a nation, had been spiritually blinded before Paul even started for Rome. 10. How do you reconcile Rom. 1:16 ("Jew first") with Rom. 10:12 ("no difference")? 11. What is the Scriptural basis for Jewish missionary work today? 12. Give two Scriptures proving that Paul received his message by a *series* of revelations. 13. Whom did Paul see in each of these revelations? 14. What one comprehensive term does he use to describe the good news he proclaimed? 15. How would you answer the contention that Paul received the revelation of the mystery in prison at Rome? 16. What passage from his later epistles indicates that "the gospel of the grace of God" and "the mystery" are inseparable? 17. Explain the relation between the two. 18. Give three Scriptures proving that Jewish and Gentile believers were one *in Christ* during Paul's *early* ministry. 19. What distinction did exist between them at that time? 20. When did that distinction cease to exist?

Chapter XIV.

THE RELATION BETWEEN PROPHECY
AND THE MYSTERY

Much harm and loss has come to the church because God's "workmen" have failed to note the distinctions and divisions in the Word of Truth. But serious harm can and does also result from a failure to recognize the *unity* of God's great plan for the ages; from a failure to observe *connections* as well as distinctions.

Extreme dispensationalists see many distinctions in the Scriptures—even distinctions which do not exist!—but they fail to see some of the most important connections. And, strange to say, in seeking to establish *non-existent distinctions* they frequently blunder back into the camp of the traditionalists and likewise fail to note some of the *most basic distinctions!*

An example of this is found in the contention that Paul, when he wrote his early epistles, had not yet come into his special Gentile ministry; that at that time he preached practically the same message as the twelve; that at that time he dealt primarily with the Jews; that his early epistles were addressed primarily to Jews and that during that time he offered the kingdom to Israel—but that *after* Acts 28 his ministry had *no connection whatever* with that of the twelve!

249

The fact is, that from the beginning Paul's *apostleship* was clearly separate and distinct from that of the twelve. He was called and commissioned far from Jerusalem, on the road to Damascus. His appointment was "not *of* men, neither *by* man," but by the glorified Lord Himself (Gal. 1:1). Moreover, he was, from the beginning, called to a different *ministry* than the twelve: *"to testify the gospel of the grace of God,"* to *"preach among the Gentiles the unsearchable riches of Christ"* (Acts 20:24, Eph. 3:8). But it must not be supposed from this that there was not, at the same time, a *connection* between the ministry of the twelve in Acts and Paul's ministry at that time, or even between the Acts ministry of the twelve and Paul's post-Acts ministry.

To begin with, Paul represented *the same God* as the twelve, against whom Israel was now rebelling. He represented *the same Christ,* whom Israel was now rejecting. And *"the salvation of God,"* which Israel had refused, was now being *"sent unto the Gentiles"* (Matt. 1:21, Acts 4:12, 13:26,46, cf. Acts 28:28).

Furthermore, the apostles at Jerusalem soon came to realize that because Israel was now refusing the risen, glorified Christ, God had chosen Paul to preach salvation to the Gentiles through Israel's fall and, in a solemn covenant, their leaders gave to Paul and Barnabas the right hands of fellowship, agreeing to confine their ministry to Israel while Paul went to the Gentiles.

Paul's ministry was not merely the starting of another program separately from the church at

Jerusalem. It was the next step in the program of God, and unless we see the *development* in the whole program we miss a great deal.

This development is best demonstrated by some of the very passages which extreme dispensationalists use to prove that Paul's Acts ministry was "a Jewish kingdom ministry" in fulfillment of the prophetic program. We deal with some of these in the following pages.

SO HATH THE LORD COMMANDED US

"Then Paul and Barnabas waxed bold, and said, It was necessary that the word of God should first have been spoken to 'you: but seeing ye put it from you, and judge yourselves unworthy of everlasting life, lo, we turn to the Gentiles.

"FOR SO HATH THE LORD COMMANDED US, saying, I have set Thee to be a light of the Gentiles, that Thou shouldest be for salvation unto the ends of the earth" (Acts 13:46,47).

Because of Paul's words: *"for so hath the Lord commanded us"* and his quotation of an Old Testament prophecy, it is contended that *this* ministry of Paul to the Gentiles still had the kingdom in view and was in no way connected with the mystery. Let us see:

When the Jews at Pisidian Antioch contradicted and blasphemed "those things which were spoken by Paul," he and Barnabas "waxed bold and said:"

"It was NECESSARY that the word of God should first have been spoken to you."

Why was this *necessary?* The answer is found in Peter's words to the multitudes at Jerusalem:

"Ye are the children of the prophets, and of **THE COVENANT WHICH GOD MADE WITH OUR FATHERS**, saying unto Abraham, And in thy seed shall all the kindreds of the earth be blessed.

"Unto YOU FIRST God, having raised up His Son Jesus, sent Him to bless you, in turning away every one of you from his iniquities" (Acts 3:25,26).

The great Abrahamic Covenant guaranteed the blessing of the Gentiles. *through* Israel; therefore *Israel first* must be saved and blessed. The *whole* prophetic program is founded on this great covenant.

This is why our Lord said to the Syrophenician woman: *"Let the children first be filled"* (Mark 7:27). This is why He said to the Samaritan woman: *"Salvation is of the Jews."* This is why He commissioned the eleven to begin their ministry at Jerusalem (Luke 24:47, Acts 1:8). And mark well: Peter explicitly states, in Acts 3:25,26, that God had sent Christ to bless Israel first *because of the covenant made with Abraham.*

As we have seen, Paul went to the Jew first, during his early ministry, confirming the fact that "Jesus is the Christ" and seeking to win his hearers to personal faith in Christ. He did this because God had not yet officially postponed the fulfillment of the Abrahamic Covenant. God was still stretching forth His hands to a disobedient and gainsaying people. He was not going to leave them with any excuse for rejecting Messiah. But let us continue with Paul's statement to the Jews at Antioch:

"It was necessary that the word of God should first have been spoken to you: BUT . . ."

Does not this "but" indicate that there is to be a departure from the prophesied procedure?

Note, however, that it was not unfaithfulness on God's part, but *their own unwillingness* to accept the fulfillment of God's promise, that caused this change in the program—a change which God, foreknowing all things, had accordingly planned in His secret, eternal counsels.

"SEEING YE PUT IT FROM YOU, AND JUDGE YOURSELVES UNWORTHY OF EVERLASTING LIFE, LO, WE TURN TO THE GENTILES."

Here let the reader carefully and candidly answer the following questions: Is salvation here being sent to the Gentiles because of Israel's acceptance of Christ, or because of her rejection of Christ? Is it going to the Gentiles on the basis of the Abrahamic Covenant or by grace? Is it going according to prophecy or according to the mystery?

There is but one answer to each of these questions. Paul at Pisidian Antioch departed from the prophetic procedure and began to do something *never once prophesied,* for the salvation of the Gentiles through Israel's *rejection* of Christ is never anywhere predicted in the prophetic Scriptures (See Rom. 11:11,12,15,25).

But why, it may be asked, does Paul then add:

"FOR SO HATH THE LORD COMMANDED US, SAYING, I HAVE SET THEE TO BE A LIGHT OF THE GENTILES, THAT THOU SHOULDEST BE FOR SALVATION UNTO THE ENDS OF THE EARTH" (Acts 13:47).

Paul does not mean here that the Gentiles are now to receive salvation according to the program outlined in prophecy, for we have already seen that the opposite is the case. The blessing of the Gentiles *through Israel* will have to wait until a future day.

The apostle simply points out here that God had "set" Christ to be "a light to the Gentiles" and "for salvation unto the ends of the earth" and that He *would* have it so, *Israel notwithstanding.* Since Israel refused to be the channel of blessing to the nations, God was now to bless the nations directly through Christ, apart from Israel, and Paul had been "commanded" to proclaim this fact.

NONE OTHER THINGS

"Having therefore obtained help of God, I continue unto this day, witnessing both to small and great, saying NONE OTHER THINGS than those which the prophets and Moses did say should come" (Acts 26:22).

Extreme dispensationalists have probably used the above passage more than any other to prove their "two body" theory. This passage, in their opinion, is conclusive proof that until the close of Acts, Paul had preached *nothing* which the prophets and Moses had not already foretold, confining his ministry entirely to the proclamation of God's prophetic purpose. Thus in effect, they have Paul preaching "the gospel of the circumcision" which, according to his own testimony, had been committed *not* to him, but to Peter (Gal. 2:7).

To teach from Acts 26:22 that Paul thus far had taught nothing that the prophets and Moses had not already foretold is manifestly contrary to the record.

254

As we have seen, neither the prophets nor Moses had foretold anything concerning the salvation of the Gentiles through the fall of Israel. Nor had they foretold *"the gospel of the grace of God,"* in which neither circumcision nor the law was to have any part. Nor had they even hinted that Jews and Gentiles would be baptized into one body by the Spirit. Nor had they said or even known anything about believers being "caught up" to heaven by "the Lord Himself." Yet all of this was proclaimed by Paul before the close of the Acts period (Rom. 11:11,12, Acts 20:24, I Cor. 12:13, I Thes. 4:16,17).

And had not Paul plainly spoken of "the mystery" and its associated "mysteries" in his early epistles? (Rom. 11:25, 16:25, I Cor. 2:6,7, 4:1, 15:51). Is the *mystery,* then, to be found in *prophecy*—that which was *"hidden"* and *"kept secret"*, in that which had been *"made known"*?

Indeed, even if we were to admit that Paul proclaimed the kingdom during his entire Acts ministry, he would then still have taught more than "the prophets and Moses did say should come," for even under the gospel of the kingdom our Lord uttered things which had been *"kept secret from the foundation of the world"* (Matt. 13:35); truths which neither the prophets* nor Moses had even known about.

What, then, did Paul mean by saying to Agrippa that until that time he had witnessed *"none other things than those which the prophets and Moses did say should come"*?

---

*It is true that our Lord Himself was a prophet, but Paul clearly refers to the prophets whom Agrippa believed (Acts 26:27).

The answer is simple when we read on:

"That Christ should suffer, and that He should be the first that should rise from the dead, and should show light unto the people, and to the Gentiles" (Acts 26:23).

In other words, Paul's testimony *that Christ had died and risen, and that He was to bring light to Israel and the Gentiles,* was nothing but what the prophets and Moses had said should come, and we find from the *preceding* context that it was because Paul had preached the risen Christ to the Jews and *"then to the Gentiles,"* that the Jews now sought to kill him.

The answer is as simple as that, and the misinterpretation of this simple passage shows how much confusion and loss can result from using one verse in disregard of its context.

THE HOPE OF ISRAEL

". . . FOR THE HOPE OF ISRAEL I AM BOUND WITH THIS CHAIN" (Acts 28:20).

The above is another passage which extreme dispensationalists frequently use to prove that Paul's Acts ministry was primarily to the Jews and that "to the end Acts deals with the gospel of the kingdom."

But what does the apostle mean by "the hope of Israel"? Does he mean that which Israel hoped *for* (i.e., the kingdom), or that which gave her *reason* to hope (i.e., the resurrection)? Does he refer to the *object* of their expectation or their *basis* for it? Those who teach the "two body" theory have

256

concluded in favor of the former. They are sure that Paul meant the promise of the kingdom when he spoke of Israel's hope.

But they are wrong. Paul had not been imprisoned for proclaiming Israel's kingdom promises. The Jews had opposed him so bitterly for *preaching to the Gentiles a risen Christ whom they were rejecting,* while Peter, who represented the kingdom promises, and sought still to bring Israel to Messiah's feet, remained free in Jerusalem.

The very point of Paul's statement here is that *the truth of the resurrection of Christ,* which the Jews so feared and hated, and which was now taking hold among the Gentiles, was actually *"the hope of Israel."*

The hope of Israel is the risen Christ. Thank God, for Israel's sake, that the Sadducees proved to be so utterly wrong when they sought to convince themselves and others that the resurrection of Christ was an impossibility and a delusion; that Christ was dead.

Had this been true, Israel would have been forever without hope. With the only One who could possibly have been their Messiah dead in a tomb, how would they have been any better off than the followers of Buddha or Mohammed?

What other hope is there for Israel? Could another son of David arise and be identified now? Could he arise in time to fulfil the time prophecies of the Old Testament? And if he could, would that mean that he must still first be "cut off," as Daniel had predicted (Dan. 9:26), before delivering his people from their enemies?

257

To fit the Hebrew Scriptures concerning Messiah, such an one would have to suffer, die, rise again and ascend into heaven before coming in power and glory to reign. But it is too late to talk about that now, for no messiah *could* appear in the time predicted, or even be identified as David's son. No, if the Christ whom Israel crucified nineteen hundred years ago is not risen and living today, then Israel is utterly and eternally without hope.

That this is what Paul had in mind when he said he was bound with a chain for the hope of Israel is clear from other passages in Acts on the same subject.

In Acts 5:31, for example, we find Peter pointing to the resurrection of Christ as Israel's hope:

"Him hath God exalted with His right hand to be a Prince and a Savior, for to give repentance to Israel, and forgiveness of sins."

Paul, of course, had a further revelation concerning the risen Christ, and proclaimed Him as Savior of Jew and Gentile alike—as the hope of fallen mankind. This is what hurt the jealous Jews. Nevertheless Paul insisted that the risen Christ was the hope of his nation too.

In Acts 23:6 we find Paul before the Hebrew council:

"But when Paul perceived that the one part were Sadducees, and the other Pharisees, he cried out in the council, Men and brethren, I am a Pharisee, the son of a Pharisee: OF THE HOPE AND RESURRECTION OF THE DEAD I AM CALLED IN QUESTION."

Note clearly that it was for *"the hope and resurrection of the dead"* that he had been *"called in question,"* and note the connection with the phrase: *"for the hope of Israel am I bound."*

In Acts 24:14,15 again *the resurrection* is *the point at issue*:

"But this I confess unto thee, that after the way which they call heresy, so worship I the God of my fathers, believing all things which are written in the law and in the prophets:

"AND HAVE HOPE TOWARD GOD, WHICH THEY THEMSELVES ALSO ALLOW, THAT THERE SHALL BE A RESURRECTION OF THE DEAD, BOTH OF THE JUST AND UNJUST."

In Acts 26:6-8 his argument is the same again. There he stands before Agrippa and carefully points out *just why* he is being tried:

"And now I STAND AND AM JUDGED FOR THE HOPE OF THE PROMISE MADE OF GOD UNTO OUR FATHERS:

"Unto which promise our twelve tribes, instantly serving God day and night, hope to come. FOR WHICH HOPE'S SAKE, KING AGRIPPA, I AM ACCUSED OF THE JEWS.

"WHY SHOULD IT BE THOUGHT A THING IN-CREDIBLE WITH YOU, THAT GOD SHOULD RAISE THE DEAD?"

Here note carefully that the *promise* referred to was that of kingdom blessing, while "the *hope* of the promise" was *the resurrection of Christ,* which was the very foundation of Paul's message. For this *"hope's* sake" Paul was "accused of the Jews." Thus it was that the apostle could say to the Jewish leaders in Rome: *"For the hope of Israel I am bound with this chain."*

That this was in fact why Paul had been *"called*

259

in question" and *"accused"* and *"judged"* and *"bound with this chain,"* is borne out even by Festus who informed Agrippa that when Paul was brought before him the Jews *"brought none accusation of such things as I supposed:*

"But had certain questions against him of their own superstition, and of one JESUS, WHICH WAS DEAD, WHOM PAUL AFFIRMED TO BE ALIVE" (Acts 25:18,19).

Thus in the book of Acts alone we have overwhelming proof as to the particular point at issue between Paul and those who had had him "bound with this chain." And that point was *not* his proclamation of the kingdom promises, but his distinctive and powerful proclamation of *the resurrection of Christ,* which, he maintained, was the hope of Israel. Had these facts been noted in time in the recovery of the Pauline message much of the confusion of extremism could have been avoided.

AS IT IS WRITTEN

Attention should also be called, at this point, to Rom. 15:8-16 where, after pointing out that *"it is written"* (Ver. 9) *"again"* (Ver. 10) *"and again"* (Ver. 11) *"and again"* (Ver. 12) that the Gentiles were to be saved, the Apostle Paul points out that God has appointed him *"the minister of Jesus Christ to the Gentiles"* (Ver. 16).

But here, as in Acts 13:46,47, we simply find again the *connection* between prophecy and the mystery.

It had indeed been prophesied that the Gentiles would one day rejoice with God's people Israel.

But, as Paul declares to the Romans, Israel herself refused Christ. How then could the Gentiles be blessed through her? It is because of this difficulty that the apostle exhorts the Gentiles at Rome:

"NOW THE GOD OF HOPE FILL YOU WITH ALL JOY AND PEACE IN BELIEVING, THAT YE MAY ABOUND IN HOPE, THROUGH THE POWER OF THE HOLY GHOST" (Rom. 15:13).

And then the apostle speaks boldly, not expounding the Scriptures he has just quoted, but declaring his authority as an apostle of Jesus Christ:

"Nevertheless, brethren, I have written the more boldly unto you in some sort [in a sense], as PUTTING YOU IN MIND, BECAUSE OF THE GRACE THAT IS GIVEN TO ME OF GOD,

"THAT I SHOULD BE THE MINISTER OF JESUS CHRIST TO THE GENTILES, ministering the gospel of God, THAT THE OFFERING UP OF THE GENTILES MIGHT BE ACCEPTABLE, BEING SANCTIFIED BY THE HOLY GHOST" (Rom. 15:15,16).

Here again we have God sending salvation to the Gentiles, *not* in the manner prescribed in prophecy, *but sending it nevertheless.* We might paraphrase the apostle's argument thus:

"That the Gentiles should glorify God for His mercy is written again and again and again. You say that Israel, through whom the blessing should flow, is rejecting Christ? Then just trust and rejoice in God, and let me speak boldly and remind you of the grace given to me, that I should be the minister of Jesus Christ to the Gentiles. And my offering up of the Gentiles is acceptable to God, too, for it is being sanctified by the Holy Spirit."

How beautiful this passage is! Those who

261

would understand the plan of God should read it again and again until the blessed truth of it is fully comprehended.

HEIRS ACCORDING TO THE PROMISE

A final word in this connection should be written for those who stumble over such phrases as "Abraham's seed" and "heirs according to the promise," applied to Gentile believers in Paul's early writings.

Is not Christ Abraham's seed? Are not we members of Christ? Do we not fall heir to *all things* in Him? True, we became heirs through God's secret, eternal purpose, when the promise *seemed* to have failed, but the fact remains that we Gentiles *have* become heirs.*

Moreover, we have become heirs "according to the promise," for the promise was to Abraham and his seed and we, being *in Christ,* are indeed Abraham's seed. Thus Israel, to whom the promise pertained (Rom. 9:4), did not become heir, while we, the members of the secret, unprophesied body have become heirs *in Christ.* This, however, does not nullify the promises made to the nation, Abraham's natural seed.

Those who stumble at such phrases as these should certainly have difficulty with many phrases in Paul's later epistles, where we read that we are "sealed with that Holy Spirit *of promise*" and made "partakers *of His promise* in Christ, by the gospel"

---

*We, however, do not inherit Christ because of the promises, but rather inherit the promises, and "all things" *through Christ.*

(Eph. 1:13, 3:6, cf. Gal. 3:14,22,29). But these passages are no stumbling block when we take proper note of the relation between prophecy and the mystery.

QUIZ

1. Give three indications that the apostleship of Paul, from the beginning, was *distinct* from that of the twelve. 2. What *connection* was there between their ministries? 3. In what solemn agreement between the Jerusalem apostles and Paul, are both the distinction and the connection emphasized? 4. Name three passages of Scripture often used by extreme dispensationalists to prove that Paul did not begin preaching the mystery until after Acts 28. 5. Why had it been "necessary" to preach the Word of God to the Jews first? 6. How did the Jews at Pisidian Antioch respond when Paul brought the Word of God to them first? 7. What did Paul do then? 8. Was this according to prophecy or according to the mystery? 9. Name three *un*prophesied truths proclaimed by Paul before Acts 28. 10. What had he preached that was in strict accordance with what the prophets and Moses had said should come? 11. What is "the hope of Israel"? 12. Explain the difference between "the *promise* made of God unto the fathers" and "the *hope* of the promise. . . ." 13. Was Paul imprisoned for proclaiming the *promise* or the *hope?* 14. Did Old Testament prophecy predict the salvation of the Gentiles? 15. Did it predict the salvation of the Gentiles through Israel's fall? 16. Has God sent salvation to the Gentiles? 17. Has He sent it in the manner prescribed in prophecy? 18. Did He send it through the twelve, under the "great commission"? 19. Did He send it in connection with Israel's *rise* or *fall?* 20. In what sense are believers today Abraham's seed and heirs according to the promise?

Chapter XV.

THE LORD'S SUPPER

Many sincere believers feel that to be consistent, those who claim that water baptism is not in God's program for this age should cease gathering at the Lord's supper too.

Here extreme dispensationalists and denominationalists stand together, their only difference being that while the former believe that *neither* the Lord's supper nor water baptism should be observed during this dispensation, the latter believe that *both* should be.

AN UNSCRIPTURAL ASSUMPTION

But both of these groups have based their arguments upon a wholly unscriptural assumption—that water baptism and the Lord's supper belong together in God's program. This is *pure tradition* and it is surprising that extreme dispensationalists, of all people, should accept it as truth.

Well do we remember how a startling misquotation of Col. 2:14 first led us into a study of this subject. A Bible teacher had quoted it thus: "Blotting out the handwriting of ordinances, that was against us, *leaving two, baptism and the Lord's supper!"* When we bégan to search the Scriptures as to this we soon discovered that water baptism *was* an ordinance, but that the Lord's supper was emphatically *not* an ordinance, in the Scriptural sense of that term.

We must be Bereans and search for ourselves to see whether water baptism and the Lord's supper are linked together as ordinances either for Israel or the body of Christ, and if we find that they are *not* so linked, we should settle it in our minds and forever be done with the unscriptural notion.

The fact is that there are definite distinctions and even contrasts between baptism and the Lord's supper.

Water baptism was an *Old Testament ordinance.*

The Lord's supper is a *New Testament celebration.*

Water baptism, like all ordinances, was "*imposed.*"

The Lord's supper was *never imposed.*

Water baptism was *a requirement for salvation.*

The Lord's supper, never!

Water baptism was associated with our Lord's *manifestation* to Israel.

The Lord's supper is associated with our Lord's *rejection* and *absence.*

Water baptism denotes an *un*finished work.

The Lord's supper speaks of the *finished* work of Christ.

Water baptism was a single act.

The Lord's supper is celebrated again and again.

Water baptism was not included in Paul's special commission.

The Lord's supper was included in Paul's special commission.

THE LORD'S SUPPER
A NEW TESTAMENT CELEBRATION

As we have seen in our discussion of water baptism, that rite was distinctly an Old Testament ordinance. The Lord's supper, however, is distinctly *a New Testament celebration.* It is disappointing to find some well-meaning extremists calling the Lord's Supper "the Passover," for surely Luke 22:14-20 proves conclusively that *after* the Passover our Lord instituted a *"remembrance"* of His death.

When Paul recounts what our Lord did and said at the Lord's supper he mentions only the bread and the wine, while at the Passover there was more than this.

The Passover, like water baptism, was an Old Testament ordinance, but the Lord's supper is as distinctly associated with the New Testament.

"FOR THIS IS MY BLOOD OF THE NEW TESTA-MENT . . ." (Matt. 26:28).

The Passover, like water baptism, spoke of an *un*finished work, for it is impossible that either the blood of beasts or the washing of water should take away sins. Both were shadows of the blood and water that flowed from the Savior's side.

Because so many stumble over the fact that water baptism was practiced even *after* the Cross,

266

we repeat that the full results of Calvary were not manifested until "due time," through the Apostle Paul. Circumcision, the sabbaths and the Levitical feasts likewise spoke of an *unfinished* work, yet they were all observed after the cross. This is simply because the time was not ripe for the unfolding of God's secret purpose and the gospel of the grace of God until the raising up of Paul, and even then its unfolding and the passing away of the old order was a gradual matter.

BUT, whereas the Passover and water baptism were *Old Testament ordinances,* the Lord's supper is *a New Testament celebration.*

The celebration of the Lord's death should never be classed with ordinances, for while these all spoke of an *unfinished* work, the Lord's supper is clearly a *celebration* of the FINISHED WORK of Christ.

At least three times the Lord's supper is stated to be *"in remembrance"* of our Lord's sacrificial work.

HOW THE NEW COVENANT
CONCERNS US

Since the New Testament, or Covenant, was specifically made with *"the house of Israel and with the house of Judah"* (Jer. 31:31), some have concluded that it can have no relation to the Gentiles and that therefore the Lord's supper should not be practiced today.

But this is an error. The Old Covenant, like the New, was made with Israel, but it vitally affects the Gentiles. See Paul's words in Rom. 3:19,20:

"Now we know that what things soever the law saith, it saith to them who are under the law: that EVERY MOUTH may be stopped, and ALL THE WORLD may become guilty before God.

"Therefore by the deeds of the law there shall NO FLESH be justified in His sight: for by the law is the knowledge of sin."

The Gentiles never were, and are not today, under the covenant of the law, but it would be a mistake to argue that the law does not affect the Gentiles, for it was given that the whole world might be brought in guilty before God.

Israel represented the world before God. Israel was the only nation with which God still had dealings after He gave up the Gentiles. When she finally fell, it meant that the whole world had fallen. If God should demand from *any* group of people the righteous standards of the Old Covenant (Ex. 19:5, 6), that group would surely be condemned. That is why the New Covenant was necessary.

After Israel's failure under the Old Covenant had become increasingly apparent, God promised to make a *new* covenant with them. This New Covenant was to be made with the favored nation alone. Jeremiah distinctly states this, as we have seen above.

And God *did* make this new covenant with Israel and Judah—*at Calvary* (Matt. 26:28). It was there that Christ procured for His covenant people what they could not attain to under the law. It was there that Isaiah's prophecy was fulfilled: *"For the transgression of my people was He stricken"* (Isa. 53:8).

It was on the basis of Calvary and the blood of the New Covenant that the kingdom blessing was offered to Israel at Pentecost, but that generation in Israel refused the blessing and the New Covenant awaits a future fulfillment.

But it does not follow from this that the New Covenant does not affect the Gentiles.

If the Gentiles come under the curse of the Old Covenant, they may also partake of the blessings of the New, for why was the blood of the New Covenant shed if not to remove the curse of the Old?

If by the Old Covenant with Israel God showed how the whole world stands condemned in His sight, then, by the New Covenant with Israel God shows how all may be justified in His sight* Heb. 2:9-16 says that Christ "took on Him the seed of *Abraham*." But why? *"That He by the grace of God might taste death for EVERY MAN."*

At Calvary God vouchsafed to Israel by solemn *covenant*: "I will forgive their iniquity, and I will remember their sin no more" (Jer. 31:34, cf. Matt. 26:28). God did *not* make such a *covenant* with the Gentiles, but what He *promised* by *covenant* to Israel, we receive *by grace*.

The reader should carefully examine Jer. 31:31-34 and note that the blessings of the New Covenant are all spiritual.° There is nothing about the land, the kingdom or the throne. Do members

---

*Note: the bare *promise* that God would make a new covenant (Jer. 31:31-34) did not make this plain. Indeed, it was not until some time after the blood of the New Covenant had been shed that its full significance was unfolded by Paul, "an able minister of the New Covenant."

°This is why Paul is never called a minister of the Abrahamic, Mosaic or Davidic Covenants, but only of the New Covenant (II Cor. 3:5;6).

of the body of Christ today receive the blessings outlined there? Yes, *all* of them. Has He not written His law upon *our* hearts? Is it not *our* desire to obey Him? Do *we* not "know the Lord"? Is He not *our* God? Are *we* not His people? Has He not forgiven *our* iniquities? Does He remember *our* sins against us?

We must not forget that *"we have redemption through His blood"*—that same *"blood of the New Covenant."* That blood saves us even while Israel gropes in blindness and staggers in unbelief.

But there are other important distinctions between water baptism and the Lord's supper.

A CELEBRATION IN HIS ABSENCE

Water baptism is clearly associated with the *manifestation* of Christ to Israel. Consider the words of John the Baptist in John 1:31:

"AND I KNEW HIM NOT: BUT THAT HE SHOULD BE MADE MANIFEST TO ISRAEL, THEREFORE AM I COME BAPTIZING WITH WATER."

In contrast to this, the Lord's supper is associated with the *rejection* of Christ and was first given to His followers to celebrate in His absence, until God should make His enemies His footstool.

It was by revelation that the Apostle Paul subsequently made known God's wonderful purpose to delay the judgment and usher in a period of grace. By revelation he declared that the Lord, in love to sinners, would remain away, an Exile, meanwhile sending forth ambassadors to offer to His enemies

270

reconciliation by grace, through faith in His finished work (Eph. 3:1-4 and II Pet. 3:3,4,8,9,15).

Every believer today should have in his heart and on his lips the message which Paul so faithfully proclaimed, and which the church has since then so grievously confused and obscured:

"Now then we are AMBASSADORS FOR CHRIST, as though God did beseech you by us: we pray you IN CHRIST'S STEAD, be ye reconciled to God.

"FOR HE HATH MADE HIM TO BE SIN FOR US, WHO KNEW NO SIN; THAT WE MIGHT BE MADE THE RIGHTEOUSNESS OF GOD IN HIM" (II Cor. 5:20,21).

It was because of the continued absence of Christ that Paul, *by revelation,* "delivered" the Lord's supper as a celebration of our Lord's death *"till He come"* (I Cor. 11:23,26).

THE LORD'S SUPPER AND SALVATION

We have seen that water baptism, both before and after the cross, was required *for the remission of sins* (Mark 1:4, 16:15,16, Acts 2:38). With the Lord's supper the very opposite is the case for only those *already saved* are invited to partake of it.

Our denominational brethren should surely recognize this distinction, for while they make baptism a prerequisite to membership in most of their churches, rarely do they make the Lord's supper a prerequisite. On the contrary, the Lord's supper is a *privilege* extended only to the saved; sometimes, indeed, only to the *members* of the particular churches in which it is "observed."

271

Like all other ordinances, *because* water baptism represented an *un*finished work it was required for salvation. No man could claim salvation without it. But contrast this with the Lord's supper.

Matt. 26:28: "FOR THIS IS MY BLOOD OF THE NEW TESTAMENT, WHICH IS SHED FOR MANY FOR THE REMISSION OF SINS."

Though our Lord's words at the table were not yet fully understood, they nevertheless mark a vital distinction between baptism and the Lord's supper.

THE LORD'S SUPPER NOT IMPOSED

Water baptism was an *ordinance*; a *yoke*. It was *"imposed."*

Heb. 9:10: "Which stood only in meats and drinks, and DIVERS WASHINGS [Gr. BAPTISMOIS], and carnal ORDINANCES, IMPOSED ON THEM UNTIL THE TIME OF REFORMATION."

This is why Col. 2:20 says:

"Wherefore if ye be dead with Christ from the rudiments of the world, why, as though living in the world, are ye SUBJECT to ordinances?"

And this is why Col. 2:9-12 shows our circumcision and baptism as having been accomplished for us by Christ, and adds:

"BLOTTING OUT THE HANDWRITING OF ORDINANCES THAT WAS AGAINST US, WHICH WAS CONTRARY TO US, AND TOOK IT OUT OF THE WAY, NAILING IT TO HIS CROSS" '(Ver. 14).

Many preachers have taught that God's children should "submit" to water baptism, but has the reader ever heard any one insist that we should "submit" to the Lord's supper? The Lord's supper can never be classed with Old Testament ordinances. It was never imposed or required for acceptance with God. On the contrary, the Scriptures clearly present it as a *celebration,* a *"remembrance,"* in which it is the believer's privilege to participate "as often" as he wishes (I Cor. 11:26), though it is taken for granted that he *will* wish to remember in this way what his Lord has done for him.

THE LORD'S SUPPER A TESTIMONY

Another sharp distinction between water baptism and the Lord's supper is that while the former was to be administered only once, the latter was to be celebrated again and again.

Without a shred of evidence or a single Scriptural proof, it is asserted by some that the purpose of water baptism is to bear public testimony to our death, burial and resurrection with Christ. But then why should believers be baptized only once? Is one testimony enough? Can we tell by looking at a person whether he has been baptized or not? If water baptism were meant for a testimony that the believer has been crucified, buried and raised with Christ, we should be baptized again and again, not just once before one group of people.

But the Scriptures do clearly teach that the Lord's supper was meant to remind believers and the world of the death of Christ.

"THIS DO IN REMEMBRANCE OF ME" (I Cor. 11:24).

"THIS DO YE . . . IN REMEMBRANCE OF ME" (I Cor. 11:25).

273

"FOR AS OFTEN AS YE EAT THIS BREAD, AND DRINK THIS CUP, YE DO SHOW FORTH THE LORD'S DEATH TILL HE COME" (I Cor. 11:26).

THE LORD'S SUPPER AND PAUL'S COMMISSION

Baptism was *not* included in Paul's special commission.

"FOR CHRIST SENT ME NOT TO BAPTIZE, BUT TO PREACH THE GOSPEL . . . " (I Cor. 1:17).

The context does not alter this fact in the least. True, the Corinthians were puffed up and carnal, and for this reason Paul was glad he had not baptized more of them. This, however, does not modify, it rather emphasizes the fact that he was not sent to baptize, and those who insist that he *was* sent to baptize, as John the Baptist and the twelve had been, should produce the evidence.

Our denominational brethren can easily prove that John the Baptist was commissioned to baptize. They can easily prove that the twelve were commissioned to baptize, but they wholly fail to produce any Scriptural evidence that water baptism was included in the great commission which Paul received by revelation. If I Cor. 1:17 means anything, it means that water baptism was *not* included in that commission. This does not mean that Paul did wrong in baptizing before Israel was set aside, any more than that he did wrong in working miracles or speaking in tongues or confirming Peter's message as God's Word to Israel.*

---

*It should be noted, however, that not until after the conversion of Paul do we have the baptism of those already rejoicing in salvation and, needless to say, Paul could not, and did not, proclaim baptism for the remission of sins as Peter before him had done.

But the Lord's supper *was* included in Paul's special commission.

"For I have received of the Lord that which also I delivered unto you, That the Lord Jesus the same night in which He was betrayed took bread." These are the words with which Paul proceeds to "deliver" the memorial of the Lord's death to them (I Cor. 11:23). This was part of Paul's distinctive message.

Paul did not have a number of *divergent* gospels. The various items of good news which he proclaimed were all part of one great message progressively developed in his epistles and called again and again, "my gospel," not "my gospels."

This is not to deny that He confirmed Peter's message. It is simply to point out that even in his early ministry his great message was not "the gospel of the circumcision" as some would have us believe, but "the gospel of the *un*circumcision" (Gal. 2:7), and that the Lord's supper belongs to this distinctively Pauline message.

THE LORD'S SUPPER AND OUR
HEAVENLY POSITION

Frankly, it is difficult for us to follow the "logic" of some of our extreme brethren who reason that since our position and our blessings are in the heavenlies, we should not partake of the Lord's supper because it is a physical celebration.

They say: "Imagine a dead man eating! Imagine one at God's right hand partaking of a supper down here!" But can this "logic" apply only to the

Lord's supper? Imagine a dead man, or one in the heavenlies, telling lies! Imagine him stealing! Imagine him travelling or held a prisoner! Yet Paul, in his *later* epistles, exhorts brethren whose position is in the heavenlies not to lie and steal, and refers to his own travels and his bonds.

Those who forward the above argument against the celebration of the Lord's supper simply forget to distinguish between our standing in Christ and our state. The apostle warns against "carnal [physical] *ordinances*," to be sure, since the mystery has been fully revealed, for now any former requirement, even if appended to faith, would be a reflection on the finished work of Christ.

But the Lord's supper was never a requirement for salvation and cannot be classed with the ordinances. Nor does Paul ever teach, indeed he refutes, the error that physical things as such are incompatible with spiritual blessings.

There are many physical privileges which, when rightly used, are translated into spiritual blessings.

We may *eat and drink* to the glory of God (I Cor. 10:31).

We may *bow our knees* unto the Father (Eph. 3:14).

We may *study out of physical books and a physical Bible* (I Tim. 4:13, II Tim. 2:15).

We may assemble with other saints on earth, generally in buildings (Heb. 10:25, Col. 4:15).

We may gather around a *physical table* and remember Christ's death with *physical food and drink,* and this table is called "the Lord's table" (I Cor. 10:21, 11:23-26).

"I NEVER FELT MOVED"

Recently someone advanced the argument to us that the Lord's supper could hardly be for this age since, as he put it: "I never felt moved at the Lord's table."

But are we to go by feelings or by faith? by the will of man or the Word of God?

Many will testify that they *were* filled with joy and peace when they were baptized with water. Does this prove that water baptism is in God's program for this age? Many have been deeply moved by the robes, the chants, the beads and candlesticks of Rome. Does this make these things Scriptural or pleasing to God? Most assuredly not. Faith rests only on the written Word of God.

Many do not feel moved at the Lord's table because it's true meaning is not appreciated. The Scriptures are as much against the legalistic manner in which many of the brethren observe the Lord's supper as they are against the practice of water baptism for today. The Lord's supper is not a mass. It is something infinitely more precious than that.

WHY THE LORD'S SUPPER

Every instructed believer today rejoices in the glorious fact that he has been baptized by the Holy Spirit into the death, burial and resurrection of

277

Christ—yea into Christ Himself; that he has been given a position *in Christ* in the heavenlies.

But has it ever occurred to the reader that to accomplish this, our blessed Lord had to be baptized into the human race—become bone of our bone and flesh of our flesh—one with us, yea one *of* us? Before *we* could be baptized into Deity, *He* had to be baptized into humanity. Before *we* could be baptized into His death, *He* had to be baptized into *our* death (Luke 12:50). To lift us from earth to heaven; to bless us with all spiritual blessings, He had to take upon Himself a physical body, to be beaten and scourged and spit upon and crucified.

God would have us remember this. He would make us more deeply conscious of it and more heartily thankful for it. This is why He has given us one solemn and precious memorial of Calvary. He would remind us again and again in this tangible way that

"You that were sometime alienated and enemies in your mind by wicked works, yet now hath He reconciled,

"IN THE BODY OF HIS FLESH, THROUGH DEATH, to present you holy and unblameable and unreproveable in His sight" (Col. 1:21,22).

And not only would He *remind us* of this stupendous fact and have us live in the light of it— He would have us show it forth to others as well.

"THIS DO IN REMEMBRANCE OF ME."

"FOR AS OFTEN AS YE EAT THIS BREAD, AND DRINK THIS CUP, YE DO SHOW FORTH THE LORD'S DEATH TILL HE COME."

278

QUIZ

1. With respect to the Lord's supper and water baptism, where do denominationalists and extreme dispensationalists agree and where do they disagree? 2. Give three proofs that water baptism and the Lord's supper do not belong in the same class Scripturally. 3. Prove from Scripture that the Lord's supper is not the same as the Passover. 4. What is the relation between the Old and New Covenants? 5. With whom were these covenants made? 6. How do both affect the Gentiles? 7. In what prophecy did God *promise to make* the New Covenant? 8. When was the New Covenant actually *made?* 9. When will it be fulfilled? 10. What was the nature of the promises under the New Covenant? 11. How do we come into the blessings of the New Covenant? 12. Show from Scripture how water baptism was an ordinance, in the Scriptural sense of the term. 13. Show how the Lord's supper is *not* such an ordinance. 14. Were John the Baptist and the twelve *sent* to baptize? 15. Was Paul *sent* to baptize? Give Scripture. 16. Was the Lord's supper included in Paul's special revelation and commission? 17. Show from Scripture how the Lord's supper was meant to be a testimony. 18. How would you answer the argument that the celebration of the Lord's supper is not compatible with our position in the heavenlies? 19. Explain why God has given us this one physical "remembrance." 20. Until when are members of the body of Christ to show forth the Lord's death in this way?

THE END

If this book has helped you to a clearer understanding of the Word of God, why not order copies for your friends?

BIBLE INDEX

BIBLE INDEX

281

BIBLE INDEX

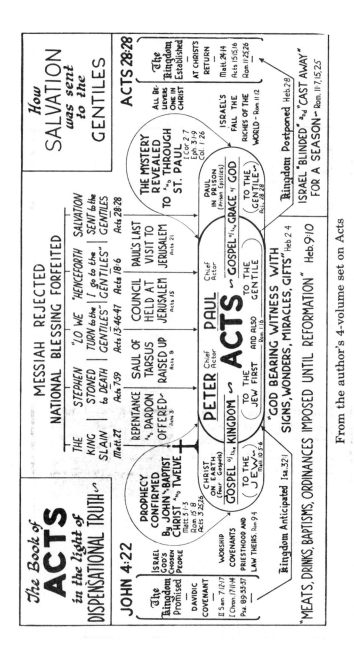

From the author's 4-volume set on Acts